THE QUEST FOR BEING

T H

SIDNEY HOOK

QUEST FOR BEING

and other studies in Naturalism and Humanism

GREENWOOD PRESS, PUBLISHERS
WESTPORT, CONNECTICUT

Originally published in 1961
by St. Martin's Press, New York

Reprinted with the permission
of St. Martin's Press, Inc., New York

First Greenwood Reprinting 1971

Library of Congress Catalogue Card Number 79-139136

ISBN 0-8371-5752-8

Printed in the United States of America

Contents

To CURT J. DUCASSE *and* WALTER T. STACE
who will mostly disagree

Introduction

Every essay is a short book and most books are long essays which could be shorter. If there were time enough every essay in this volume of essays could have been expanded into a volume but I have preferred to leave them in their previously published form, in order to embrace a larger number of problems than would otherwise have been possible. With the exception of the essay which gives the collection its title, and two others, these essays have been written for the philosophical layman and have been published in literary reviews.

Philosophical labels today are extremely misleading, partly because most philosophers are interested in piecemeal analysis of specific problems and partly because the meanings of the large terms which designate schools of thought are in dispute. If I were permitted to define the point of view from which these problems are approached, I should call it experimental or pragmatic naturalism. According to this philosophy the furniture of heaven and earth, the way things are and the way they behave, are best described by the scientific disciplines when the latter are conceived as continuous with, although sometimes critical of, common-sense experience. The philosopher has no special sources of insight in this domain. He has, however, an important and perennially useful task. Employing sharp conceptual tools, he can help clarify problems and untangle the paradoxes which result as the language of common sense struggles to keep abreast of the growth of new scientific knowledge.

The distinctive contribution of the philosopher, aside from his activity as a logical and linguistic analyst, is to be found in his conception of man. Here, too, he must be familiar with the findings of the psychological and social sciences whose underlying pattern of inquiry is common with that of the natural sciences. But what he brings to bear on this knowledge is a conception and vision of man, of a way of life, thought, and social action which recommends itself by its anticipated fruits in experience. The philosopher's distinctive function, therefore, is moral both in its critical and creative modes. At the very least, the philosopher should make men critically aware of their fundamental commitments and the consequences of their commitments. At his best, he projects a vision of human excellence, of what men may become, rooted in a firm knowledge of the limiting conditions of nature, and a sober assessment of the possibilities of development open to men in an unfinished universe.

The essays contained in this book have appeared over a wide span of years. I have left them stand except for certain minimal changes required in the interest of accuracy concerning details of the passing scene. Had I rewritten them the tone of some of the essays would have been different but not the substance of their argument. Although grouped around different themes, they may be read in any order depending upon the reader's interest.

The first essay was presented as the opening paper of the Third East-West Philosopher's Conference in Hawaii in 1959. Essays Nine and Thirteen were published in the *Journal of Philosophy*, in 1953 and 1934. Essays Three and Eleven were respectively my contributions to a *Festschrift* for John Dewey, *John Dewey: Philosopher of Science and Freedom*, which I edited in 1949, and a *Festschrift* for Morris R. Cohen, *Reason and Freedom*, edited by Baron and Nagel in 1951. Essay Ten was part of the collection *American Philosophers at Work* which appeared in 1955. Essays Two and Seven were published in *Commentary*, 1958 and 1960. Essay Seven was originally delivered as the Nineteenth Free Garvin Lecture at the Church of Our Father, Unitarian, in Lancaster, Pennsylvania, December 18, 1959. Essays Four, Five, Six, Eight and Twelve appeared in the *Partisan Review*, 1943, 1950, 1956, and 1958. In Essay Six, I have reprinted, with his agreement, Dr. Ernest van den Haag's criticism of my position on religion because it sharply focuses certain issues which have become increasingly pertinent in recent years. I have always found my disagreements with him fruitful.

I am happy to acknowledge the kind permission of editors and publishers to reprint these contributions.

S.H.

South Wardsboro, Vermont
September 1, 1960

Philosophy and Human Conduct

That philosophy counts in human affairs is acknowledged by governments as well as by landladies. Few governments until recent times have been indifferent to the philosophic ideas professed by their citizens and especially by the teachers of their citizens. And it is hardly fortuitous that all groups in possession of power have been biassed in favor of philosophical ideas which celebrate eternity rather than those which glorify change. Even when power manifests itself most nakedly it often seeks to clothe itself in philosophic thought. And although such thought may rightly be characterized as a rationalization, it would be hazardous to dismiss rationalizations as inconsequential. Human beings have lived and died by their rationalizations.

On a more mundane plane few would deny the insight in G. K. Chesterton's remark that it is more important for a landlady to know her boarder's philosophy than the contents of his trunks. For the reference is obviously to the boarder's moral principles. But the insight becomes highly problematic when instead of moral principles the reference is to the boarder's epistemology or meta-

THE QUEST FOR BEING

physics. The withers of most landladies would be completely un-wrung at the news that their boarder had surrendered his belief in the *Ding-an-sich* for the view that a thing was a complex of sense-data.

This suggests the necessity of making a few preliminary distinctions in order to sharpen our question. If philosophical ideas play a role in determining social practice then it is simply tautologous to proclam that some ideas have relevance to conduct. But the fact that some ideas and beliefs are efficacious in experience is not by itself evidence that *philosophical* ideas have the same role. For belief that scientific and technological ideas are implicit plans of action which have momentous bearing on the affairs of experience may be coupled with the view that philosophical ideas have no such bearing at all. For example, Bertrand Russell has maintained in a book in which he declares political *theory* to be one of the three dominant causes of political and social change that: "The belief that metaphysics has any bearing upon practical affairs is, to my mind, a proof of logical incapacity." [1] That in subsequent writing Russell asserts that some philosophies are dangerous because of their influence on practice, that the epistemology of empiricism is more congenial to liberalism than to conservatism, and that "the only philosophy that affords a theoretical justification of democracy in its temper of mind is empiricism," [2] indicates some confusion on Russell's part on the matter. Nonetheless in principle there is no inconsistency in holding the view that ideas count in practice but not philosophical ideas.

Since I shall contend both that (a) ideas in science and technology, and (b) ideas in philosophy are important determiners of conduct, I begin with a brief consideration of the view that all ideas are epiphenomenal, that they are the effects of certain ultimate causes and are never themselves proximate causes of effects. If this position is valid, it follows that philosophical ideas are fanciful notions or vapors thrown up by the movements of things and social forces, surface patterns of foam on the waters of the deep. If, on the other hand, the position is invalid, this does not by itself establish the validity of (b). It shows only that it may possibly be true.

1

It requires considerable intellectual sophistication to deny causal influence to ideas in human affairs. For aside from instinctive and habitual conduct, what we do is largely determined by what we believe. Even habitual conduct often presupposes that certain beliefs have been accepted as true in the past. The world we live in is an interpreted world. The evidence for this is so massive that no one but philosophers would doubt it. Ideas are sometimes stronger than the strongest natural impulses. We know that human beings have starved to death in the sight of nourishing food because they believed certain animals to be sacred or certain plants poisonous. Nor is it necessary for ideas to be true to have determining significance for conduct. Witches do not exist. But how many unfortunate creatures have been brought to a miserable end because of the belief in the existence of witches? To be sure one may believe in witches and not burn them but put them to work on useful tasks. This testifies only to the influence of other ideas about witches. It still remains true that if we did not believe in witches, thousands of innocent women would not have been tortured to death.

The view that ideas have no influence on human conduct is hardly intelligible in the light of the liberating consequences sometimes anticipated as resulting from the enunciation of that view. But it may be instructive to examine some of the grounds offered for the belief in the inefficacy of ideas. The most important ground offered is that ideas are events either in a man's biography or in a culture and like all events have necessary causes. But that ideas have causes is not incompatible with the proposition that ideas have consequences. If it were, then since "the causes" of ideas are themselves caused by antecedent events, these "causes" would have to be denied efficacy. It would then be illegitimate to say that ideas were *their* consequences. In other words, once we recognize the operation of proximate causes of our ideas, we can no longer call into question the possible efficacy of ideas which are themselves caused.

A second reason for questioning the practical import of ideas is that they and the behavior patterns which define them are not sufficient to explain their alleged effects. Multiple causes and multiple factors, limiting objective conditions, are invariably present. Historians of ideas often assert that "the time must be ripe," "possibilities open," "the stage set," "the situation prepared" before ideas can take hold. All this may be true but it only indicates that ideas are not omnipotent and that they cannot explain everything about a situation. Men are creatures of interests, habits, passions as well as thought. Unless it is argued that a resultant effect would have occurred anyhow, independently of the presence or absence of ideas, causal imputation cannot be denied to ideas.

From two diametrically opposed, yet related, points of view, the efficacy of ideas in history has been denied. The dialectical idealism of Hegel as well as the dialectical materialism of Marxism, in their standard versions, render ideas otiose for different reasons. In Hegel the world is conceived of as embodied Reason, developing to be sure, but developing out of time. The real is *already* rational. At most human thinking recognizes the immanent necessities in things in order to proclaim them necessary, reasonable and therefore good rather than to transform or change them. "Reason is already in the world," says Hegel, just as God is in the world, and the progress of thought is the progress of recognition of the fact.

What is true for human ideas generically in Hegel is true for philosophical ideas specifically. In his famous lines in the preface to his *Philosophy of Law,* he writes:

> The task of philosophy is to comprehend that which exists for that which exists, is Reason. Just as every individual is a child of his time so, too, is philosophy an expression of its time in thought. . . .
> Philosophy always comes too late to teach the world what it should be . . . When it paints its gray upon gray, a form of life has already become old and with gray and gray life cannot be rejuvenated but only understood. The owl of Minerva takes its flight only when the shades of twilight have fallen.[3]

In Marxism the mode of economic production takes the place of the Hegelian developing *Begriff* or concrete universal as the basic cause of historical change. Human beings are moved by ideas but these ideas are epiphenomenal (or superstructural); they have neither autonomy nor independent force. Strictly speaking there is no such thing according to orthodox Marxists as a history of ideas but only a history of modes of production whose needs create the interests which reflect themselves in the construction of morality, religion and philosophy. In *die deutsche Ideologie,* Marx and Engels write:

> In complete opposition to German philosophy which descends from heaven to earth, we here mount from the earth to heaven. We do not take our point of departure from what men say, imagine, conceive nor from men as they are described, thought about, imagined or conceived in order to arrive at men in the living flesh. We start from real, active men. We present the development of their ideological reflexes and echoes as products of their real life-processes. Even the fantasies in the human brain are the necessary sublimates of the life processes which are tied to material presuppositions of an empirical and verifiable character. Morality, religion, metaphysic, and other ideology and their corresponding forms of consciousness herewith lose their semblance of independence. They have no history, they have no development. Human beings in consequence of their material production and material intercourse transform their existence and therewith also their thinking and the products of their thinking. It is not consciousness which determines *life* but life which determines consciousness.[4]

Neither Hegel nor Marx, as customarily interpreted, can consistently defend their positions in denying causal efficacy to ideas. In Hegel this is apparent in his denunciation of the mischievous effects of what he regards as mistaken ideas. When he turned against the ideas of the French Enlightenment, it was because he held it and its mode of thinking responsible for practices and events which threatened the security of the German states. Instead of leaving to God and the Absolute or *die List der Vernuft* the correction of the liberal ideas of Fries and his school, Hegel approved of police measures against them. If philosophical ideas are ineffectual by their very nature, why is it necessary to suppress them?

In Marx's case although all other ideas merely sanctify the social *status quo* by interpreting it differently, his own ideas were offered as a means of revolutionizing it. Although he says "not criticism but revolution is the driving force of history and also of religion, philosophy and all theory,"[4a] his own criticisms and ideas are advanced as the *preface* to revolution, as a means of rallying the

masses to action. The failure of revolutions to develop where objective conditions are ripe for them is attributed to the influence
of traditional ideas or to absence of proper political organization
which in part depends upon correct ideas of organization.

Even aside from their inconsistencies both Hegel and Marx fail
to do justice to the complexities of the so-called fact of "reflection"
or "expression." Ideas and ideals may "reflect" or "express" social
forces or conditions or national interests. But they may reflect or
express in different ways. A philosophy which pleads for human
freedom and one which justifies caste or class discrimination may
both be properly described as "reflecting" or "expressing" existing
institutions but this leaves unexplained their differential meanings
and effects. Burke's philosophy is a reflection of the French Revolution but so are the writings of Robespierre, de Constant, St. Just
and de Maistre. No set of ideas *merely* reflects or expresses given
conditions. To the extent that it is believed or commands influence, it *strengthens* or *weakens* these conditions. And since social
relations always show some fluidity, since some choices and alternatives are always open, the *mode* of expression or reflection becomes
a contributory factor, if not always decisive or even weighty, in
determining the movement of affairs.

2

It is not enough to vindicate the efficacy of ideas in social and
practical affairs. The question is whether what is true of ideas in
science, technology, and every day intercourse is true of philosophical ideas. Those who grant that ideas are influential in human
affairs but deny that philosophical ideas play the same role as other
ideas do so on four generic grounds. They maintain (1) that philosophical ideas, insofar as they can be distinguished from others, are
transcendental or non-empirical and therefore have no differential
bearing or relevance on human behavior; (2) that there is no observable personal connection between the philosophy a man holds,
his theory of reality, and, say, his social views or his views on any
practical matter; (3) whatever other connection exists is demon-
strably not one of necessary entailment; and since it is logically
possible to combine belief in any theory of reality with any practice, there is no problem; (4) and finally, if there are causal con-

nections between philosophical ideas and practices either one may be the cause of the other or both may be caused by some other state of affairs.

Granted then that ideas, as John Dewey was fond of observing, are the most practical things in the world. Can we say this or something similar to this about philosophical ideas? At first glance it seems that we may say this only if philosophical ideas are cognitive and make knowledge claims, and only if these knowledge claims can be shown to be about empirical matters and therefore have consequences, direct or indirect, for practice. But it is possible to challenge the cognitive character of all assertions in philosophy. Independently of this, one may challenge the relevance of philosophical assertions to life on the ground that even if they do have cognitive meaning, their validity is compatible with all social systems and human practices no matter how contrary the latter are to each other. The motto of the old *American Journal of Speculative Philosophy* used to read: "Philosophy can bake no bread, but she can procure for us God, freedom, and immortality." What philosophy, so conceived, can procure for us is no mean thing but how does it bear in any specifiable way on human conduct? Suppose we believe God exists and that everything happens by His will. What follows for practice? Nothing specific because everything *after* the event can be construed as happening by Divine Will. Despite the village atheist: there is no inconsistency in praying "Thy Will Be Done" in a church whose steeple flaunts a lightning rod to divert a bolt from on high. To the pious both the bolt and the ingenuity to divert it happen by the will of God. Similarly, human beings may differ over the justification and nature of various punishments, but acceptance or unacceptance of metaphysical freedom of the will is compatible with all positions taken. The belief in immortality is closer to an empirical proposition although few of those who believe in immortality are clear about the nature of the immortal self. Usually what takes place is an extrapolation of the complex of feelings, hopes, fears and desires of the existing self to another state independently of the material conditions upon which the existing self seems to depend. But by itself a belief in immortality does not involve commitment to a specific course of conduct unless it is associated with other beliefs of a factual nature, say, in Heaven or Hell or with moral beliefs in a

path of Salvation and a schedule of duties to be observed in this
life. It is hard to see what specific practice the belief in immortality
per se commits one to in life. But where the belief in immortality
takes the form of a belief in reincarnation (*samsara*), where this
belief is allied with the doctrine of *karma* or a cosmic law of
justice or retribution, and where it is assumed that the status in
the hierarchy of future reincarnated being is a function of piety
towards and observance of caste duties in the present state of
existence—then it may be argued with some plausibility that upon
the acceptance of some propositions of philosophy—(those of
natural theology)—an entire mode of social life depends, and not
merely the baking of bread. At the very least, belief in some philosophical propositions, in some historical situations where traditions
of otherworldliness are deeply rooted, would be necessary conditions for social stability and the domination of one class over
others. To be sure it has been argued that these religious and
philosophical beliefs arose at a time when it was necessary to con-
solidate existing social institutions. But even without raising the
question of causal priority, the fact that these beliefs had definite
influence on the practical behavior of those nurtured on them
seems incontestable. To the extent that reform movements like
Buddhism and Jainism in the East and Protestantism in the West
break with dominant traditions many social practices associated
with these traditions are repudiated.

The most important point I wish to make here, however, and
which I shall develop later, is that if transcendental philosophical
or religious beliefs are denied relevance to practical conduct because they are compatible with all varieties of empirical behavior,
this overlooks the possibility that the connection may not be
theoretical or cognitive but attitudinal. That is to say from the
statements "Everything is Mind," "All is Feeling," "Reality is
Will," "Everything is Vanity (or Illusion)," nothing differential
in the way of cognitive belief may be inferred and the *differences*
between experiences may be surreptitiously acknowledged by adjectival distinctions. Nonetheless these assertions may express attitudes, commitments, evaluations which have a bearing upon conduct none the less effective for being vague, discontinuous or
episodic. As with so many other things the influence of ideas on

behavior is a matter of more or less, not an affair of either-or, all
or none.

3

The most common reason for denying that philosophical ideas
and social practices are integrally related is that the philosophical
ideas of individual thinkers and their social views and/or practices
are often different from what we should expect if there were an
organic connection between philosophy and practice. For example,
empiricism and materialism are associated with liberalism and
radicalism but Hobbes was a royalist, Hume a Tory, and Santayana
sympathetic to Fascism. On the other hand, idealism has been associated with conservatism but T. H. Green was a Liberal and
Felix Adler, like many others influenced by Kant, was a great ex-
ponent of social reform. The most outstanding rationalist and
idealist in America, Brand Blanshard, is a free-thinker and democratic socialist. One can find many other illustrations. The empiri-
cist Francis Bacon was politically reactionary, the non-empirical
rationalist, Spinoza, was a liberal in social and political affairs and
an eloquent advocate of tolerance. The same absence of connection
holds for outstanding individuals who were not professional philosophers. The radical William Blake professed to being a Berk-
leian immaterialist while that Tory's Tory Samuel Johnson scoffed
and kicked when Berkeley's views were mentioned.

All these instances seem to me to establish conclusively that
there is no personal psychological connection between personality
or temperament as this is expressed in social or political life, and
philosophical belief. This does not deny that complex causal influences are at work in determining a man's beliefs even about the
most recondite things as well as his daily behavior. But unless there
is specific empirical evidence to warrant it, we are not justified in
assuming that the same set of causes determines both his personal
philosophy and his personal practice, or that one is the cause of
the other. Two men of the most diverse temperaments may subscribe to an identical set of theoretical propositions. Two men
equally fanatical in temperament may be at each other's throats
doctrinally. The same man without a perceptible change in personality pattern may embrace at different times in his career con-

trary brands of fanaticism. Two men who subscribe to the same set of philosophical beliefs may differ in their political and social allegiance whereas two men who differ fundamentally in their philosophic beliefs, *e.g.,* Dewey and Russell, may support the same social and political program.

But all this is beside the main point which asserts not that there is a general connection between the *personal* social and political commitments of philosophers and their philosophies but that the *significant connection is to be found between social movements and philosophical doctrines.* Such connections are *historical,* not primarily psychological or personal. A doctrine or a theory may be put to social uses quite different from those the individual author of the doctrine or theory intended or approved of. Ideas and doctrines have historical effects rarely explicable in terms of personal intent. The rise of experimental science is undoubtedly part of the intellectual movement which contributed to the liberation of Western Europe from medievalism. But this was certainly not the intent of Catholic scientists like Galileo and others. Bacon was personally a time-serving royalist and extreme conservative but his doctrine that knowledge is power and his critique of the idols of the human mind inspired the French Encyclopedists and contributed to undermining social institutions and prejudices which were personally congenial to him.

Hobbes for our purposes may serve as an ideal case. Certainly, he was a conservative. But his views about the nature and grounds of sovereignty were flatly incompatible with the doctrine of divine rights. They had a chilling effect on the royalists whom he personally supported. It was as if they put the person of the King in the shadow of the gallows or execution block.[5] Hobbes' appeal to the principle of self-interest struck his fellow conservatives as seditious, and his belief, restated in many different ways, that "in sum all actions and habits are to be esteemed good or evil by their causes and usefulness in reference to the commonwealth," as a standing invitation to social criticism of all institutions including the absolute monarchy. For all of Hobbes' transparently sincere *personal* willingness to serve them, the conservative forces and movements of his time and subsequent times could not *use* his doctrines. On the other hand, it was the liberals in subsequent generations who developed his implicit utilitarianism, his anticlericalism, his secular and scientific approach to political issues. Hobbes' doctrines are part of the same family tree as those of Bentham and the other leading figures of philosophical radicalism. And we shall see below why this is so.

4

I have previously quoted Russell's remark "the belief that metaphysics has any bearing upon practical affairs is, to my mind, a proof of logical incapacity." What Russell obviously means is "the belief that metaphysics has any *logical* bearing upon practical affairs is . . . a proof of logical incapacity." It is quite true that no metaphysical proposition (except where disguised value judgments are involved), entails anything about practical affairs since there seems to be nothing contradictory in holding the view that "Reality is X" equally with the view that "Y should be done" or "Y should not be done." But there may be some connection, as we have seen, which is other than one of "entailment"; in ordinary discourse we speak of many different kinds of "necessary connection" where necessary is not a strict logical relation. If we insist upon the presence of strict entailment relations before we relate thought to conduct we will have to rule out the influence of all ideas—even scientific and technological ideas—upon human conduct. It is not logically contradictory to assert that "x is a poisonous substance" and "I should eat it." To insist on relations of logical entailment in assertions bearing on human conduct seems to me to betray a fundamental lack of common sense. It would lead not only to what C. D. Broad calls silly philosophy but to views that are plain silly. It is as if someone were to argue that if *all* we knew about an individual whom we wanted to hire as a bodyguard was that he was a member of Murder, Inc., pledged to commit crimes, we would not be warranted in considering him unfit for his post because it would not be logically impossible for such an individual to be a secret member of the F.B.I.[6] It is not *logically* impossible for something to be both a pig and to fly. But if anyone gave this as a reason for mounting a pig to take off into the blue we would question his sanity.

From a strictly logical point of view there is no reason to infer that a belief that one possesses absolute and infallible truth or that one is the recipient of a uniquely revealed message necessitates a policy of intolerance towards those considered to be in error or lost in heresy. As important as the belief in absolute truth may be, the belief that freedom to err is part of the vocation of the free man whose personality has an absolute value, is not incompatible with it and some of us are familiar with individuals who hold both beliefs. A revelation that one has received a unique truth from on high may be compatible with another enjoining believers to permit others, without persecuting them, to find their own path to salvation or damnation. Nonetheless I think it would be pretty generally admitted that the belief that one group, class, party or church possesses absolute and infallible truth about things that matter is more likely to encourage patterns of intolerant conduct towards those who disagree with these alleged truths than the belief that no human being possesses absolute truth and that we are all fallible. Similarly a belief that we are the exclusive custodians of a unique revelation from God is more likely to encourage patterns of fanaticism and religious intolerance than the belief that God's revelations are continuous and not restricted to one individual or group.

If one believes that the world of sensuous experience is illusory, that time is unreal, that in some sense everything is one and separation the result of a finite perspective, it is still possible to be curious about the forms illusion takes, the apparent difference of things, and the qualities of experience which mislead us into thinking that time is both objective and important. But by and large, any culture where such beliefs are widely held will be one in which science is not likely to develop, technology will be limited to gratification of needs necessary for life, inventiveness will not be encouraged and institutionalized. Why, indeed, should anyone be interested in disinterested study of the details of the Book of Nature if it is not considered to be a Book of Truth?

In all of these illustrations, and they can be easily multiplied, there is a certain social connection between doctrine and practice which is less than logical, more than personal, and other than casual.

5

Our task is not yet done. Grant, for the moment, that there is some determinate connection between organic theories of society, which teach that the welfare of all groups, classes and individuals is inherently harmonious, and the special interests and needs of a bureaucratic class to maintain existing power relations; between atomistic or individualistic theories of empiricism and movements of social reform, decentralization and opposition to the constraints of tradition; between theories of renunciation, rejection of and withdrawal from the world, and conditions of social chaos and disorder—this does not by itself establish where the causal primacy lies. The orthodox Marxist view assumes that there is a one way dependence of philosophical views on political and socioeconomic conditions and that if there is no clear line of causal connection between them then *both* can be shown to be consequences of an earlier set of social conditions.

I do not see how it can be established *a priori* which way the causal connection runs. Although orthodox Marxists claim that they are espousing merely a heuristic hypothesis they have done very little to test it in a critical or scientific spirit. But the decisive point is this. Even if it were the case that philosophical beliefs arose to meet a social situation or to further an interest, in some cases it is clear that they subsequently influenced social developments, so that one can legitimately assert that the history and practical life of a culture in important respects would be unaccountable without reference to them. This is apparent both in the case of the philosophy or social ethics of Christianity and of modern democracy.

There have been many attempts to enunciate the Christian "ethos" but it seems to me that the best warranted formulation is to be found in the work of the famous German scholar, Ernst Troelsch: "The lasting and eternal content of the Christian Ethos," he maintains, "recognizes differences in social position, power and capacity, as a condition which has been established by the inscrutable Will of God; and then transforms this condition by the inner upbuilding of personality and the development of the mutual sense of obligation into an ethical cosmos." [7] Whatever the social conditions were which gave rise to the Christian Ethos, it is clear that this Ethos played a powerful role in practical affairs in two ways. First it tended to reconcile and gloss over conflicts of social interests, and by legitimizing existing power relations contributed to stabilizing society. Secondly, for those who accepted this Ethos it made life supportable or endurable even if their status was that of the slave or serf. It generated a kind of spiritual buoyancy, a confidence and cosmic hope which prevented those on whom the hard and cruel chores of the world fell, from being dragged down by their sufferings and weariness into apathy or despair [8] or from being goaded into a continuous state of resentment and periodic revolt. Whether early Christianity be conceived as a this-worldly spiritual revolutionary movement or an otherworldly compensatory revolutionary movement, it is noteworthy that the frequency and intensity of slave revolts decreased sharply with the Christianization of the Roman Empire.

That modern democratic theory and practice is a child of the developing European capitalist economy is believed not only by Marxists but by the school of Hayek and von Mises who draw different political conclusions from this alleged causal dependency. But an unprejudiced analysis of the impact of the democratic faith upon the development of Western society establishes its independent influence upon social, political, and economic life. The affirmation and reaffirmation of the democratic faith, particularly as a consequence of two wars in which the slogans of democracy became common coin, played a powerful role in the extension of democratic practices in the United States. The U.S. Supreme Court's desegregation decision reversing previous decisions on racial questions is a weighty piece of evidence that principles of social philosophy can be effective. To be sure, conditions must be ripe before the principles become operative. But conditions may be ripe, and yet, without appropriate belief, they may never mature. Sometimes what human beings believe is an index or a part of the ripeness of conditions. What is true of the appeal and impact of the democratic ideal in the United States is true of its spread as a slogan, a rallying cry, a set of abstract principles, in most regions of Asia and Africa.

Yet for all the "reciprocal influence" of philosophical ideas and ideals on events and practices, it does not yet establish the view that all philosophical ideals have this function. That, broadly speaking, ethical ideals, or propositions have an influence on behavior may be granted. But have ontological or epistemological ideas either a direct influence on behavior or a mediate influence through their alleged influence on ethical ideals? The philosophy of dialectical materialism is a good test case. It is an open question whether the programs which led to the Russian October Revolution and the construction of the economy of socialism in one country are compatible with belief in the theory of historical materialism as Marx and Engels interpreted it. There can hardly be any doubt, however, that these programs followed from Lenin's interpretation and revision of Marxism. With some modifications I believe a plausible case can be made for the contention that the Bolshevik-Leninist political ideology or theory is still the most fruitful guide to Soviet practice. But despite the official pronouncement that dialectical materialism is the logical basis of communism and the guide to the theory and practice of the Soviet regime, no one has succeeded in showing in a single instance the influence of the so-called laws of dialectic or the other general principles of dialectical materialism, upon any *specific* Soviet practice. That is to say, despite official pronouncement to the contrary, the laws of dialectic provide no guide to any specific judgment or practice. It is true that sometimes the philosophy of dialectical materialism has been invoked to condemn some theory in astronomy, biology, chemistry, physics, or psychology. But in no case has any analysis shown that the laws of dialectic are actually incompatible with the proposition condemned. Indeed, in every case a more plausible explanation can be found why one proposition was approved and the other rejected by the Politbureau; for example, in Lysenko's case the hope that his theories would increase the wheat yield; in other instances, the desire to sustain the intellectual authority of Marx-Engels-Lenin's views on nature and science because of the key place that their political doctrines held in the Communist program. In other words were the Communists to abandon all belief in the laws of dialectic tomorrow, nothing of moment would be altered; no one could show why anything should be different except that scientists and other scholars and teachers need no longer profess allegiance to them. This obviously would not be the case if

the Communists abandoned their theory of the state or their views
of the class struggle, or the nature of capitalism.

6

That the philosophical views of some groups are associated with,
and influence, their social practices is easier to establish for some
periods of history than that there is *always* a determinate connection between philosophical theory and practice, in the sense that
once we know *in the abstract* what philosophy a group supports
we can predict what their social practices will be or on which side
they will line up with respect to practical issues like trade unionism, the relation between church and state, birth control, or a
world state. Here I believe that every assertion of universal connection is false whether it be Hegelian or Marxian; and if we take
the historical approach, which both schools urge, to the connection
between philosophy and culture, we can establish the absence of
any universal connection. Many other things in addition to philosophical belief may determine practical commitment so that even
when the philosophical beliefs are the same, other factors like
national interest, religious traditions, and sectional ties may be the
overriding considerations. A theory of predestination accepted by
a marginal class of down and outers will manifest itself in quite
different behavior patterns from those observed in bourgeois com-
fortable Calvinist circles in which the same theory is also an
article of faith. This suggests the possibility that although a philosophical belief may *tend* to influence conduct in a certain direction, it may be counteracted by the effect of other factors which
determine action.

In line with this possibility I should like to venture an hypothesis about the relation between philosophical views, when these
are conceived in a certain way, and social practices. I understand
by philosophical views, as distinct from purely scientific views,
interpretations of existence from the standpoint of value. Values
may not be rooted in interests but whenever serious conflicts of
value arise they involve or are related to interests—and to the extent
that the content of interests is social to social interests. No plausible
account of the history of Western culture (perhaps of Eastern cultures, too), can be written which does not recognize the enormous

role of conflicting group and class interests in the struggle for
political power and the distribution and control of economic
wealth. It is obviously to the interest of those groups or classes
which enjoy the dominating position in society and command the
posts of strategic power, to attenuate, moderate, and whenever possible conceal conflicts of interest. Otherwise society would be in
a state of chronic civil war in which the very advantages of domination would be imperiled. The interest of any class or group in
power is, in other words, to conceal conflict of interests, to develop
and reinforce attitudes, habits and beliefs which make the customary appear the natural, the reasonable, and the necessary. Every
vested interest will shy away from an experimental or empirical
approach which will test slogans and principles by performance,
examine causes and consequences of social policies, and expose to
the light the interests which are furthered or repressed by them.

Consequently, we should expect that those who are in positions
of social authority and power would be predisposed to support
views and attitudes which tend to rationalize the social status quo.
Those who wish to reform or revolutionize the existing order will
support views and attitudes which tend to reveal the roots of
interest under the trees of accepted theory and bring to light the
conflicting interests whose vitality and growth and satisfaction are
frustrated by existing social institutions. They will adopt this outlook until they themselves come to power when, if they develop
vested interests of their own, they will tend to shift towards a modification of their doctrines. The first group, the "in-group," will be
inclined to support a philosophical outlook which is organic,
hierarchical, idealistic, which stresses that every thing has its necessary place in the universe and therefore every man his necessary
station in society with fixed duties. Or it will be sympathetic to
philosophies that give great scope to revelation, intuition, authority, and tradition, providing that the necessity of some institution to interpret them is conceded. The second group, the "out-
group," will tend to be empirical and experimental, materialistic
or naturalistic, insisting upon reducing large and grandiose abstractions about social peace, harmony and unity to denotative
differences in practice.

This hypothesis in its general outline is not novel except possibly for the explicit reference to social interest. We have seen

that Russell maintains that the empirical theory of knowledge, which he identifies with scientific outlook, "is the intellectual counterpart of what is, in the practical sphere, the attitude of Liberalism," [9] and that it is the "only philosophy that affords a theoretical justification of democracy," but he gives no convincing reason why this should be so. Our hypothesis would explain it.

The works of John Dewey are studied with reference to the social implications of philosophical positions. He is perhaps the most notable contemporary philosopher who has stressed the relation between philosophy and social action. His most pointed attempt to trace the specific relation between the philosophy of Kant —its dualism of "the world of sense and mechanism and the world of the supersensible and purpose"—and the culture of Imperial Germany must be regarded as a failure.[10] Nonetheless he feels convinced that "one can say with considerable assurance that a hierarchically ordered and subordinated state will feel an affinity for a philosophy of fixed categories while a flexible democratic society will, in its crude empiricism, exhibit loose ends." [11] The reason for this affinity is that an organic view tends to minimize the significance of specific conflicts of interests by showing that all interests are servants of one general interest which is both all inclusive and harmonious.[12]

Even more emphatic in this connection is the memorable passage in John Stuart Mill's *Autobiography:*

> The notion that truths external to the mind may be known by intuition or consciousness, independently of observation or experiences, is, I am persuaded, in these times, the great intellectual support of false doctrines and bad institutions. By the aid of this theory, every inveterate belief and every intense feeling, of which the origin is not remembered, is entitled to dispense with the obligation of justifying itself by reason, and is erected into its own all sufficient voucher and justification. There never was such an instrument devised for consecrating all deep-seated prejudices.[13]

A similar motivation accounts for Locke's earlier criticism of the doctrine of innate ideas.

If our hypothesis is tenable, there are certain things which we should be prepared to expect. It is unlikely that "the official philosophy" or the dominant philosophy in any culture riven by strong conflicts of interest will be experimental. To the extent that materialism allies itself with scientific method in social affairs, it is unlikely that materialism will ever be a regnant philosophy in such a culture. The Soviet Union is not an exception. The Marxist philosophy which functioned essentially as a critical instrument to lay bare the political and social interests behind ideologies, and their connections with the mode of economic production, became transformed when it was elevated to the rank of official state philosophy of the Soviet Union, into a shamefaced variety of objective idealism. In that role it functions just as much as an ideology as any of the dominant philosophies in previous ages, preaching, for example, that "a unity of interest" existed between the workers and peasants during the very times when the peasants were being expropriated from their holdings. That is why although in the Soviet physical sciences an empirical and experimental approach, within certain limits, is accepted, in the social sciences it is not tolerated.

We should further expect that close relations will exist between the dominant or official philosophy and the dominant or official religion of a period although there will be differences in the *manner* in which the rationality or acceptability of traditional values is defended.

Our hypothesis will also explain why most specific metaphysical assertions are irrelevant to social practice. For although assertions like "Reality is Will or Feeling or Matter" may express personal judgments of value, in the sense that those who hold them thereby indicate their interest in, or preference for, some special feature of experience, it is difficult to show their bearing on existing social interests.

There are, however, certain obvious difficulties with this hypothesis. The first is that sometimes a group struggling to further its interests against the existing power complex may invoke the ideal of the dominant philosophy and religion. Where this is the case one would expect the philosophy of the opposition to contain more empirical elements than the official creeds they oppose, to pay more attention to the facts of social experience. The history of religious movements illustrates a similar tendency. Although the religious dogmas are common, the interpretations vary. The social and political opposition tends to liberalize the theology. So in England the Cromwellians against the Crown and the Levellers against both.

The Left Hegelians were more empirical than the Right Hegelians despite their common jargon. Nonetheless this phenomenon—the use of the same philosophical tradition for different social purposes —weakens the force of the assertion of the relation between philosophical doctrine and social allegiance.

A more formidable objection to this hypothesis about the social bearing of philosophical doctrines is formulated by Professor Feuer [14] who believes that psychoanalytical motivation is the key to the kind of view which flourishes. He calls attention to the fact that whereas the revolutionists of the eighteenth century were *intuitionists* and *a priorists*, Burke, who opposed them, was an historical and empirical conservative. Although detailed studies are necessary to explore these connections, I venture the judgment that Burke in his *Reflections on the French Revolution* did not take an empirical approach to history but a fetishistic one. He is really an *a priori* traditionalist using the language of historical tradition. An appeal to history is an appeal to a succession of events which contain all sorts of changes, including revolutions. An empirical approach would have indicated the conditions under which revolutions were justified and when they were not; but the upshot of Burke's *Reflections* was that revolutions were never justified in any circumstances.

The case of the revolutionary natural law intuitionists of the Eighteenth Century is much more difficult. I am convinced, however, that in Locke, in the French materialists, and especially in Jefferson, "natural rights" were really synonymous with "moral rights" and that moral rights are justified by an implicit utilitarianism which, despite the historical fiction of the social contract, places chief emphasis upon present-day consequences. Literally taken, of course, this Utilitarianism is incompatible with the belief that certain rights are absolute or "inalienable," since any right, if unlimited, may have disastrous consequences upon the community. Nonetheless, it is obvious that the language of inalienable rights was never literally taken. Otherwise we could hardly explain the practices defended in their name. The easy assumption was that the rights of life, liberty, property, and happiness were always compatible with each other. When it was discovered that they were not always compatible, they were in fact treated as "alienable." Historically, the right to private property was given precedence over the others. With the extension of the franchise and the growth in power of the masses other rights conceived as necessary to human happiness and welfare, were, on occasions, given legislative, if not judicial, priority. The right to property was more clearly grasped as only one among other human rights. The upshot of all this seems to me to be adequately expressed by Morris R. Cohen, who after a life-long study of natural law and natural rights, concluded with the observation: "Ultimately, then, the essence of all doctrines of natural rights is the view that any established or proposed social order or institution must defend itself before the *bar of human welfare.*" [15]

Several things should be noted about our hypothesis. Even if it is sustained, it does not justify sweeping statements about philosophical positions and social commitments. Certainly there is little evidence that most technical doctrines in philosophy, about which philosophers are professionally concerned, have any relevance to problems of social importance unless they are extrinsically coupled with differences in attitude or with differences in opinion about fact. Further, the revelance of philosophy to social practice is to be tested wherever policies involving values and the formation of values are being formulated. In this connection the study of philosophy of education and the habits of thought and action stressed in educational institutions are highly pertinent. Whatever else philosophy of education is, it concerns itself with the ends of education. The liberal and democratic outlook is associated with emphasis upon finding out, upon the right to challenge, to inquire and dissent, upon the authority of objective methods, upon self-discipline. The conservative outlook stresses the acceptance of tradition, respect for authority, the security of results won rather than the adventure of doubt, and discipline imposed from without. An investigation of the values stressed in educational systems at different periods in the past, and of the relation between these educational objectives and the philosophy embraced by those who exercised the decisive roles in fashioning and guiding the educational systems, would provide some empirical test of the hypothesis.

Finally, the hypothesis is not arbitrary in that there are reasonable grounds for expecting a connection to be present. A community is liberal and/or democratic to the extent that all the interests present within it are represented, to the extent that they have an opportunity legally to oppose the majority decisions when it goes against them, and to become the nucleus of a new majority. The assumption is that until men become angels there will be not only disagreements among them about how to implement their common interests but that there will also be objective differences of interests among them. The only alternatives to democratic society are the despotism of a minority, malevolent or benevolent, or anarchy which is the reign of a thousand despots. The democrat assumes *vis-à-vis* the despot, especially the benevolent despot, that most men in the open light of clash and criticism of interests are better judges of their own interests than anyone else. *Vis-à-vis* the anarchist, the democrat assumes that men have more significant interests in common than the interests which divide them even if it be little more than a desire to live in peace with one another's conflicting interests. What is common to all forms of empiricism is the belief that truth is an affair of observational consequences. Although the hypothesis may burn out to be false, it is not unreasonable to assume that where men are willing to test their beliefs not by their alleged presuppositions, but by their observable consequences, they will probably be more willing to compromise their demands, to negotiate differences, to take the standpoint of the other, to live together and help each other to live rather than to fight and die together.

This connection, I repeat, is only plausible. It has been challenged by several thinkers who, although they believe it true that empiricism in philosophy has practical consequences, maintain that the practical consequences, if logically drawn, would be not liberalism or democracy but totalitarianism. In each case, I believe the contention mistaken even for those traditional schools of empiricism which mistakenly identified ideas with images or impressions and ignored the initiating role of ideas as hypotheses or plans of action. Since, however, we are dealing with an empirical assertion in the history of ideas, the truth of the matter must be determined not primarily by argument but by patient historical inquiry. It cannot be stressed too strongly that the question of the connection between philosophical ideas and social practice or human conduct is not a philosophical question but an empirical question. Even if it were true that the abstruse and recondite consequences of a philosophical position, if drawn, would require

in the interests of logical consistency some modification of a practical attitude, this is not evidence of historical connection.[16] Even
simple logical consequences are sometimes not drawn in historical
experience and practical affairs: the subtle complex consequences
hardly ever. Men who make history, fortunately or unfortunately,
are not mathematical logicians. Intelligence in human affairs requires something more than a passion for consistency. The springs
of action are impulse and desire, ambition, hope and fear. Intelligence by exploring the meanings of belief may govern, moderate,
strengthen or check the springs of action. Whoever, therefore,
would trace the influence of large and general ideas on human behavior must find the paths of connection between human interest
and human thought.

Moral Freedom
in a Determined World

1

In the last year of the Weimar Republic, when ordinary criminals were sometimes more philosophical than the judges of Hitler's Third Reich subsequently proved to be, a strange case was tried before the tribunal of Hannover. The evidence showed that one Waldemar Debbler had been guilty of burglary, and the prosecutor proposed two years of penal servitude. Whereupon the prisoner rose and said:

"Gentlemen, you see in me the victim of an unwavering destiny. So-called freedom of decision does not exist. Every human action in this world is determined. The causes are given by the circumstances and the results inevitable. By my inclinations of character, for which I am not responsible, since they were born in me, by my upbringing, my experiences, I was predetermined to become what I am. If you, gentlemen, had a heredity similar to mine and had been subjected to the same influence as I, you would also have committed the burglary in this particular situation. With this theory

I am in good company. I refer you to Spinoza and Leibnitz. Even St. Augustine and, later, Calvin attributed all human actions to the immutable decree of destiny. As I have only done what I had to do, you have no moral right to punish me, and I therefore plead for my acquittal."

To which peroration the court answered:

"We have followed the prisoner's reasoning with attention. Whatever happens is the necessary and immutable sequel of preceding causes which, once given, could not be other than it is. Consequently the prisoner, by reason of his character and experience, was destined to commit the burglary. On the other hand, destiny also decrees that the court, as a result of the submitted testimony, must judge the prisoner guilty of burglary. The causes —the deed, the law, the nature of the judge—being given, the sentence of guilty and punishment follows as a natural consequence."

When asked whether he accepted the sentence, the prisoner declared: "Destiny demands that I appeal." To which the judge replied: "That may be. However, destiny will see to it that your appeal is rejected."

This story, for whose authenticity with respect to exact detail I will not vouch, confuses the concept of determinism with that of fatalism. It confuses an event whose occurrence depends upon, or is caused by, what the individual in this particular situation desires and does, with an event whose occurrence does not depend upon any event antecedent to it, and which would occur no matter what the antecedent event was. It confuses conditional necessity with unconditional necessity, what is *predetermined* with what is predictable with reference to certain laws and initial data. It further fails to distinguish clearly between the concept of punishment and the concept of moral responsibility. Nonetheless, in its appeal to a double standard of judgment it illustrates a defect which appears in the writings of more sophisticated philosophers who have returned to the theme of determinism and moral responsibility in recent years.

Those philosophers who have thought that progress in philosophy consists in part in showing that the traditional problems of philosophy are either pseudo-problems, or a confusing mixture of psychology, logic, and sociology, have been rudely awakened from their complacency by a revival of interest in the question of free will, determinism, and responsibility. It had been widely assumed that the whole problem of whether the *will* is free had been replaced, in consequence of the writings of Hobbes, Locke, Hume, Mill, and the modern naturalists and positivists, by the problem of the *conditions* under which men's actions are free. The general solution had been that *men* are free when their actions are determined by their own will, and not by the will of others, or by factors which lead us to say that their actions were involuntary. To the extent that conditions exist which prevent a man from acting as he wishes (*e.g.*, ignorance, physical incapacity, constraint used upon his body and mind) he is unfree. This view accepts the postulate of determinism as valid, regardless of whether a man's action is free or coerced—in one case his action is determined by his own volition, in the other not. The fact that my volition, say, to undergo an operation, is caused by a complex of factors, among which the existence of sickness or disease, or the belief in the existence of sickness or disease, is normally a necessary condition, does not make my action less free. After all, it would be absurd to suggest that my action in undergoing an operation would be free only if there were no cause or reason to undergo it. If one insisted on undergoing an operation when one knew there was no cause for the operation, one would normally be regarded as insane. That there would be a cause for the decision, for the insistence on the unnecessary operation, would not affect our judgment of it. On this view, the distinction between free and unfree acts, sane or insane acts, lies in the specific character of the causes at work, not in the presence or absence of causes.

What has been until recently considered a commonplace is now in several quarters described and repudiated as a wild paradox. That an action can be characterized as both "determined" and "free," or "determined" and "responsible," is denied from two different points of view. The first view accepts determinism, indeed insists on it, because of the findings of modern medicine and psychotherapy, and then argues the invalidity of judgments of responsibility in any and every case. The second accepts the validity of the principle of responsibility, but denies the validity of the postulate of determinism or of its universal applicability.

2

Those who believe that one cannot legitimately square the doctrine of determinism with the acceptance of responsibility argue generally as follows: an individual is neither responsible nor blamable for his actions unless he could have acted differently from the way he did. Given the sum total of conditions which preceded his action, the latter is in principle always predictable or determined, and therefore unavoidable. But if an action is unavoidable, then no one can be held morally responsible for it.

The usual retort to this is to point out that an act is determined, among other things, by a wish or desire or volition for which we shall use the generic term "choice." Consequently it is sometimes true to say that if an individual had chosen differently, he would have acted differently. To which the rejoinder comes that this is merely an evasion. If every event is in principle predictable and therefore determined, then the choice itself, given all the antecedent conditions, is unavoidable. An individual cannot be held morally responsible for his choice if it could not have been other than it was. And even if it were true that his choice now was a consequence of an earlier choice, which *if* it had been different *would* have led to different present choice and action, that earlier choice *could not* have been different, given its antecedent conditions, and so on for any other choice in the series. And since the choice could not have been different, we cannot blame the person choosing since he is not morally responsible. He is "a victim of circumstances."

There is a certain ambiguity in the writings of those who, accepting the principle of determinism, criticize the attribution of moral responsibility to individuals or the judgment of blameworthiness on their actions. Sometimes their criticism has an air of high moral concern. They imply that under certain circumstances, which they often spell out in advance, individuals are being improperly considered responsible. They inveigh against the injustice of improperly blaming those who, because their desires and choices are determined, are the victims not the agents of misfortune. This plea is sometimes forensically very effective, as the legal career of Clarence Darrow shows. Defending the accused in the Leopold-Loeb murder case, which is now enjoying a revival in popular concern, he said in his closing address to the jury, after quoting Housman's poem, the soliloquy of a boy about to be hanged, "I do not know what it was that made these boys do this mad act, but I know there is a reason for it. I know they did not beget themselves. I know that any one of an infinite number of causes reaching back to the beginning might be working out in these boys' minds, whom you are asked to hang in malice and in hatred and injustice, because someone in the past has sinned against them."

One does not, of course, look for precision in an *ex parte* plea. To a determinist, what difference does it make whether human beings are begotten by others, whether they reproduce by fission or by spontaneous generation in test tubes? In any case the process is determined. Of course we did not choose to be born. But suppose we did choose to be born: would that make us more responsible? The choice to be born would not be any less determined. And if the argument is that in a determined world, where our choices are bound to be what they are, it is unfair to blame anybody for any action to which that choice leads, how would we be better off, *i.e.*, more responsible, if we chose to be born? And if it is unjust to tax anyone with sinning who is not responsible for his being born, is it any more legitimate to speak of his being sinned against? If children cannot sin against parents, neither can parents sin against children.

Darrow's inconsistencies are less surprising than the fact that some sophisticated philosophers have adopted pretty much the same position.[1] They fortify it with complex and subtle elaborations of the findings of psychoanalysis as these bear upon the motives and compulsive behavior of men. Yet the logic of their argument makes all the evidence of psychoanalysis irrelevant to the question of blame and responsibility. For if every psychoanalytical theory were discarded as false, the life of mind would still be determined if one accepts the postulate of universal determinism. The piling up of the data which exhibit the specific mechanism of determination adds only a rhetorical force to the position. Further, it is one thing to imply that the concept of moral responsibility is empty, that although in fact no individuals are morally responsible, there are conditions or circumstances under which they could be legitimately held responsible; it is quite another thing to hold that the concept of moral responsibility is completely *vacuous,* that no matter what the specific conditions are under which men choose to act, it would still be inappropriate to hold them morally responsible or blame them. And it is this view *i.e.,* that moral responsibility is a vacuous or unintelligible expression, which seems to me to be entailed by those who urge Darrow's position, for they never seem able to indicate the rule or conditions for its proper use. If one cannot indicate any possible situation on a deterministic view under which actions can be blamed, the term "blame" is cognitively meaningless.

Nonetheless, the paradox of the position is that those who hold it, blame us for blaming others. Just as the burglar in our story makes an appeal whose sense depends upon there being alternatives, that is upon the possibility of making or not making that specific appeal, so some philosophers find us blameworthy for not acting on the recognition that in a determined world in which no one chooses to be born, no one can be held at fault.

3

I think it will be pretty generally admitted that whether a person could or could not have acted differently (or have chosen to act differently), it is a fact that we do blame him for an action which is evil, if it is apparent that he is the cause of it. Whether we *should* blame him for the action is a question which we cannot decide without reflection, *i.e.,* cannot decide until we discover whether what is apparently so, is actually so. "We should think in each case before we should blame" is a maxim universally agreed upon by all writers in this age-old discussion. But if "should blame" is an unintelligible expression, then so is "should think." If anyone interposes and objects that the belief that a person could not have acted (or chosen) differently under the circumstances entails the view that it is impermissible "to blame" or "to hold responsible," then by the same logic the belief that a person could not have thought differently entails the view that it is impermissible to say that "he should" or "he should not have" thought as he did. A philosopher who took that alleged entailment seriously would not only have to abandon the expressions "should have blamed" and "should not have blamed"—and restrict himself to asking whether "we *will*" or "we *will not*" blame—(an entirely different kind of question from the one which provoked the discussion originally)—he would have to forswear the use of "should" and "should not" in every other normative context.

This is not, as we shall see, merely a dialectical or debating point. It cuts the nerve of the argument of those who believe, like Darrow, that their position necessarily makes for greater humanity and kindliness. As a matter of fact, such a position often makes for sentimentality—the refusal to blame or punish where blame and punishment may prevent actions which are undesirable. It often leads to pity for the criminal as a victim, not of a special set of particular circumstances which might have made it harder for him than for others to refrain from committing a crime, but as a victim of any circumstance in general (referred to as heredity and environment or the sway of the law of causality). This is sometimes carried to the point where there is not sufficient pity or compassion left for the criminal's victims, not only for his past victims but his future ones and the victims of others whose action the criminal may inspire. To blame and to punish, of course, are two distinct things logically (except when blame is considered a form of punishment), but psychologically there is a great reluctance to punish if one believes blame is absent. Darrow argued on the abstract *a priori* grounds of universal determinism that all men were blameless, and with his dramatic pleas often won acquittals, not on the specific evidence, but despite it. Yet surely, if needless pain and cruelty are evils, then punishment which prevents or deters actions likely to result in much greater pain and cruelty than it imposes on the guilty, is obviously the lesser evil. Without being a saint, one can forgive the pain a criminal causes to oneself; but not even a saint can claim that this therefore justifies him in forgiving the criminal the pain he causes others.

In passing I should like to comment on some peripheral points, confusion about which seems to have encouraged the view that belief in the incompatibility of determinism and moral responsibility is a mark of enlightenment. The first is that if one holds human beings blameless, one will necessarily treat them more humanely and eliminate capital punishment. But actually the issue of capital punishment has nothing to do with the question of determinism and responsibility. The valid argument against capital punishment is that its abolition makes the rectification of occasional injustice possible. But such an argument presupposes precisely what Darrow and those who think like him deny, *i.e.*, that it is blameworthy to punish an innocent man. And as for the humanitarian aspect of the situation, although Darrow won the Leopold-Loeb case with a plea for imprisonment of the criminals rather than their execution, the judge in announcing sentence declared: "Life imprisonment, at the moment, strikes the public imagination less forcibly than would death by hanging; but to the offenders, particularly of the type they are, the prolonged suffering of years of confinement may well be the severest form of retribution and expiation."

It may be argued that nonetheless there is a psychological if not logical connection between the view that determinism strictly entails the absence of moral responsibility and the abandonment of retributive punishment. This can be challenged on many grounds. From Augustine to Calvin and their latter-day followers, the torment of eternal damnation is assigned and approved independently of moral responsibility. It is not related of the oft-cited Puritan who piously observed to his son when they saw a man being led to the gallows: "There but for the grace of God go I," that he opposed retributive punishment. Nor could the determinist of this kind say that he morally *should* repudiate retributive punishment since he cannot help believing it. On the other hand, if it is retributive punishment which is the target of the analysis, there is no necessary logical connection between a belief in moral responsibility and approval of retributive punishment. Certainly those determinists who assign responsibility to actions only when there is reason to believe that blame or punishment will modify future conduct are hardly likely to defend retributive punishment which is directed exclusively to the past.

4

Although the concept of moral responsibility in a deterministic system is neither empty nor vacuous, it is far from having a clear meaning in ordinary usage and experience. Before discussing it further I wish to comment briefly upon the position of those who accept the validity of the concept of moral responsibility, but believe they must therefore contest the belief in the postulate of determinism. Now it may be granted straightaway that we cannot prove that all events have sufficient causes, such that given these causes the events must occur. This is a postulate which we accept because of its fruitfulness in enabling us to predict and control our experience. Nor is it necessary to assume on the basis of this postulate that we can predict in principle the occurrence or emergence of all qualities of events. What is absolutely novel in experience cannot be derived either deductively or inductively from the qualities of the initial conditions or given data from which, together with general laws, we predict future events. Nonetheless we know enough about human behavior under everyday as well as laboratory conditions to make a reasonable induction that, given certain antecedent conditions, certain choices will be made (or even more strongly, certain choices are unavoidable). That we cannot always infallibly predict how people will choose is no more a decisive consideration against the belief that with more knowledge we can increase the accuracy of our predictions of human choices, than the fact that we cannot always infallibly predict the behavior of things is a decisive consideration against reliance upon the laws of physics. Now those who hold that the belief in moral responsibility entails an acceptance of indeterminism do not believe that *nothing* in the world is determined. They admit that some events, including some choices, are determined. And of the choices they believe undetermined, they are prepared to grant that certain *necessary* conditions of their occurrence exists. They deny that these undetermined choices follow from any set of *sufficient* conditions.

The difficulty with this view, as I see it, is that the distinction between determined and allegedly undetermined choices does not always correspond with the attributions we make or refuse to make of moral responsibility. It is sometimes said that in human relations the prediction that an individual will choose a certain course of conduct, if publicly made, has a consequence which may affect his choice. Suppose I predict that you will refuse to give alms to the beggar. You therefore set out to disprove my statement. Knowing this will be your reaction, I make a fresh prediction that you

will give alms because I say you won't. Realizing I am now count-
ing on your being shamed into giving alms, you truculently may
refuse to do so. And no matter what further prediction I make,
that prediction will have an effect which presumably I cannot rely
on. Therefore, concludes Maurice Cranston, from whom I borrow
the illustration, "that is why I say predictions made to you about
you are impossible." [2] Karl Popper and D. M. MacKay have argued
in a similar vein that "any proffered description of your choice
would automatically be self-invalidating." The law of determinism
even for macroscopic phenomena breaks down.

I do not believe such predictions are impossible, but let us grant
the point for the sake of the argument. Now consider two situations. In the first I make a successful prediction about you but not
to you, concerning your behavior or choice at the sight of a beggar
in great distress. Here the choice or action is determined. In the
second, I make an unsuccessful prediction to you about you, in
relation to the beggar. Here your choice is allegedly undetermined.
But now would anyone seriously maintain that you were not
morally responsible for the action which I successfully predicted,
but you were morally responsible for the action which I failed to
predict because it was unpredictable? Unless other factors are
introduced, it seems to me that you would hold yourself, and be
held by others, equally responsible for your action with respect
to the beggar in distress, quite independently of the success of the
prediction, independently of whether I made the prediction *to*
you or *about* you to someone else. The predictability or unpre-
dictability of the choice seems irrelevant to the question of its moral
responsibility. And all this aside from the fact that it is highly
disputable whether predictions made to you about you are in principle unconfirmable. All of us have seen human beings cleverly
and unscrupulously manipulated by individuals who make predictions of their behavior to their face and shrewdly calculate the
reactions to the predictions. A man who dares another to jump
knowing that the person dared hardly ever resists a dare and that
the leap in question is very hazardous, may be guilty of murder.

The great difficulty with the indeterminist view in most forms
is the suggestion it carries that choices and actions, if not determined, are capricious. Caprice and responsibility are more difficult to reconcile than determinism and responsibility, for it seems

easier to repudiate a choice or action which does not follow from one's character, or history, or nature, or self, than an act which does follow. Consequently, the more thoughtful indeterminists are those who do not deny the operation of determining forces or tendencies altogether, but insist upon a certain kind of determination which manifests itself in addition to, or over and above, the factors extrinsic to the particular situation in which the choosing individual finds himself. For example, they believe that the free action is not the habitual action, not the coerced action, not the instinctive or impulsive action, but the action which is determined by reflection. And as we shall see, there is a sense in which ordinarily we do characterize an action as responsible, depending upon whether it was intended, and if intended, upon the character and extent of the reflection which preceded it. But so long as "reasons" are not disembodied entities but express reflective choices of men in nature, there is nothing here at which a determinist need boggle. On the contrary, he may define the locus of moral freedom and responsibility in the capacity of the human creature, using his insight and foresight, to modify his preferences and control his inclinations whenever they conflict or lead to "actions involving others."

Not only indeterminists who recognize moral responsibility, but some determinists who regard it as an empty concept, write as if a person would be responsible if he could "ultimately and completely shape or choose his own character." Surely the notion of ultimately and completely shaping or choosing one's own character is more difficult to grasp than any it would illumine. Since every decision to shape or choose one's character, to be responsibly attributed to oneself, must be one's own, and therefore is already an indication of the kind of person one is, the notion that one can ultimately and completely shape or choose one's character seems to be unintelligible. C. A. Campbell in a stimulating article [3] distinguishes between a choice which is the expression of a formed character, and therefore determined, and a choice of a self. But aside from the difficulty of separating self from character, it is hard to understand why we should be more willing to accept responsibility or blame for the decision of a raw or pure self that has no history, than to accept responsibility or blame for the choices of our formed characters.

5

We return now to consider some of the difficulties which the determinist faces who attributes blame or responsibility to himself or others. If all actions are in principle predictable or unavoidable, how can he blame the actor? If every judgment of "ought" or "should" implies a "can" or "could," and if of every act we can say (once given its antecedent conditions) that it cannot or could not have been avoided, why blame, why praise, why, indeed, in a determined universe, pass any moral judgment whatsoever, whether it be on a petty sneak-thief or on a Hitler or Stalin?

I shall try to show that the difficulty lies uniquely in the use of the concept of blame, not of praise, and not of moral judgment *per se*. The difficulty in the concept of blame is that ordinary usage is itself confusing, that the confusion requires a reconstruction of our use in such a way as to bring out more consistently and systematically the pragmatic character of judgments of blame. I do not believe that if we guide ourselves by ordinary usage we can make ends meet, because in this instance ordinary usage is vague and inconsistent.

First of all, although it may be difficult to square the belief that all choices are determined with judgments of blame and responsibility, I do not see that there is any difficulty in squaring the belief that all choices are determined with the moral judgment that these choices, and the actions to which they lead, are good or bad. Pain is evil, and an intentional action which imposes unnecessary pain, or a desire to impose unnecessary pain, is wicked. After all, we blame persons only for those acts of omission or commission which we condemn. If such actions were not initially or antecedently judged good or bad, we could not blame anybody for failing to do the one, or failing to prevent the other. No matter whether an action is determined or undetermined, accidental or intentional, I can still pronounce it good or bad. We may not blame the child whose actions cause the house to burn, or the maniac who kills those who minister to his wants; but we can and do deplore and condemn these actions as bad. And I believe that this is legitimate from the standpoint of any analysis of the meaning of "good" or "bad" which philosophers have offered, except the Kantian analysis. So, too, although there are difficulties about feelings of "remorse" similar to those about judgments of blame, I can only feel remorse about something I regret, and the qualities of the action I regret are what they are, independently of whether the action is determined or not.

It is sometimes said that if it is unwarranted to pass judgments of blame on actions that are predictable or unavoidable, it is also unwarranted to pass judgments of praise. I am not so sure of this, because of the broader semantic range of judgments of praise. When we praise a person for his or her beauty, talent, intelligence, charm, personality, warmth, etc., etc., we do not have in mind at all whether or not the person could help being or doing that which evokes our praise. Formally, we can always praise a person for not committing an act that we would blame, and in this sense the logic of the judgments is symmetrical. But aside from such cases, and some others in which praise seems to be justified because an individual might have acted differently, e.g., in which he fights against odds instead of running away, there is an indefinitely large number of situations in which we unembarrassedly praise, regardless of whether the person can help being as he is or acting as he does. And when judgments of praise do not have this character, they may plausibly be regarded as having the social function of inducing individuals to do what we regard as desirable and to forgo doing the undesirable. But if it is possible to carry out such an analysis without difficulty for judgments of praise, is it possible to do so for judgments of blame and attributions of moral responsibility?

The facts of responsibility must be distinguished from their justification. By facts of responsibility I mean that in every society there are social relations or institutional arrangements which are regarded as binding on human behavior, for violations of which human beings are called to account. When individuals are called to account, this involves the possibility that sanctions may be applied. These facts of responsibility are an anthropological datum—varied and multiform. In some cultures children are held responsible for their parents; in others, parents for children. Leaving aside questions of legal responsibility, or rather legal liability, which are often only matters of social convenience and rules of the road, the justification of responsibility is a moral question. Should a child be held personally responsible for the sins of its

father, not only for the Biblical three generations, but even for
one? Should a parent ever be held responsible for the misdeeds of
his children? Now those who hold that determinism is incompatible with reasoned judgments of blame presumably do not
mean to deny the existence of the facts of responsibility. They
simply contest the justification of the facts—not the justification of
any specific fact of responsibility, but the possibility of any justification whatsoever on the determinist view. If this were true, then,
since social life is impossible without recognition of some kind of
responsibility in behavior, the whole basis of social life would
appear utterly unintelligible, or if justified, only by some extrinsic
consideration that had no moral relevance. But, as our illustration
shows, there are obviously good reasons why in general we regard
it as more justifiable to blame parents up to a point for the misdeeds of their children than to blame children for the misdeeds of
their parents. First, we know there is some causal connection between the training or absence of training which parents give their
children and the children's behavior outside the home, a causal
connection which is not reversible; second, and more important,
we blame parents for their children rather than children for their
parents, primarily because in this way we can get more desirable
conduct on the part of both parents and children. We influence
the future by our judgments of blame and, to the extent that they
are not merely judgments of spontaneous admiration or excellence,
by our judgments of praise as well.

6

There are some obvious difficulties with this interpretation of
judgments of blame. For example, as C. A. Campbell observes, we
can influence the future behavior of infants and animals by punishment, but we certainly do not blame them when we are reflective. On the other hand, we do not seem to be able to influence
the future behavior of the hardened criminal, but we certainly do
blame him. Further, how explain remorse, as distinct from regret,
for actions committed long ago?
Because the behavior of children and animals is modifiable by
appropriate reward and deprivation, we punish them, even though
we may hesitate to use the term to identify what we do. We do not

"blame" them, however, even when we find it necessary to punish, because blame is directed to volitions, or, if we do not believe in volitions, to intentions. If children's actions reveal intentions or if we suspect, as we sometimes do, that animals have intentions, we count upon the sting of our blame to prod them to different behavior. Otherwise there is no point in blaming. But, it is objected, this only tells us whether our blame is effective rather than deserved. The blame is "deserved" if the action we wish to correct is bad, and the worse the action the more deserved—provided the blame has point in the first place. When we distribute blame— as when we say "I blame you more than I do him"—it is because we believe that the intentions (or volitions) of the one had a greater role in the commission of the act, or could have a greater role in preventing similar actions in the future, than the intention of the other. We must be able to answer the question; what is the use of blaming any individual? before we can properly distribute blame among individuals. I can see no earthly use of blaming an individual save directly or indirectly to prevent the undesirable act from being repeated in the future. This is the justification for blame in a determined world.

Another element enters into the picture. The more rational an individual is, the more susceptible he is to understanding and giving reasons, the more blameworthy we hold him—not because the intelligent man's choice is less determined than that of the stupid man's but because the choice, which is determined among other things by insight into reasons, is generally more informed, more persistent, and more decisive in redetermining the stream of events. We blame children more as they approach the age of rationality, not because they come into possession of a soul, not because they become more subject to causal laws, but because the growth of intelligence enhances the subtlety, range, and effectiveness of their choice. And if animals could think or respond to reasons, we would blame them, too, because we could build up within them a sense of blame, shame, and responsibility. A sense of blame, shame, and responsibility has a sound therapeutic use in the moral education of men.

Why, then, do we blame the hardened criminal for his actions, when the continued life of crime makes blame and punishment almost as inefficacious in his case—so it is said—as in the case of an alcoholic, a dope addict, or a kleptomaniac? I believe here that most people in blaming a hardened offender are blaming him for the entire series of his actions and not only for his latest action; what revolts them is the cumulative series of evil things done; and they make the mistake of running these evils together, as if it were one great evil which one great blame or punishment might effectively forestall in the future, if not for the offender in question then for others. If, however, one were to isolate the latest dereliction of the hardened offender, and show that no blame or punishment one can devise is more likely to modify his conduct than blame or punishment can prevent an alcoholic addict from drinking or a kleptomaniac from stealing or a pyromaniac from arson, then I believe blame of the hardened criminal would be pointless. We would tend to regard him as criminally insane, confine him without blaming him.

It is sometimes said that we can legitimately blame only when the person blamed has failed to do his duty or live up to an obligation, and that wherever a person has a duty, wherever we say he "ought" to do something, then he in fact "could have" done so. As I have already indicated, I am not at all sure that our actual usage of terms like "blame," "duty," or "ought" in life and law bears this out. In some contexts "ought" clearly does not entail or even imply "can." "A, the contestant in a quiz, ought to have answered x instead of y to question z" is perfectly intelligible and leaves completely open the question whether he could or could not answer question z, or even see question z. Even in strictly moral situations, when I say "Since he was on guard duty, he ought not to have fallen asleep," I am not sure that I am implying necessarily that this particular soldier could have stayed awake, although I am undoubtedly referring to the general capacities of soldiers. But it is undoubtedly true that the evidence that this particular soldier had not slept for seventy-two hours and was assigned to guard duty by mistake, or that he suffered from sleeping sickness, leads to the judgment that he is not as blameworthy as a sentry who had had normal sleep and enjoyed perfect health. That the actions of both sentries, given the antecedent conditions, were determined or predictable, although in one case it was easier than in the other, seems irrelevant. Yet in one case we say that the sentry could not help falling asleep, and in the second we say he could help it. This produces the appearance of paradox. But if one is challenged to explain the judgment, he would probably say that no matter how hard the first sentry tried, it would not have helped him stay awake, whereas if the second sentry had tried, thoroughly rested and thoroughly healthy as he was, he could have remained awake. The distinction between what one can and what one cannot help doing is perfectly intelligible to a determinist, even though in concrete situations it may be difficult to determine which is which. Normally we do not go beyond that distinction. To the question: could he help trying? we normally reply in the affirmative, and expect the burden of proof to rest upon the person who claims that the second sentry could not help not trying because say (a) either he had been doped or (b) hypnotized. In both cases we are prepared to make allowances or excuses for anything which seems to be an external constraint upon choice or volition. But merely because an action is caused, it is not therefore excused.

Our ordinary common-sense judgments are here rather faltering, because the criteria of what is an external constraint as distinct from an internal constraint, and the distinction between an internal constraint which has originally been set up by an outside agency and one which develops naturally within the system, are vague. The progress of science affects our moral judgment of wrongdoers by uncovering the *specific* factors which tend to make the *wrongdoing* uncontrollable by the volition or decision of the agent involved. If one believes that alcoholism is a disease which operates independently of what one wishes or of how one tries, one will judge differently from the way one will if alcoholism is regarded merely as a bad habit. In law as in common sense, the individual is expected to take responsibility for what is self-determined, for one's character or the kind of person one is, even though no one is completely self-determined. If A develops a fateful passion for B, given A's character, then although there may seem to be a tragic inevitability about the course of the affair, we normally do not expect A to duck responsibility by claiming that he could not help being born, or could not help having the character he has. However, if A, as in Tristan and Isolde, is the victim of a love potion administered by others, we are likely to feel and judge quite differently; for in that case it is not A's choice, but someone else's choice, which coerces his own. The cause was of a compelling kind.

I venture to suggest that in all these cases the difference in our response does not depend upon our belief that in one class of situations the individuals are free to choose and in another they are not, but on the belief that, where responsibility and blame are appropriate, the uncompelled choice had some determining influence on the action, and that *our* judgments of responsibility and blame will have some influence upon the future choice of actions of the person judged, as well as on the actions of all other persons contemplating similar measures.

7

I believe that considerations of this character are acted upon in many different fields of experience, and that where we excuse human beings from responsibility, it is not because of a belief in determinism generally, but only because specific investigation reveals specific causes which are interpreted as of a "compelling" nature. Here is a person who is suffering from a very violent skin eruption accompanied by general malaise. Inquiry reveals that he is allergic to every variety of sea food. Now if he continues to eat sea food, we properly regard him as responsible for his plight. If he continues to bemoan his condition, we are inclined to think of him as a self-indulgent whiner who either does not know what he wants or wants to eat his eels but with impunity. However, if on the basis of independent evidence, we are convinced that he really wants to get rid of his allergy and its effects, then we suspect that perhaps some hidden hunger for iodine or some other element plentiful in sea food compels him despite himself to persist in his food habits. We no longer blame him. His craving for iodine is like the thirst of a diabetic. But if iodine in some other form is available, we expect him to take it. If he refuses, we revise our judgment once again. Given the antecedent conditions, the choice, of course, was unavoidable. But wherever it is possible to alter these conditions by informed action, *that* particular choice can no longer be regarded as unavoidable.

The law, when enlightened, offers perhaps the best illustrations of the relevant distinctions, especially in considering cases of those suspected of insanity. The McNaughton Rules, which until recently guided judges in Anglo-American countries, have been

severely criticized for being too narrow in their conception of what
constitutes responsibility in adults charged with crime. As far as
they go, however, they recognize the distinction between a voluntary and an involuntary act. They exonerate a person of diseased
mind from responsibility. Where the death sentence obtains, this
means that the person of diseased mind cannot be executed. But
these Rules conceive of mental disease primarily as "a defect of
reason." A person of diseased mind is one who does not know what
he is doing, or who did not know that what he was doing was
against the law. Although humane at the time they were formulated, the McNaughton Rules no longer reflect what we know today, or believe we know, about mental disease. According to these
Rules, the "Mad Bomber of New York," whose actions showed that
he knew very well what he was doing and that what he was doing
was against the law, would have to be declared sane although he
fervently believed that what he was doing—planting bombs in
public places—was an appropriate way of getting even with the
Consolidated Edison Company. Anyone found insane under the
McNaughton Rules certainly could not have his behavior influenced by blame or punishment, since he does not know what he
is doing and whether it is legal or not. Today insanity is considered
a disabling emotional disorder; even if the unfortunate person has
sufficient wit to know that he is violating the law, he may still be
so emotionally disturbed as to be "beyond influence" by any threat
of blame or punishment. Because an "emotional disorder" is a
vaguer and more comprehensive term than knowledge or a defect
of knowledge, it is more difficult to apply, particularly when individuals plead temporary insanity or uncontrollable impulse. But
in all cases the rough-and-ready test is whether blame and punishment would tend to influence future behavior in similar situations.

This also explains why in the absence of a case history of emotional disorder we are, or should be, rightly suspicious of pleas
that at the time a crime was committed the individual did not have
sufficient power to prevent himself from committing it. "Tem-
porarily insane" sounds like insanity made to order. Nonetheless,
both in law and morals we do recognize situations in which, as the
Scottish phrase goes, a person is guilty but with diminished responsibility. This may range from actions of self-defense to actions
provoked by gross infidelity. It may be argued, however, that in

many of these situations of "diminished responsibility," in which the subject is unquestionably sane, a severe sentence may have the effect of increasing responsibility.

One of the obvious absurdities of the view that judgments of blame and responsibility cannot be squared with an acceptance of thoroughgoing determinism is that it wipes out or ignores the relevance of distinctions between the sane and insane, and undercuts the basis of rational legal and moral judgment with respect to intentional and unintentional actions. It suggests that the difference between the criminal and non-criminal is *merely* a matter of accidental power, that the difference between the sane and insane, the responsible and irresponsible, is only a question of majority and minority. It even goes so far as to call all moral terms into dispute. In the words of Clarence Darrow, "I do not believe that there is any sort of distinction between the moral condition in and out of jail. One is just as good as the other. The people here [in jail] can no more help being here than the people outside can avoid being outside. I do not believe that people are in jail because they deserve to be. They are in jail simply because they cannot avoid it, on account of circumstances which are entirely beyond their control and for which they are in no way responsible." To analyze this seems as cruel as dissecting a butterfly, except that its contradictions and sentimentalities have been incorporated in the attitudes of many social workers. But all we need ask is what sense the word "deserve" has on Darrow's view. If no action can *possibly* merit deserved punishment, on what ground can any punishment be justifiably considered "undeserved"? Once more we ask: if the people in jail can no more help being there than the people outside of jail can help being outside, how can those outside help jailing those on the inside? And, if they can't help it, why condemn them?

The belief that because men are determined they cannot be morally responsible is a mistaken one. Not only is it a mistaken belief, it is a mischievous one. For far from diminishing the amount of needless suffering and cruelty in the world, it is quite certain to increase it. It justifies the infamous dictum of Smerdyakov in *The Brothers Karamazov:* "All things are permissible," if only one can get away with them. One of the commonest experiences of teachers, if not parents, is to observe young men and women whose belief that they can't help doing what they are doing, or failing to do, is often an excuse for not doing as well as they can do, or at the very least better than they are at present doing. When we have, as we often do, independent evidence that they are capable of doing better, is it so absurd to hold them at least partly responsible for not doing better? Do we not know from our own experience that our belief that we are responsible, or that we will be held responsible, enables us to do things which had previously seemed beyond our power?

I do not think that the theories of psychoanalysis contradict the belief that moral responsibility is a valid concept of psychological experience. If they did it would be only additional evidence of their unempirical character. At any rate some psychoanalysts agree with Franz Alexander, who writes: "The fundamental principle, however, no matter what practical disposition is made [of the criminal delinquent] is that every person must be held responsible for the consequences of his acts." He concludes that this sense of moral responsibility is not only indispensable to society, but to individual growth. "A person reared according to the principle of responsibility will eventually internalize this feeling of responsibility towards others as a responsibility towards himself as well."

I must confess, however, that I find psychoanalytic literature full of inconsistencies on the subject, most of them present in Freud. For example, Freud's answer to the question: "Should a person be held responsible for his dreams, which are the products of unconscious forces over which he has no conscious control?" was, "Who else but the dreamer should be responsible for his dreams?" This seems to me a clear equivocation. The question speaks of *moral* responsibility. Freud replies in terms of causal attribution. Certainly if in a sleepwalking dream an individual did something hurtful or mischievous, no reasonable person would hold him morally or legally responsible.

What often passes as irremediable evil in the world, or the inevitable ills and suffering to which the flesh is heir, is a consequence of our failure to act in time. We are responsible, whether we admit it or not, for what it is in our power to do; and most of the time we can't be sure what is in our power to do until we attempt it. If only we are free to try, we don't have to claim also to be free to try to try, or look for an ultimate footing in some prime metaphysical indeterminate to commit ourselves responsibly. Proximate freedom is enough. And although what we are now is determined by what we were, what we will be is still determined also by what we do now. Human effort can within limits re-determine the direction of events even though it cannot determine the conditions which make human effort possible. It is time enough to reconcile oneself to what is unalterable, or to disaster, after we have done our best to overcome them.

There are some people—even some philosophers—who, observing the human scene, declare themselves unable to give an intelligible meaning to judgments of human responsibility. They say: "It's all a matter of luck." This is no more sensible than saying, "Nothing is a matter of luck," even if "luck" has an intelligible meaning in a determined world. It is true that we did not choose to be born. But from this it only follows that we should not blame or punish anyone merely for being born, whether he is black or white, male or female. It is also true that we choose, most of us adults who are sound of limb and mind, to keep on living. And if we do, we bear a contributory responsibility for remaining in the world. The Stoics, who so lamentably confused physics and ethics, were right in pointing out that most of us are free to leave "life's smoky chamber." It is not true that everything which happens to us is like "being struck down by a dread disease." The treatment and cure of disease, to use an illustration that can serve as a moral paradigm of the whole human situation, would never have begun unless we believed that some things which were did not have to be; that they could be different; and that *we* could make them different. And what we can make different, we are responsible for.

With respect to judgments of blame and responsibility, the pragmatic theory stresses not the multiplication of such judgments, but only their use as means of individual help and social protection. It eschews the automatic judgment of blame and responsibility, in order to devote itself to the difficult task of discriminating in the light of all the relevant scientific evidence what it is reasonable or unreasonable to expect from a human being in the situation in which he finds himself. It also expresses a certain human ideal of man as a contributing maker or creator of his own destiny, rather than as a passive creature of fate. Sickness, accident, or incapacity aside, we feel lessened as human beings if our actions are always excused or explained away on the ground that, despite appearances, we are really not responsible for them. For whoever treats us this way is treating us like an object or an infant, or like someone out of his mind. Our dignity as rational human beings sometimes leads us to protest when an overzealous friend seeks to extenuate our conduct on the ground that we are not really responsible, that we are either too stupid to know, or too lost in illusion, really to intend to do what we actually have done. There are times when this unfortunately is only too true. But there are also times when we burst out and declare that we really are responsible, that we know what we are doing and are prepared to take the consequences. As bad as the priggishness of the self-righteous is the whine of the self-pitying. To the extent that the priggishness and the whine follow from mistaken beliefs about blame and responsibility, they are both avoidable. In the end, but only in the end, our character is our fate. But until the end, it is a developing pattern on which we work with whatever courage and intelligence we have. To that extent we make our character.

The Ethical Theory
of John Dewey

*"In morals there are immediate goods, the desired,
and reasonable goods, the desirable."*—DEWEY

The sterility of most discussions of the nature of value has long been a source of complaint. One of the causes of this sterility, it seems to me, is that the approach to human values has not been sufficiently empirical, even on the part of some theories that regard themselves as empirical. Another reason is that too much emphasis has been placed upon preliminary *definitions* of value. As distinct from attempted definitions of qualities and relations in other fields, such discussions have usually turned into an analysis of the nature of definitions—sometimes into an analysis of analysis—as if this were a necessary preliminary both to a definition of value and to subsequent investigation of the relationships between values and the conditions of their discovery.

Most philosophers are ready enough to admit that in other fields definitions should be laid down at the conclusion of investigations, or, when a subject matter has been sufficiently organized to permit some control over the adequacy of the definition. But this procedure has rarely been followed by philosophers in the field of value. Among the things a definition of value must be adequate to is, of course, common usage. But common usage, it seems clear, is not the only control over adequacy, if only because common usage is inconsistent and may change overnight because of other changes, for example a dictator's decree, which all investigators into the nature of values agree are irrelevant to what they are trying to understand. The problem then becomes what kinds and occasions of common usage are relevant. Unless it is assumed that there is some natural language sense, universal in extent, which can be disclosed by peeling away different layers of conventional usage, we cannot justifiably ignore the possible relevance of such questions as: *why* do people speak as they do? *what* events in their experience account for this one or that particular usage? *what* observational tests enable us to determine what they mean? This takes us outside of verbal usage to other human behavioral facts. Otherwise we remain in the predicament of trying to get insight into the nature of ethical behavior, merely by examining what are allegedly the rules of good linguistic usage and, indeed, of *English* usage. Imagine what would happen if at the United Nations someone were to attempt to criticize the ethical pronouncements of representatives of other countries on the ground that they were illegitimate or prohibited by the standards of good English usage!

This situation would hardly arise in other fields of study in which questions of conflicting usage arise. There is a clear sense, for example, in common usage in which *both* "position" and "velocity" can be attributed at the same time to anything that moves. When the physicists declare that under certain conditions it is illegitimate to attribute both of these predicates at the same time to a given particle, they are apparently running counter to common usage. Nothing would seem to be more futile than to dispute their statement, as some seem inclined to do, on the ground that it violates common usage. The question which should concern us is: What in the experimental situation leads them to say what they do?

Corresponding in ethical discussion to the attempt to get back of the question of correct usage in other fields, is reference to the empirical facts of moral behavior, including the facts of conflict and disagreement as well as those of agreement. Any credible theory of value must do justice not only to how people talk but to how they behave in other ways. It is not necessary to begin with a pre-

cise definition of the meaning of value any more than an investigation of color theory begins with a definition of color or biological
investigation of the nature of frogs begins with a definition of
frogs. It is enough to begin with an assorted selection of colored
things or frogs or value facts and then to formulate some conception of the quality or thing in question, which will enable us to
organize more effectively our other knowledge about it and facilitate the subsequent process of inquiry and systematization. Ultimately the test of a good definition—and all definitions are in some
sense analytic—is whether it makes it easier to relate in a significant
and fruitful way our existing knowledge without establishing semantic or other blockages to the discovery or recognition of new
knowledge. Definitions are adequate or inadequate, not true or
false like the primary statements of observation with which knowledge begins and always ends. But the fact that they are justified or
controlled by the consequences of their use gives them a cognitive
status that purely arbitrary nominal definitions do not have.

The most obvious empirical fact often disregarded in current
discussion is that questions about specific values in human experience arise out of problematic situations. Such questions arise when
habitual responses are insufficient to sustain the free flow of experience or when these responses are challenged by others and we
grope for a guide or justification. This is a commonplace, but if it
is *dismissed* as a commonplace, as if it had no further bearing upon
judgment of value, subsequent discussion has removed itself from
the most important element of *control*.

The fact that questions of evaluation arise out of problematic
situations is not a discovery of John Dewey. It is recognized in the
classic formulation of the fundamental problem of ethics: What
should we do? When we ask such a question we are implying that
the answer will be a proposed decision, a decision to do not something in general but something specific from a number of alternative modes of action all relevant to the problem that evoked the
question, and that a satisfactory answer will indicate *why* one
proposed decision is to be selected rather than others. The good
of that situation will be the realized object of the decision.

In making such a judgment of value are we making empirical
cognitions that are certifiable by the methods of scientific or rational inquiry? Or are such judgments merely judgments of feel-

ing, true or false, depending upon whether we have them or not? Or are they no judgments at all, but merely or primarily expressions of attitude or commands?

Before answering these questions a number of observations must be made about what such a situation involves. First of all, whenever we are mature enough to make a decision or even begin to be puzzled, we never start *de novo* or from scratch. We carry with us a heavily funded memory of things previously discovered to be valuable, ends or goods to which we feel committed as prima facie validities. The list will not be the same for everybody or for any one all the time, but it will contain values like health, friendship, security, knowledge, art, amusement in their plural forms. It will also include certain general rules like thoughtfulness, honesty and truthfulness, which are the conditions of any social life in which human values are systematically pursued and sufficiently enjoyed to make social peace preferable to civil war.

Secondly, the situation is one that demands a choice between incompatible alternatives, not the application of a fixed universal rule to a concrete case, which could be done perhaps by a complex calculating machine.

Third, the choice involved in moral deliberation is between conflicting ends of a kind that will determine or redetermine the character or disposition of the agent. That is why there is no sharp decision between knowledge relevant to moral situations and other types of knowledge. Any problem of choice may become a moral problem when our own relatively permanent dispositions of character are involved, because they bear on relationships which involve other human beings. Any act acquires a moral character as soon as it has consequences for others that could have been foreseen.

Fourth, the resolution of any concrete problem is a conclusion about what is most worth while doing here and now, in this place and this time. We *assume* that certain ends of action are valid in the course of our deliberation and that certain consequences of the means used in removing the conflicts between ends are satisfactory. Now we can go through the verbal motions of challenging these consequences as themselves satisfactory. If we justify *them* by reference to further consequences, we can raise the same question over and over again. So long as the discussion remains on the plane of a purely theoretical possibility, there seems to be a danger of an

infinite regress. But the point cannot be too strongly emphasized
that ethical discussions are forced upon us by life situations and
their concrete problems. They do not grow out of talk. We do not
in *fact* ask why? why? why? unless there is some genuine perplexity,
some genuine need or difficulty which seems to coerce us into making a choice. It simply is *not* the case, and the adequacy of the
whole empirical approach to ethics depends upon recognizing it,
that before we can justify to ourselves a decision in the light of
consequences, we must justify these consequences, and the consequences of these consequences, and go on until we reach some consequence or other which in fact serves as an anchor ledge for the
whole, and which itself is forever beyond the possibility of being
challenged. In human experience there are no beginnings and
there are no final endings to the succession of moral problems. We
always find ourselves, and this is recognized not only by Dewey but
by other writers, like Stevenson, "in the middle course." There are
no ultimate values or judgments of value that are self-certifying in
the sense that they can never be reasonably challenged to justify
themselves.

Fifth, every envisagement of a possible decision in relation to a
problem is an incipient first step in the formation of a favorable
or unfavorable attitude to the objects involved. In one sense all
statements of fact in relation to problems put our body in a state
of motor readiness, but a statement about what should be done in
a problematic moral situation, because it expresses a special concern or urgency, has a quasi-imperative force. It is a preeminent
judgment of practice designed to move us and others to action.
There is not only a quasi-imperative force in the meaning of the
proposed ethical judgment, but an emotive influence as well. As
Dewey puts it: "A moral judgment, however intellectual it may
be, must at least be colored with feeling if it is to influence behavior."[1]

These verifiable characteristics of the problematic ethical situation will have a bearing upon the analysis of the meaning and
validity of value judgments. If they are true, then it will be clear
why immediate enjoyments as experiences which are merely *had*,
generate no problems even when different people have them. They
do not need to be warranted because their existence cannot be challenged, but only indicated either by a word or by a sound. There

may be a problem as to whether the proper word is being used to indicate them, for example, when someone is using a foreign tongue, or whether the sign of the enjoyment or suffering has not been masked for purposes of social amenity. But no problem of *valuation* attaches to them. It is in this particular sense that it is true to say: "Concerning tastes there is no disputing." Coffee tastes pleasant to me, it does not taste pleasant to you. No argument can alter the facts. Never is there a *conflict* of attitudes towards coffee as an experienced taste here and now. The difference in attitudes might become a conflict in attitudes when some such question is asked as: Should we order coffee again? Is coffee a more enjoyable drink than tea? If all a person means to assert by "coffee is good" is that at the moment he finds the coffee pleasant-tasting—and he knows that this is his meaning—it is an observable fact that he will never dispute with someone else who says: "Coffee is not good," if he understands this expression to mean that at the moment the other person finds it unpleasant-tasting.

But there is another sense in which we can, according to Dewey, very well dispute about tastes. This is the sense in which we ask: is this *truly* or *really* or *objectively* a good thing? and we find that our judgment of value is significantly denied or that it can be mistaken. Dewey uses the expressions, italicized in the previous sentence, interchangeably with what is genuinely "valuable" or "desirable." And he believes that whenever something enjoyed or desired is questioned, it becomes necessary to give adequate or relevant grounds for regarding what is desired as desirable or what is enjoyed as enjoyable.

In the first sense "the Good is that which satisfies want, craving, which fulfills or makes complete the need which stirs to action." [2] In the second sense, the good as something to be justified by thought "imposes upon those about to act the necessity for rational insight, or moral *wisdom*." Dewey goes on to add, "For experience shows that not every satisfaction of appetite and craving turns out to be a good; many ends *seem* good while we are under the influence of strong passion, which in actual experience and in such thought as might have occurred in a cool moment are actually bad."

This position has been the occasion of acute criticism by Professors Stevenson and White which I propose to examine. Since

Professor Stevenson's view is much closer to Dewey's than is Professor White's, I shall discuss the latter first.[3]

The nub of Professor White's criticism is that whereas "x is desired" is an empirical statement, "x is desirable," on Dewey's analysis, is not an empirical statement in the sense in which "x is desirable" and "x ought to be desired" are synonymous terms. Professor White argues that Dewey, like Mill, has been misled by the suffix ending of "desirable," *able,* except that Mill made the error in a cruder form by thinking that "desirable" is like "soluble," whereas Dewey makes the more subtle one of thinking it ("desirable") is a disposition-predicate like "objectively red"[4] or objectively hot, fluid or heavy. The difference between "soluble" and "objectively red" is that to say "x is soluble" is to say that it is capable of being dissolved. And if there are *any* conditions under which x dissolves, we can say it is soluble. One dissolution, so to speak, is as good as a million. For objectively red (or the other qualities) this is not true. Something may appear to be red without being objectively red, although everything which is objectively red will under determinate conditions appear red. "X is objectively red" is synonymous with "x looks red under normal conditions"[5] to normal people, but the fact that something appears blood red in the light of a garish sunset, is not sufficient for us to call it objectively red.

Dewey grants that "x is desired" does *not* mean "x is desirable." Indeed, he insists on this. Otherwise there would be no problem for evaluation. But his mistake, according to Professor White, is to assume that "x is desirable" is equivalent to "x is desired under normal conditions." But "x is desired under normal conditions" is no more *normative* than "x looks red under normal conditions." On this analysis there is as much sense in saying "x ought to be desired" as "x ought to appear red."[6] Dewey would assert the first, but certainly not the second. But he should assert the second, so the criticism runs, if his analysis of the first were sound. Since neither he nor anyone else would do so, his analysis of "desirable" is unsound.

The relevant passages are from Dewey's *The Quest for Certainty:*

The formal statement may be given concrete content by pointing to the difference between the enjoyed and the enjoyable, the de-

sired and the desirable, the satisfying and the satisfactory. To say
that something is enjoyed is to make a statement about a fact,
something already in existence; it is not to judge the value of that
fact. There is no difference between such a proposition and one
which says that something is sweet or sour, red or black. It is just
correct or incorrect *and that is the end of the matter*. But to call an
object a value is to assert that it satisfies or fulfills certain conditions [p. 260].

If one likes a thing he likes it; that *is* a point about which there
can be no dispute:—although it is not easy to state just *what* is liked
as is frequently assumed. A judgment about what is *to be* desired and
enjoyed is, on the other hand, a claim on future action; it possesses
de jure and not merely *de facto* quality. It is a matter of frequent experience that likings and enjoyments are of all kinds, and that many
are such as reflective judgments condemn [pp. 262–3].

To assume that anything can be known in isolation from its connections with other things is to identify knowing with merely having some
object before perception or in feeling, and is thus to lose the key to
the traits that distinguish an object as known. It is futile, even silly,
to suppose that some quality that is directly present constitutes the
whole of the thing presenting the quality. It does not do so when the
quality is that of being hot or fluid or heavy, and it does not when
the quality is that of giving pleasure, or being enjoyed. Such qualities
are, once more, effects, ends in the sense of closing termini of processes
involving causal connections. They are something to be investigated,
challenges to inquiry and judgment. The more connections and inter-
actions we ascertain, the more we *know* the object in question. Thinking is search for these connections. Heat experienced as a consequence
of directed operations has a meaning quite different from the heat that
is casually experienced without knowledge of how it came about. The
same is true of enjoyments. Enjoyments that issue from conduct directed by insight into relations have a meaning and validity due to
the way in which they are experienced. Such enjoyments are not re-
pented of; they generate no after-taste of bitterness. Even in the midst
of direct enjoyment, there is a sense of validity, of authorization,
which intensifies the enjoyment. There is solicitude for perpetuation
of the *object* having value which is radically different from mere
anxiety to perpetuate the *feeling* of enjoyment [p. 267].

The difficulty in Dewey's position, according to Professor White,
is that whereas statements like "x is desired," "x appears red,"
"x is objectively red" are all *de facto,* statements like "x is desir-

able," which are analogous to "x is objectively red," suddenly take
on *de jure* status, too. By a kind of transubstantiation the factual
becomes normative. "Here we have generated a normative or *de
jure* proposition by performing a suitable operation on merely
de facto propositions," [7] the complaint runs.

To begin with, it should be pointed out that Dewey is drawing
what he calls a "formal analogy" between the two kinds of qualities. He nowhere actually says that "x is desirable" is synonymous
with "x is desired under normal conditions." What formally cor-
responds to "normal conditions" where values are concerned is
"understood in the light of its causes and consequences." Where
what is desired, say a craving for a certain food, is understood in
the light of its cause, say a pathological state of the organism, it
will have a bearing on the desirability of the desired. Where what
is desired is understood in the light of its consequences, on health,
fortune, etc., that, too, will have a bearing on desirability. Consequences are usually the most important; but the desirable is that
which is desired *after reflection* upon relevant causes and consequences. What gives the desired desirability is that it is reaffirmed
in the light of its actual and possible connections. This means that
it takes on a *new* character, desirability, without losing the old one,
being desired. That this is possible is evident from the fact that in
many other situations, things take on new qualities in new relations—corn becomes a food, gold money, etc.

The crucial difference, however, overlooked in Professor White's
analysis of "desirable" and "objectively red" is that the problematic
situation in which we seek to find what is really good or desirable is
one that requires a "genuine practical judgment" in answer to the
question: what should I do or choose? whereas the analysis of
"seeming red" and "objective red" has been conducted without
reference to any practical problem of choice. Complete the analogy
and introduce a situation in which it becomes *important* to distinguish between apparent and real color, and *"objectively red"* acquires a normative status that "apparently red" does not have.
Apparently red is not good enough in matching draperies or in any
other situation in which we want to know what color we are really
choosing. Only the "objectively red" will do. Professor White believes that this is a *reductio ad absurdum,* because it would follow
that *all* true scientific statements would have a *de jure* quality.[7a]

Not at all, unless he maintains that as scientific they all bear
per se upon immediate practical problems of what should be done.
But the propositions of science are theoretical until they are applied
in some practical situation—a tautology which in this connection
has significance because it marks a definite distinction in function.
Dewey's contention is that every true proposition *in use* in a concrete situation provoking choice does have a normative status, because wherever relevant it determines in some degree what we
should choose. But the great body of scientific propositions at any
time are not in use.

This view seems very paradoxical to Professor White. "Take,
for example, the statement that the table upon which I am working now is actually brown. In what sense is this normative?" he
asks. The answer is: in no sense, because he has uttered a detached statement in the blue unrelated to any problem of choice.
This example is trivial, but it is easy to think of situations in which
a man's life may depend upon knowing (in medicine and other practical disciplines), what the real or objective property of a substance
is. But let him ask: What color of cloth or ornament should I choose
for this table? And at once the actual color of the table, if he wishes
to choose wisely, becomes a normative element for his action.
(The analogy between the analysis of the normative scientific statement and the normative ethical statement is formal. It does not
mean that the normative scientific statement is an ethical statement, since not all problems of practical choice are ethical.)

What Professor White has established is that in any *theoretical*
argument we cannot reach a conclusion with an "ought" term unless one of the premises contains an "ought" term. If this is the
decisively relevant point, then any naturalistic account of "ought
to be desired" would have to be ruled out—a position which he
leaves open—and not only the specific one Professor White rejects.
But a "phenomenological" account of the nature of the problematic ethical situation will show that "theoretical" propositions when
relevantly introduced, do acquire from their context a directive and
practical status on our decision which they do not have in isolation.

A disregard of the living context of the practical judgment—
and all evaluative decisions are practical judgments—leaves us with
the truism that from any set of matter of fact propositions, no
conclusions about what should be done follow. If there is no

"ought" or "should" in the premises of the "detached" argument, no "ought" or "should" is entailed in the conclusion. But within a context in which something must be *done,* the "ought" of the decision or conclusion is, so to speak, ultimately derivative from the urgencies of the problem, and supported or justified by the factual statements about the probable consequences of doing one thing or another to meet the situation. The normative element in the conclusion is in a sense provided by that which distinguishes the situation as a practical one from one that is purely logical or theoretical. The underlying premise is: that should be done which appropriately meets the needs and requirements of the situation, broadly conceived to include the demands and expectations of the community or traditions in which we find ourselves. Then, by ordinary scientific means, we discover that the probable consequences of *this* act, meet these needs and requirements and conclude it should be done. The underlying premise of the argument is not an explicit statement at all, but the situation itself.

Charles Beard, the late American historian, was fond of saying that no aggregation of facts by themselves determined any policy. Of course, literally construed, this is quite true. Statements of facts by *themselves* without reference to the problem-situation and its conflict of ends, on which the facts bear, determine nothing. Certainly, they do not *logically* determine anything. But if by policy we mean not a course of action to realize an *already decided upon end* (which would mean that the moral problem had been settled), but a course of conduct that defines what the end should be, and some proximate means of achieving it (as when we say that the U.S. needs a foreign policy); and if "determine" means providing evidential grounds, it is hard to see what else could determine policy except the aggregation of relevant facts from different fields. What we ought to do in any particular situation is that which we choose to do *after* reflection upon the relevant consequences of proposals framed to meet the needs of the situation.

The underlying criticism of Dewey's theory of value by Professor White, it seems to me, does not depend upon the latter's rejection of the parity of analysis between the disposition-predicates "desirable" and "objectively red." What he really believes is that Dewey's theory of value has nothing to do with ethics, because the ethical "ought-to-be" imposes a kind of obligation foreign to all

empirical statements. It is this antecedent acceptance of the separation of natural good and moral good, of the entire realm of empirical findings in anthropology, economics, law, psychology, politics, etc., from what is binding in a special moral sense which is
challenged by Dewey's theory according to which, without reducing the *concept* of right to good, morals are as wide as the area of
everything which affects the values of human living.[8] This separation is challenged not only by Dewey's theory but by the historical
record which shows that judgments of morally right and wrong,
despite theoretical pronouncements to the contrary, do, in fact,
change with wider understanding of biological and social phenomena.

There is another variant of Professor White's criticism of Dewey's theory which should be briefly considered. According to this
criticism, knowledge of the causes and consequences of our desire,
and of what is desired, does not make the desired desirable unless
among the consequences there are some other desirables. Unless
we can get back to some rock-bottom desirable in itself, the position is circular.[9] Again the failure appears to me to result from
disregarding the facts of actual moral situations. Of course, there
are other desirables that have to be taken into account in assessing the consequences of proposed modes of conduct in a problematic situation. These desirables are assumed or *postulated* as
valid because they summarize previous experience. That is what it
means to say that we no more start from scratch in ethical inquiry
than in any other kind of inquiry. The knowledge that the desired
has consequences, which we have reasons to believe desirable, when
added to relevant knowledge of the causes of our desire, makes
what is desired desirable. The important point here is that the
knowledge which makes the difference is knowledge of fact, of the
non-value facts (usually causes) and of the value-facts (usually consequences), won by ordinary scientific methods and investigation.
The value-facts which are introduced as data can, of course, be challenged, but that is another problem. "Should he take a vacation or
continue this piece of work?" someone asks. Among the consequences is the discovery that if a vacation is not taken, he will
probably have a nervous breakdown. This is assumed undesirable.
But why is this undesirable? This is another problem entirely, and
to be a genuine one, must be taken very concretely. In the course

of settling it, he may discover other value-facts. Unless he pre-
serves his health, his children will suffer. This is bad. Why is it
bad? Another problem, in the course of the solution of which he
discovers that his children are so much a part of his life that it
would be sadly altered if anything serious happened to them. One
can keep on asking questions until the inevitable one is reached:
"Is life itself worth living?" But must we really answer that question, too, and an indeterminate number of others, in order to be
able to answer the question we started from? No one can seriously
maintain this. Whether life is worth living *may* arise as a specific
question and is answerable one way or the other. But it is not relevant to most of our ethical problems.

Professor Stevenson's position is much closer to Dewey's than
that of the previous critic. Not only does he believe that ethics
"must draw from the *whole* of a man's knowledge," denying the
separation between empirical evaluations and moral obligations;
he forswears any attempt to find "ultimate principles" or "otherworldly norms." Some chapters of his brilliant *Ethics and Language,* especially the chapter on "Intrinsic and Extrinsic Value,"
are substantially along the same lines as Dewey's ethical theory.
His main difference from Dewey is on the place and significance
of emotive elements in ethical language and behavior. And here it
becomes hard to determine how important the differences are,
since Professor Stevenson professes to be interested only in the
analysis of ethical language and asserts that the theoretical differences between Dewey's position and his own reflect Dewey's
concern as a moralist.

There is one general criticism, however, which Professor Stevenson makes of Dewey's theory as a piece of analysis, which is central.
This is that Dewey, although less so than most critics, neglects the
role of emotive meaning as a factor in the determination of ethical
issues. And by words possessing emotive meaning are intended those
non-descriptive words which by expressing attitudes have a persuasive function on conduct. Stevenson's view is that descriptive
meanings—roughly the reasons we give for an ethical position—may
influence beliefs, but beliefs do not by themselves always determine
attitudes, even if they are beliefs *about* attitudes. Where they seem
to do so, it is always because they are wedded to some emotive
meaning, whose presence is just as relevant for the understanding

of ethical judgment as the cognitive meaning of the supporting reasons. For Dewey, anything "worthy" of being done—which is the meaning of "should be done"—depends for its justification completely upon the cognitive reasons or "factual evidence available." These, and these alone, make the normative or practical judgments valid. Every ethical judgment for Dewey is a "recommendation," a proposal, a prescription. Therefore, their function is quasi-imperative. For Stevenson, if this is true, it cannot follow only from its cognitive support and the emotively laden meanings of the cognitive terms in the problematic situation, but from some relatively independent factor of irreducible emotive meaning. It therefore becomes necessary to examine Stevenson's theory a little more closely.

In some ways it is curiously difficult to assess the precise difference between Dewey and Stevenson. But concerning two of these differences, it is possible to speak with some assurance. First, for Dewey a term that functions in a typical context of human communication can only influence conduct if it has some cognitive meaning. Whatever its emotive effects, they are dependent upon direct, peripheral, or suggested cognitive meaning. Stevenson seems to believe that some terms possess independent emotive meaning, although he asserts that what is distinctive about his position does not really depend upon this particular thesis. So far, however, he has not been able to present any indisputable illustration of terms that have persuasive, emotional force that do not depend upon the hearer or reader taking them as descriptive signs, too. The nearest he has come to establishing the existence of independent emotive meaning is in the use of expletives like "Damn!" or "Hell!" and the more strongly expressive four-letter words.

It is one thing to use such terms as abstract illustrations: it is quite another to observe how they function in a living context. In the latter case, these terms are read in the light of the whole situation. A man who misses his train or who, instead of hitting a nail square on the head, hits his thumb square on the nail, conveys a rather definite meaning, no matter what kind of language he uses. Even syntactically nonsensical expressions are taken as signs designating certain states of affairs if they are not considered as detached from, but as related to, their actual uses. In this connection one is reminded of De Man's story of the date vendor of Constantinople who did a brisk trade hawking his wares with repeated cries of "Hassan's dates are larger than they are!" to the impotent envy of his fellows. It is safe to say that either Hassan's dates were *in fact* larger than those of his competitors, or that his hearers thought they had heard him say something very much like it. What is meaningful in ethical discourse cannot be determined merely by the form of a linguistic expression alone. It is necessary to observe the wider context of interest, situation, and activity in which the expression is used. When this is done, there seems little evidence for the belief in the existence of independent emotive meaning.

Although Dewey insists that the purpose of an ethical judgment is to influence conduct, he refuses to regard this purpose as a constituent element of the meaning of the ethical judgment, or to give to the emotive elements of discourse an equivalent function in the legitimate determination of ethical issues. Dewey does not deny that emotive means are employed to resolve conflicts any more than he denies that brass bands, hypnotic suggestions, and physical coercion are effectively employed for the same purpose. But he denies that all modes of effecting agreement are ethically relevant. Mere agreement on attitude does not settle an ethical issue independently of how the agreement is achieved any more than mere agreement settles a scientific issue. Only when someone is persuaded by argument, when the grounds or reasons of an action have become one of the psychologically efficient causes of the action, do we feel that persuasion on an ethical issue has been appropriately effected. That is why, according to Dewey, we disallow the relevance of emotive elements in ethical situations, even if they seem to influence or redirect attitudes, when we are considering the truth or falsity of judgments of value.

According to Dewey, evaluative decisions are made not only in ethics but in all fields of human activity, including science. Although the subject matter of the natural scientist differs from that of the moralist, when he is trying to make up his mind about what hypothesis to approve of, he is seeking, like the moralist, to find grounds for a decision which also will express his attitudes. A scientist who is making an evaluative decision about whether he should commit himself in the way of belief—with its corollary of experimentation—to one or another theory of light or disease may be emotively concerned or affected by the things he is investigating.

But he would not regard these emotive elements as in any way relevant to the weight of evidence which determines his appraisal.

In any situation where an evaluative decision is to be made, "x is valuable," for Dewey, may roughly be analyzed as "I will choose or approve of x after reflection on the relevant consequences of my choice. The relevance of the consequences is determined by their bearing on the situation which has provoked my indecision and on the interests which constitute the relatively permanent core of my self." Professor Stevenson asserts that such an analysis is incomplete because it leaves us with an indeterminate number of unrelated predictive judgments. The result is that we can never specify what ethical sentences mean; nor can we account for the distinctively quasi-imperative meaning of ethical terms.

I submit that Professor Stevenson has overlooked the continuous control of the problematic situation itself upon the number and kind of predictive judgments which are ethically relevant. We don't predict for the sake of predicting, or about everything, but in order to meet the particular challenge set by the particular problem. The predictions are the foreseeings and forewarnings that constitute wisdom. They will vary with the kind of problem. They will be different if I am trying to determine whether to support a strike or report an act of cruelty to the SPCA. But they will not be unlimited. We do not need reference to emotive meaning to help unify all cognitive elements involved. The problematic situation serves as the unifying reference. Many things that may be causally relevant to our emotive attitudes may be logically irrelevant to the ethical judgment. Indeed, although in Dewey's theory we cannot tell in advance the precise amount of knowledge we need in order to justify our making a well-grounded evaluative decision, on Stevenson's theory it is hard to see how anything can be ruled out as irrelevant as a reason for an ethical judgment. "Any statement," he says, "about *any* matter of fact which *any* speaker considers likely to alter attitudes may be adduced as a reason for or against an ethical judgment." [10]

The judgment of what should be done has all the intellectual weight of its supporting reasons. At the same time, it derives its quasi-imperative function not so much from any dependent emotive meaning as from the fact that it is formulated in a situation of stress to resolve a perplexity. We feel caught in a problem that has to be met, and every ethical judgment has the force of a proposed resolution.

When we go from a situation of personal decision to one of conflict between two individuals or classes, the emotive theory of ethics seems to rest on the strongest grounds. For in such cases, the relative distinction between disagreement in attitude and disagreement in belief seems justified even though we recognize that an attitude towards an object expresses an implicit belief about it and a belief about an object involves an implicit attitude towards it. But I agree with Professor Stevenson that this does not make beliefs and attitudes identical. The question is how they vary with each other. In so far as disagreement in attitude is rooted in disagreement in belief, the scientific methods by which we reach agreement in belief are sufficient to effect ethical resolution. In so far as disagreements in attitudes are not rooted in differences in belief, then all agreement in belief will be unavailing to settle an ethical issue. Agreement in practice in such cases, Professor Stevenson holds, can be reached, if at all, by use of emotive meanings if not by stronger methods.

Now there are a number of observations about attitudes and beliefs which seem to me to be true, and which suggest that the role of belief in ethical affairs is perhaps more important than we are at first inclined to think in face of the manifest ethical disagreements of social life. First, in any concrete situation of ethical disagreement, if one knows what an individual's empirical beliefs are about that situation, one can almost always in fact tell what his attitudes will be. Indeed, some social psychologists measure a person's attitudes by his indication of beliefs—although this is very rough since the reliability of statements about beliefs must be checked. Personally, I have never known a case of ethical disagreement which did not seem to turn on differences in belief that were admitted by all parties to be relevant. Second, in cases of ethical disagreement, to assert that an individual's beliefs depend *only* upon his personal attitude or interest, is usually construed as a charge of prejudice which everyone seems concerned to deny by pointing to the evidence on which his judgment rests. It is assumed that his interests are always involved, but it is expected that the *evidence* will be disinterested, and that what it will show is that the judgment is not being made *exclusively* in behalf of the individual interest. Third, in cases where disagreement in attitudes seems to persist where there is agreement in belief, it will almost always be found that the beliefs on which there seems to be agreement are not held with the same degree of assent. They may vary from highly tentative surmise to absolute conviction. Consequently, the weight they have in determining attitudes differs—so that in effect we have disagreement in belief. Fourth, where disagreements in attitudes are not resolvable by agreement through beliefs, if they are compromised—the compromise can be shown to rest on agreement on another set of beliefs, viz., that the consequences of compromise are better in specifiable respects than those of conflict.

I mention these things because they suggest to me the possibility of accepting everything Professor Stevenson says about agreement and disagreement between two or more persons or classes without accepting his entire emotive theory of ethical terms. What he seems to assume is that any normative ethics on a naturalistic basis, which believes that ethical sentences have descriptive meanings, must give conclusions that are not only objectively true, but *universally* true, and since no one can establish *in advance* that an objective universal morality can be established holding for all interests, he believes that the descriptive theory of meaning is untenable. Once we surrender this assumption, however, and recognize the possibility of a relativism, which is, nonetheless, genuinely objective, then I see little pragmatic difference between saying—irrespective of all their other not inconsiderable differences—what Dewey, Perry, Santayana, possibly Lewis, and other naturalists in ethics are saying, and what Professor Stevenson seems to be saying. If the good is defined in relation to human need or interest (or preference, desire, satisfaction)—if, in other words, the nature of morals is conceived as having any relation to human nature—then every statement about the good or better in any situation has a descriptive meaning, and in principle is decidable in reference to the needs and interests involved. The nature of human nature, and more particularly the presence of shared interests in a shared experience, or the possibility of such shared interest, becomes relevant at every point. Whether, as Dewey claims, there exists "a psychological uniformity of human nature with respect to basic *needs* . . . and of certain conditions which must be met in order that any form of human association must be maintained,"¹¹ is an empirical question to which the answer is difficult but not inaccessible to study. Surely we know that men are not always aware of what their interests are, and that their interests (or attitudes) often change in the light of the knowledge of their causes and consequences. Since intelligence is also natural to man, in situations of conflict we can use the method of intelligence to negotiate differences by seeking a more inclusive interest to enable us either to live with our differences, to mitigate them or to transcend them, and thus convert value conflicts into compatible value differences. This is the constructive moral function of intelligence, which to be effective must be given institutional form—educational, economic, political.

No one who soberly looks at history would wish to assert that all disagreements among human beings must yield to negotiation through intelligence, that we can be certain that men *are* sufficiently alike to work out ways of becoming more alike, or sufficiently alike to agree about the permissible limits of being different. The unwillingness to use intelligence where there is a possibility of using it, does not gainsay the fact that if it had been used, certain shared interests might have been—sometimes we can say *would* have been—discovered.

It is important to point out, however, that it is easy to exaggerate the non-negotiable differences among men, and to convert by theoretical fiat the occasions of disagreement into irresolvable ultimate differences of value attitudes. Most disagreements among men, Professor Stevenson has shown in a remarkable chapter of his book, are about focal aims, major or lesser, and not about allegedly ultimate values concerning which in Western culture, at any rate, most human beings *profess* to agree, to a point where Franco speaks of the "brotherhood of man under God" and Stalin speaks of "freedom."

We must recognize the possibility of a situation arising in which a man has been convinced by reasoning that "x is good" in a descriptive sense, and thereupon shows a greater desire to destroy it. He may have other interests, however, including an interest in peace and survival, which may lead him to restrain his desire to destroy x. And if he is intelligent enough to see that x is really good, his intelligence may suggest the *possibility* of finding an x which furthers a wider, common good. But even if this is not so, I do not see that it impugns the objectivity or truth of the original statement that "x is good" any more than Galileo's statement as to what could be seen about Jupiter's satellites through his telescope was less true because some Aristotelians refused to look through it.

There are two generic alternatives. One of them is illustrated by the Grand Inquisitor in Dostoyevsky's *Brothers Karamazov* who justifies his totalitarian society to Christ returned on earth by arguing that it is the only system that will bring happiness to the poor benighted creatures whom God has created. "There are three powers," he says, "three powers alone able to conquer and to hold captive forever the conscience of these important rebels for their happiness—these forces are miracle, mystery, and authority." I believe it is possible to prove him mistaken about the nature of man, the nature of human happiness, and the methods of achieving it. But his willingness to give grounds for his position, to examine consequences, already sets up a hope for agreement. Contrast this with a situation somewhat nearer the hypothetical case described in the previous paragraph—the apologia of the Inner Party Leader in George Orwell's novel, *1984,* in which the leader differentiates himself from all other totalitarian groups past and present, declaring: "Power is not a means, it is an end. The object of persecution is persecution. The object of torture is torture. The object of power is power." Here there is no attempt to relate needs and consequences, no presence of rational intent. To the extent that the Grand Inquisitor offers reasons on which his attitudes are presumably based, he belongs to the moral community; the Inner Party Leader does not. If he is a man, he is a sick man. If he is not a sick man, then he must be contained or fought.

Granted, then, that there is an element of the *arbitrary* in the source of our moral judgment—a view which, if I am not mistaken, is one of the animating insights of the emotive conception of ethics—I do not see the necessity of carrying what is arbitrary into the moral judgment itself under the flag of the emotive theory. What is arbitrary or non-rational about man is his nature—a statement that would be just as true if he had the nature of an angel or a tiger. But what follows from his nature is not arbitrary in the same sense, particularly not his judgments of evaluation about what is *good* for that nature. Such judgments are empirical cognitions, and rational or irrational because tested and controlled by the outcome of experience.

That man has intelligence is as much a fact about his nature as that he has needs and desires which he seeks to satisfy. And since the successful satisfaction of these needs depends upon the knowledge of all sorts of conditions and consequences, there is no problem about justifying the use of intelligence to the extent that any man has it. He has a natural interest in intelligence because the prospering of all his other interests depends upon it.

Reflection on the social nature of the self, the success of experimental methods in the natural sciences, the costs and ineffectiveness of other methods in human affairs carries us a long way in justifying the use of intelligence in settling *conflicts* between groups and classes. But the *advocacy* of the use of such methods in situations where others may prefer to use different methods, the *proposal*, in the face of differences, to sit down and reason together, can be interpreted as a *decision* not to give ethical status to non-rational persuasive methods of effecting agreement like "emotive meaning, rhetorical cadence . . . stentorian, stimulating tones of voice, dramatic gestures . . . the use of material rewards and punishments," [12] unless preceded or accompanied by rational grounds.

In other words, we seem to have been implicitly defining "ethical agreement" as one reached through agreement on beliefs by rational means.

This looks very much like a *"persuasive definition"* in Professor Stevenson's sense—perhaps a "persuasive definition" in reverse. Instead of giving a new conceptual meaning to a familiar word, it reinforces an old meaning in current use, and is tantamount to a recommendation to use and continue using rational methods to resolve conflicts until evidence of bad faith or the *actions* of others make it impossible. And so long as this does not commit us to "the emotive theory of meaning," we should not be very concerned to deny it, for almost every critic of the emotive conception of ethics seems to be committed to some such persuasive definition. This is clear in Dewey's case when he tells us that "as far as non-cognitive, extra-cognitive factors enter into the subject-matter or content of sentences purporting to be *legitimately* ethical, those sentences are by just that much deprived of the properties sentences *should have* in order to be *genuinely* ethical." [13] I believe that it can be shown that almost all writers on ethics have said something similar although they have differed on the precise analysis of what rational method consists in.

From this I conclude that the use of the definition, persuasive or not, is innocent because it expresses what is normally meant by *ethical* agreement when conflicts arise, and that to the extent that it has an influence on conduct, it would make for "an attitude of rationality" in the face of value conflicts.

PART 2

The New Failure of Nerve

In the famous third chapter of his *Four Stages of Greek Religion* Gilbert Murray characterizes the period from 300 B.C. through the first century of the Christian era as marked by "a failure of nerve." This failure of nerve exhibited itself in "a rise of asceticism, of mysticism, in a sense, of pessimism; a loss of self-confidence, of hope in this life and of faith in normal human efforts; a despair of patient inquiry, a cry for infallible revelation: an indifference to the welfare of the state, a conversion of the soul to God."

A survey of the cultural tendencies of our own times shows many signs pointing to a new failure of nerve in Western civilization. Its manifestations are more complex and sophisticated than in any previous time. It speaks in a modern idiom and employs techniques of expression and persuasion that reflect the ways of a secular culture. But at bottom it betrays, except in one respect, the same flight from responsibility, both on the plane of action and on the plane of belief, that drove the ancient world into the shelters of pagan and Christian supernaturalism.

There is hardly a field of theoretical life from which these signs of intellectual panic, heralded as portents of spiritual revival, are lacking. No catalogue can do justice to the variety of doctrines in which this mood appears. For purposes of illustration we mention the recrudescence of beliefs in the original depravity of human nature; prophecies of doom for western culture, no matter who wins the war or peace, dressed up as laws of social-dynamics; the frenzied search for a center of value that transcends human interests; the mystical apotheosis of "the leader" and élites; contempt for all political organizations and social programs because of the obvious failure of some of them, together with the belief that good will is sufficient to settle thorny problems of economic and social reconstruction; posturing about the cultivation of spiritual purity; the refurbishing of theological and metaphysical dogmas about the infinite as necessary presuppositions of knowledge of the finite; a concern with mystery rather than with problems, and the belief that myth and mysteries are modes of knowledge; a veritable campaign to "prove" that without a belief in God and immortality, democracy—or even plain moral decency—cannot be reasonably justified.

Liberalism—not the nineteenth-century ideology or social theology of laissez faire which was already moribund before the First World War—but liberalism as an intellectual temper, as faith in intelligence, as a tradition of the free market in the world of ideas is everywhere on the defensive. Before the onrush of cataclysmic social and historical changes, large sections of the intellectuals and clerks of the Western world are abandoning the hard-won critical positions of the last few centuries. In the schools, the churches, and in the literary arts, the tom-tom of theology and the bagpipes of transcendental metaphysics are growing more insistent and shrill. We are told that our children cannot be properly educated unless they are inoculated with "proper" religious beliefs; that theology and metaphysics must be given a dominant place in the curriculum of our universities; that churchmen should cultivate sacred theology before applying the social gospel; that business needs an inspired church that speaks authoritatively about absolutes—this by the editors of *Fortune;* that what is basically at stake in this war *
is Christian civilization despite our gallant Chinese, Moslem, and

* This essay was written in 1942 and published in 1943.

Russian allies; that the stability of the state depends on an *unques-
tioned* acceptance of a unifying dogma, sometimes identified with
the hierarchical authoritarianism of Catholicism, sometimes with
democracy; that none of the arts and no form of literature can
achieve imaginative distinction without "postulating a transcendental reality." Obscurantism is no longer apologetic; it has now
become precious and wilful. Fundamentalism is no longer beyond
the pale; it has donned a top hat and gone high church.

The primary evidence of the new failure of nerve is to be found
in an attitude underlying all of the views and movements enumer-
ated, and many others as well. It exhibits itself as a loss of confidence in scientific method, and in varied quests for a "knowledge" and "truth" which, although they give us information about
the world, are uniquely different from those won by the processes
of scientific inquiry. Often, with no great regard for consistency,
these uniquely different truths are regarded as "superior" to the
common garden variety truths of science and good sense. They are
the self-proclaimed governors of the moral and theoretical economy. Their function is to point to man's natural and supernatural
end and to prevent science, competent to deal only with means,
from stepping out of bounds.

This distrust of scientific method is often concealed by statements to the effect that science, of course, has a certain validity
in its restricted sphere and that only the pretensions of scientific
philosophy, naturalism, empiricism, positivism—not to speak of
materialism—are being criticized. Yet it is not to the actual procedures of scientific inquiry that such critics go to correct this or
that formulation of scientific philosophy. Instead they invoke the
claims of some rival method to give us knowledge of what is
beyond the competence of scientific method. Occasionally they
boldly assert that their substitute method gives a more reliable
and completer knowledge of the matters that the sciences report
on, particularly about the behavior of man and the history of
society. What an eloquent revelation is contained in Reinhold
Niebuhr's words: "Science which is only science cannot be scientifically accurate." [1]

Distrust of scientific method is transformed into open hostility
whenever some privileged, "private" truth pleads for exemption
from the tests set up to safeguard the intelligence from illusion.

The pleas for exemption take many forms. They are rarely open and direct as in the frenzy of Kierkegaard who frankly throws overboard his intelligence in order to make those leaps of despairing belief which convert his private devils into transcendent absolutes. Usually these pleas are presented as corollaries of special *theories* of knowledge, being, or experience. There are some who interpret science and discursive knowledge generally as merely confirming what we *already* know in a dim but sure way by other modes of experience. If the methods of scientific inquiry do not yield this confirmation, they are held to be at fault; some other way must be found of validating and communicating primal wisdom. Others maintain that scientific method can give us only partial truths which become less partial not by subjecting them to more careful scrutiny but by incorporating them into a theological or metaphysical system whose cardinal principles are true but not testable by any method known to science. Still others openly declare it to be axiomatic that every experience, every feeling and emotion, directly reports a truth that cannot be warranted, and does not need to be warranted, by experiment or inference.

These, bluntly put, are gateways to intellectual and moral irresponsibility. They lay down roads to a happy land where we can gratify our wishes without risking a veto by stubborn fact. But of the view that every mode of experience gives direct authentic knowledge, it would be more accurate to say that it carries us far beyond the gateways. For in effect it is a defense of obscurantism. It starts from the assumption that *every* experience gives us an authentic report of the objective world instead of material for judgment. It makes our viscera an organ of knowledge. It justifies violent prejudice in its claims that if only we feel deeply enough about anything, the feeling declares some truth about the object which provokes it. This "truth" is regarded as possessing the same legitimacy as the considered judgment that finds no evidence for the feeling and uncovers its root in a personal aberration. After all is it not the case that every heresy-hunting bigot and hallucinated fanatic is convinced that there is a truth in the feelings, visions, and passions that run riot within him? Hitler is not the only one for whom questions of evidence are incidental or impertinent where his feelings are concerned. If the voice of feeling cannot be mistaken, differences would be invitations to battle, the

ravings of an insane mind could legitimately claim to be prophecies of things to come. It is not only as a defense against the mar-
ginally sane that we need the safeguards of critical scientific method.
Every vested interest in social life, every inequitable privilege,
every "truth" promulgated as a national, class or racial truth, like-
wise denies the competence of scientific inquiry to evaluate its
claims.

Those who hold this view sometimes seek to avoid its consequences by admitting that not every experience or feeling is as
valid as every other, any more than every scientific judgment is
as valid as every other. But this does not alter the logic of their
position. The relative validity of different scientific judgments is
established by methods of public verification open to all who
submit themselves to its discipline, whereas the relative validity
of feelings is decided by another private feeling.

Not infrequently the demand that the revelations of feeling,
intuition or emotion about the world meet scientific canons of evidence is rejected as an arbitrary legislative decree concerning what
visions are permissible and what may or may not exist. The complaint is made that such a demand impoverishes imaginative resources and blights the power to see new and fresh visions without
which preoccupation with method is nothing but a word-game of
sterile minds. As far as the seeing of visions and the winning of
new truths are concerned, such an interpretation is nothing short
of grotesque. The essential point, when the question of knowledge or truth arises, is whether we have seen a vision or been a
victim of a delusion; or, to avoid the appearance of question-
begging, whether we have beheld a trustworthy or untrustworthy
vision. Some people claim to see what we know is not there. If
seeing were believing, or if all seeing were evidence of what could
be believed, independently of the conditions under which the seeing
took place, it would be easy to keep men perpetually duped.

The intelligent demand for evidence need not paralyze the pio-
neers of truth who catch glimpses of what until then may be un-
dreamed of. Nor does the progress of science demand complete and
exact confirmation of an hypothesis at the very outset, but only
enough to institute further inquiries. The history of the sciences
is sufficient evidence that the discipline of its method, far from
being a bar to the discovery of new knowledge, is a positive aid in

its acquisition. What other discipline can point to the acquisition of new knowledge or to truths about existence that command the universal assent of all investigators?

Nor is it true that scientific method or the philosophy of naturalism, which whole-heartedly accepts scientific method as the only reliable way of reaching truths about man, society, and nature, decrees what may or may not exist. It concerns itself only with the responsibility of the assertions that proclaim the existence of anything. It does not forbid but explores and tests. It does not jeer at the mystical swoon of dumb rapture; it denies only the mystic's restrospective cognitive claim for which no evidence is offered except the fact of a trance. It does not rule out on *a priori* grounds the existence of supernatural entities and forces. The existence of God, immortality, disembodied souls or spirits, cosmic purpose or design, as these have customarily been interpreted by the great institutional religions, are denied by naturalists for the same generic reasons that they deny the existence of fairies, elves, leprechauns, and an invisible satellite revolving between the earth and moon.

There are other conceptions of God, to be sure, and provided they are not self-contradictory, the naturalist would be unfaithful to his own philosophy if he refused to examine the evidence for their validity. All he asks is that the conception be sufficiently determinate to make possible specific inferences of the *how, when,* and *where* of His operation. The trouble with most conceptions of God which differ from the conventional ones is that either they are so vague that it is difficult to tell what they mean, or else they designate something in experience for which a perfectly suitable term already exists.

Unfortunately, for all their talk of appeal to experience, direct or indirect, religious experientialists dare not appeal to any experience of sufficiently determinate character to permit of definite tests. There is a certain wisdom in this reluctance. For if experience can confirm a belief, it can also disprove it. But to most supernaturalists the latter is an inadmissible possibility. We therefore find that the kind of experience to which reference is made is not only unique but uniquely self-authenticating. Those who are not blessed by these experiences are regarded as blind or deaf and, under certain circumstances, dangerous to the community. But is it not odd that those who worship Zeus on the ground of a unique experience should deny to others the right to worship Odin on the ground of a different unique experience?

Scientific method cannot deny that the secular and religious spokesmen of the supernatural hear voices, but it cannot accept these voices, as they are reported, as valid testimony about the world of fact or the world of value. It judges the truth of what is heard by what it logically leads to in the realm of empirical behavior. It seeks to draw what is reported about this world or any other into some community with the limited but precious store of responsible assertions that constitute knowledge. The attack upon scientific method, in order to be free to believe whatever voice speaks to us, is a flight from responsibility. This is the dominant characteristic of the failure of nerve.

The causes of the failure of nerve in our time are multiple and obvious. Economic crises, world war, a bad peace, tragically inept statesmanship, the tidal waves of totalitarianism, tell the story of the twentieth century. These are the phenomena that are behind the interrupted careers, the frustrated hopes, the anxiety, the sense of being lost and alone, the growing bewilderment, fear and horror—that feed the theology of despair and the politics of wish. It is important to remember this. The "arguments" of those who have been panicked into embracing the new varieties of transcendental consolation may be met a thousand times over. But not until a democratic, freedom-and-welfare-planning economy is built out of what is left of our world, in which stable traditions can absorb the conventions of revolt of political man and the experiments of growth of individual men, will these intellectual excesses subside from epidemic to episodic proportions. Until then it is necessary to prevent intellectual hysteria from infecting those who still cling to the principles of rational experiment and analysis.

There is still another source of the new fusion of super-agony and superstition. This is the inability of those liberal, labor, and socialist movements which have prided themselves on being scientific and which have lost one social campaign after another, to supply a positive philosophy, that would weld emotion and scientific intelligence, as a new rallying ground. Wilsonian idealism is dead although some do not know it, syndicalism is a fascist changeling, and orthodox Marxism is bankrupt. The grand visions of the socialist prophets have given way to petty political horse trading or pathetic confidence in the good will of individual statesmen. The left lives from day to day in a world going from bad to worse.

Into the breach has stepped the motley array of religionists filled with the élan of salvation and burdened with the theological baggage of centuries. This is the one respect in which the new failure of nerve basically differs from the old. The failure of nerve of the early Christian era sought to convert the soul to God in order to withdraw it from all concern with the world. Today the churches are so much of this world that their other worldliness is only a half-believed prophecy of man's inescapable destination rather than an ideal of personal and social life. As interpreters of divine purpose, they have now become concerned with social healing, with the institutions of society and with the bodies of men, as necessarily involved in the healing of individual souls. The world-order is to become a moral and religious order. Plans for the postwar world and for social reconstruction are coming from the Pope as well as from the humblest Protestant sect. They are now at flood-tide. The Churches bid well to replace political parties as sounding boards, if not instruments, of social reform.

It is characteristic of the tendencies hostile to scientific method that they reject the view that the breakdown of capitalism and the rise of totalitarianism are primarily the result of a conjunction of material factors. Rather do they allege that the bankruptcy of Western European civilization is the direct result of the bankruptcy of the scientific and naturalistic spirit. The attempt to live by science resulted in chaos, relativism, Hitlerism and war. The latter are treated as superficial evils destined to pass like all of God's trials. But the radical evil is a scientific attitude which sacrificed true understanding for prediction and individual salvation for social control.

That science was king in the social life of the Western world, that modern ills are the consequences of our attempt to live by scientific theory and practice—these assumptions border on fantasy. No convincing evidence has ever been offered for them. On the contrary, the chief causes of our maladjustments are to be found precisely in these areas of social life *in which the rationale of scientific method has not been employed*. Where is the evidence that any Western State ever attempted to meet scientifically the challenge of poverty, unemployment, distribution of raw materials, the impact of technology? Attempts to grapple with these problems in relation to human needs in a rational and scientific spirit have run squarely against class interests and privileges which cut savagely short any inquiry into their justification. What has controlled our response to basic social problems have been principles drawn from the outworn traditions or opportunist compromises that reflect nothing but the shifting strength of the interests behind them. In either case the procedure has had little to do with the ethics and logic of scientific method. It is only by courtesy that we can call them principles at all. Drift and improvisation have been the rule. Enthusiasm for the bare *results* of the physical sciences—which undoubtedly did reach a high pitch in the nineteenth century—does not betoken an acceptance of a scientific or experimental philosophy of life in which all values are tested by their causes and consequences. The cry that a set of "laboratory techniques" cannot determine values in a philosophy of life betrays the literary man's illusion that the laboratory procedures of the natural sciences are the be-all and end-all of scientific method instead of restricted applications of it in special fields.

The truth is that scientific method has until now been regarded as irrelevant in testing the values embodied in social institutions. *If* one accepted the religionists' assumption that values can be grounded only on a true religion and metaphysics, together with their views about the ideal causation of events, it could be legitimately urged against them that the bankruptcy of civilization testifies to the bankruptcy of *their* metaphysics. For if science is irrelevant to values, it cannot corrupt them; and if theology and metaphysics are their sacred guardian, they are responsible for the world we live in.

The social principles of Christianity have had almost two thousand years in which to order the world on a moral basis. It is not likely that anything new can be discovered from its principles or that its social gospel will succeed better in eliminating war, social distress, and intense factional strife, than it did during the historical periods in which religious institutions enjoyed chief authority. And when we examine the behavior and doctrines of different religious groups as they meet the trials of our world today, the impression is reinforced that there is no more unity of purpose among them, no more agreement in program and direction of effort, than among their secular brethren. But whereas the latter *may* rely upon a method by which to limit, adjudicate and negotiate the differences among them, the former *must* absolutize their differences if they are consistent.

It is an obvious fact that all religious groups, with the exception of some Protestant churches in America, have been able to find support of their own national governments in prosecuting the war compatible with the sacred principles of Christianity. Some of them have even professed to be able to derive the necessity of such support from sacred doctrine. Cardinal Verdier of France and Cardinal Hinsley of England have declared the war to be a religious crusade; so have some of the German bishops on the other side who have blessed Hitler's arms and prayed for his victory; while the Pope himself is still neutral in respect to it. J. Maritain at the time of the Nazi-Soviet Pact declared that the war against Hitler was a just war but not a religious one. He also asserted "it is entirely understandable" that the German bishops should support their government; indeed, that it was naive to be scandalized by the divisions among religious groups on the war. Today the just war has become transformed in M. Maritain's eyes into a "religious" war. Yet no matter how they characterize the war, religious groups do not contest the validity of opposite statements made about the war by other national religious groups who take their point of departure from the *same* religious premises.

Now this is extremely odd. No one would tax theologians with insincerity. But if it is true that a religious principle or dogma is compatible with two contradictory positions in respect to the defeat of Hitlerism, then the principle or dogma in question is irrelevant to the nature of the war. And since it is true that the defeat of Hitlerism is of the very first importance for the social reconstruction of Europe, we are justified in entertaining a lively suspicion of the relevance of Christian principles to such reconstruction, if at the same time they can reconcile themselves equally well to Hitler's victory or defeat.

The only implication that can be drawn from this strange state of affairs is that religious groups are seeking, as they always have, to make of God an instrument of national policy. One of two things: Either national policy can be defended as good or just without theological sanctions or dogmas, in which case the interposition of religion obscures issues: or the defense presupposes religious dogmas, in which case, to countenance a different national policy, is to betray *religious* dogma. The German Bishops who admonished the Catholic soldiers in a Pastoral Letter to give their lives *"in obedience to the Fuehrer"* should have been denounced as bad Catholics. Before Catholics, Protestants and Jews urge the acceptance of their dogmas as necessary preconditions for intelligent belief in democracy and anti-Hitlerism, let them convert their own churches to democracy, and denounce religious neutrality before Hitlerism for what it is, connivance with the enemy. This is their sector of the battle. But, better still, let them take their theology out of politics.

On the very question of the war itself the Protestant Churches of America are split wide open although this is somewhat concealed by the unanimity of interest in problems of postwar reconstruction. Yet no matter with what voice the Churches speak on the issues of the day, they do so not as other associations of citizens who must face demands of empirical evidence, but as guardians of a revelation which gives them unique knowledge of man and his destiny.

Religion can escape showing its credentials concerning the inspiration of its knowledge but not concerning its validity. For the reliability of any knowledge is tested in the necessities of intelligent action. That test, together with the varying counsel of the Churches on specific social policies, is sufficient to indicate that there is no unique religious knowledge or religious guidance. When Church pronouncements about the nature of the world are not irrelevant or clearly false, they can be more plausibly derived from positions that Churches usually characterize as unbelieving. When the claims to unique knowledge are exploded, the last resort of religionists is the assertion that religious beliefs, and only religious beliefs, can supply that dynamic faith without which secular defense of the good society is ineffectual, unable to imple-ment its own humanist ideals.

The defense of religious faith takes many forms. Most of them are variations on the theme that if the beliefs of faith were false, the world would be a terrible place: therefore they must be true.

Or since the beliefs of faith are consoling, they cannot be false. Sometimes the argument rises a little higher. Because not everything can be proved, since even science must make assumptions, some faith in something is unavoidable if one is to believe or do anything. Therefore faith in the absurd is justifiable. But only our faith, not the other fellow's! On its most sophisticated level, faith is defended not as a specific belief but as an attitude of wisdom and resignation towards the human situation. When it is realized that such faith is not distinctively religious at all, either there is a relapse into metaphysical double-talk about faith also being a form of knowledge or religion is defined so that all people who have faith or passion, *i.e.,* who are not yet dead, are regarded as religious and committed to religious beliefs. But when religious belief is a universal coefficient of all other beliefs, it is irrelevant to them. This may be seen most clearly in the theology of Reinhold Niebuhr.

Reinhold Niebuhr is one of those men of whom Emerson said they were better than their theology. A radical and honest intelligence, he brings to bear upon specific problems of social change a scientific attitude and rare courage, that make his discussions always illuminating. But not a single one of the positions that Niebuhr takes on the momentous issues of social and political life is dependent on his theology. One may accept his rather reactionary theology, which is an eloquent combination of profound disillusionment in human action and a violent belief in human ideals, and deny all his secular views. Or one may accept the latter, as so many of his friends do, and regard the former as moving rhetoric that breathes passionate conviction about something whose very sense is in doubt. Indeed, if we look closely at Niebuhr's theology, and take it out of the language of myth and paradox, we find that whatever is acceptable in it to critical thought is an obscure retelling of what was known to the wiser unbelievers of the past.

Consider, for example, Niebuhr's conception of religion. It is "the primary and ultimate act of faith by which life is endowed with meaning. Without that act of faith life cannot be lived at all." [2] To be alive is to be religious, and the atheists, the irreligious, the agnostics, have been converted by definition: they all have religion. This is innocent enough so long as we never lose sight of the differences between religions or *what* men believe in, and so long as we realize that, although life cannot be lived without some acts of faith, death may be the consequence of other acts of faith, *e.g.,* faith that pneumonia can be cured by absent treatment. What Niebuhr must now show as a theologian is that the faith necessary for life is necessarily faith in God. This he completely fails to do. Instead by another essay in redefinition—one not so innocent—he equates the meaning which is the object or reference of *any* faith, with God. "There is no action without religious orientation and no religion without God." [3] To be alive is not only to be religious, it is to have faith in God even if we deny his existence. This is still not the end. Niebuhr must now as a *Christian* theologian show that the God we affirm in action is the God of revealed Christianity who is transcendent to the world and yet intimately connected with it. This is accomplished in his Gifford Lectures by describing man as a "self-transcendent spirit" consumed by a metaphysical anxiety and hunger which can only be appeased by belief in the symbolical (not literal!) truth of the Incarnation. Insofar as arguments are employed instead of exhortation they are fallacious. For example: what is unique about the human spirit cannot be derived from man's animal nature; nor is it an expression of reason. Therefore, infers Niebuhr, man is a child of God who can only comprehend himself "by a principle of comprehension which is beyond his comprehension." One mystery calls to another and the plain fact that what is distinctive about human traits has its origin and fruit in the social and cultural matrix is considered only to be dismissed by a question begging interpretation of man's capacity to transcend his immediate interests.

Man, Niebuhr asserts, is not only a creature of God, he is a sinner. He is an inevitable sinner and yet cannot escape responsibility for his sins. He is a sinner because he forgets that he is a creature of God, because he thinks he is more than he is, knows more than he does, because, in short, he is not God. When he is contritely aware of his sinfulness, of its inevitability and his responsibility for it, grace descends upon his soul and he receives remission from sin.

There is a simple moral homily that can be tortured out of

this oxymoronic language but it is completely spoiled by Niebuhr's theology.

What Niebuhr is telling us is that every effort, every movement of man in warding off evil or achieving good, leads him to "the sin of imperialism in action." Whether we are selfish or righteous, the tincture of sin is present. For we absolutize the relative, dogmatize insight, eternalize the fleeting, take the part for the whole. Man deludes himself into believing that he sees the infinite from a finite perspective, and that he transcends self-interest and selfishness in his conceptions of impartial justice. All of his ideals, including his God, he makes in his own image. In his struggle to achieve his limited ideals, as if they were absolute, he consequently is guilty of fanaticism whose evils may be not less than those he set out to rectify. Man must therefore accept some supernatural standard to curb the conflicts of partial truths, each claiming to be the whole truth.

What is here correctly perceived as a problem still remains a problem, for Niebuhr's solution is stultifying. The conflict of absolutes is to be settled by appeal to another absolute which on Niebuhr's own theology is necessarily injected with human finitude! This is a romantic and violent solution of a human predicament already violently distorted to begin with. Niebuhr writes as if all men were naturally romantic theologians, victims of a fantastic logic according to which, if God did not exist, *they* must be God. He ignores the entire tradition of scientific and naturalistic philosophy that has never claimed divinity for man nor infallibility for his judgment. The doctrine of original sin turns out to be nothing more than the discovery that man is a limited creature. But this is no more justification for believing he is essentially evil than that he is essentially good. For these are qualities that depend upon the use man makes of his limitations. Naturalist philosophers have urged men to understand the causes of their limitations, so that by reducing the margins of ignorance and increasing their scientific knowledge, they may be less limited. The whole enterprise of scientific method with its self-corrective procedures cuts under the dogmatism, absolutism and fanaticism of Niebuhr's theological man at the same time as it gives us conclusions that are sufficiently reliable to overcome some specific limitations. Niebuhr would frighten men out of their mistaken belief in omnipotence by a fairy tale about a creature that is absolutely omnipotent. The humility it induces is one of fear, not the humility which is fostered by knowledge of human limitations and ignorance. His wisdom does not carry further than the caution that no claim is completely justified, but he is helpless before the problem of determining the degree and extent of its justification, so necessary in order to get on with the problems in hand. Whenever Niebuhr tackles these problems, he deserts his theology.

It is true that intellectual pride is an expression of "original sin" insofar as we make a claim to know what we do not know and overlook the natural and historical origins of reason. Niebuhr is very eloquent about the dangers of intellectual pride. "Fanaticism is always a partly conscious, partly unconscious attempt to hide the fact of ignorance and to obscure the problem of skepticism." And again: "The real fact is that all the pretensions of final knowledge and ultimate truth are partly prompted by the uneasy feeling that the truth is not final and also by an uneasy conscience which realizes that the interests of the ego are compounded with this truth."[4] True, but Niebuhr should address these words not to naturalists but to theologians, for in the history of thought it has been the naturalists who have exposed the pretensions of final truths and who have uncovered the nerve of interest behind the absolute values of church, state, and conscience. Science has known its dogmatism, too. But the cure of bad science is better science, not theology.

On many specific issues of scientific inquiry Niebuhr is one with us. Despite his extravagant rhetoric, he does not believe in blowing out the candlelight of intelligence and wallowing in the dark night of the soul in an effort to make mysteries more mysterious. The only point at which Niebuhr seems to use his theology is in situations where values and partial interests are locked in mortal combat.

But does an appeal to the absolute really help us here? Is any war so fanatical and bestial as a religious war in which the conditioned values of social and personal interests take on the awful authority of unconditioned claims? Is might right when it is divine might? Is not the God of faith always the God of limited, erring and partial men? If we must have an absolute, let us look for it elsewhere. Against Niebuhr's myth of a private and mysterious absolute, we counterpose the public and self-critical absolute of reflective intelligence or scientific method in its most comprehensive sense. By evaluating claims in the light of their causes and consequences, it makes clear the interests from which they spring, and the meaning of what they propose. By guiding us to the construction of a social order whose institutions provide for the negotiation and compromise of claims on the basis of the completest knowledge available, it promises not absolute security but greater security. It does not pretend to make men gods but to treat more intelligently the problem always at hand. It is not incompatible with action, even with revolutionary action on a large scale. Nothing is won forever but something may always be won. How to get men to accept this absolute method—and to test it by its fruits, not only in the realm of nature but of human affairs— is a specific problem of scientific politics and education concerning which theology can tell us nothing.[5]

Niebuhr's theology has a grand irrelevance to the specific patterns and problems of social life, although psychologically it breathes a defeatism more congenial to Toryism than to his own political progressivism. The same cannot be said of other varieties of theological doctrine which are tied up with a Church as Niebuhr's is not and which take the historical content of revelation more literally than he does. This is most evident in the social and political implications of Roman Catholicism.

Political events bearing on the prospects of its survival have made it necessary for the Catholic Church to strike a new tune in democratic countries. Its leading spokesmen are seizing every occasion to assure us that the last and best defense of democracy and freedom is a Christian social order. By "freedom," they explain, is meant "freedom in its true Christian sense," and by "true Christian," they are careful not to explain, is always meant "Catholic." Any catalogue of Church activities in these countries will reveal that it is increasing in power and influence. It is in the van of attack against the best liberal traditions of American culture and education, particularly in the field of education. What is not understood so well is the fact that its official *doctrinal* teachings, although compatible with a "hierarchical, authoritarian democracy," are also compatible with the denial of freedoms, and of religious toleration, which are essential to the democracy we know.

Christian morality is Catholic morality and the Christian state is bound before God and man to carry out the precepts of morality as interpreted by the Church, which insists that the salvation of the soul is its chief concern, and that outside of the Church there is no salvation. Insofar as it is weak and its communicants in a minority, the Church tolerates modern freedoms and liberties. Where it is strong enough, it has doctrinal authority to suppress them, particularly the propagation of "false" religious teachings by other groups that may undermine "true" Catholic belief. On *prudential* grounds a Catholic state may continue to tolerate modern freedoms and religious heresies. But if it chooses to follow the line of suppression, it can do so on the ground of high *principle*.

That these are not recondite inferences of a suspicious critic of church history is shockingly evident in the Papal Encyclical, *Libertas,* of Leo XIII. That some American churchmen are faithful to this doctrine is just as clear. Fathers Ryan and Boland in their authoritative *Catholic Principles of Politics* explicitly say that if professing Catholics constituted a majority of the population in the United States, the state they would set up "could not permit non-Catholic sects to carry on general propaganda nor accord their organizations certain privileges that had formerly been extended to all religious corporations, for example, exemption from taxation." [6] Although we are assured that this is not likely to happen, we are informed that principled justification is at hand were it to happen.

If this remains Catholic doctrine and is not replaced by "the heresy of Americanism," it testifies not to a failure of nerve but just to plain nerve—brazen and provocative. To match it we must go to the literature of the Communist Party which, demanding unabridged civil rights for itself under existing society, tells us that under the proletarian dictatorship, "all the capitalist parties—Republican, Democratic, Progressive, Socialist, etc.—will be liquidated, the Communist Party functioning alone as the Party of the toiling masses." [7]

As the self-constituted shepherd of all men's souls, the Catholic Church demands as great a control over social and political life as any totalitarian party, for as Pope Leo XIII made abundantly clear, it alone can determine what is subject to the power and judgment of the Church as affecting the salvation of the human soul. Consequently, when the Catholic Bishops who constitute the Administrative Board of the National Catholic Welfare Conference list the chief evils that imperil supernatural religion in this country as "false doctrine, immorality, disbelief, and reborn paganism," it is not hard to see what they refer to. False doctrine is Protestantism, or any religious faith except the true one; immorality is civil marriage, divorce, birth control, any civil freedom that violates a sacrament; disbelief is modern philosophy, any heresy that contradicts the heresies canonized as *philosophia perennis;* reborn paganism is any morality which is not grounded on revelation and any political theory that advocates the separation of church and state. There is a sting of death to the free spirit in every measure the Church proposes to take to safeguard its dogmas.

Partly as a result of Catholic agitation and partly as an expression of spiritual despair, many influential Protestant groups have echoed the call for a society organized on Christian foundations. It is questionable whether all who employ the phrase know what they mean by a Christian society. But whatever it means, it must refer either to Christian organization or Christian dogma. Would a Christian society based on Protestant dogmas, assuming the Protestant sects could agree on any, lead to a state similar in anti-democratic outline to Catholic clericalism? The evidence of history and the logic of the position suggest that, at most, it would tolerate different religious beliefs but not *the freedom of disbelief.* The state could no longer be regarded as neutral to religion. Education would have to be purged of all freethinkers to prevent them from examining the "truths" of religion as critically as the truths of other branches of knowledge. This conclusion is implicit in the recent writing of Professor W. Hocking. The new orthodoxy would find new ways to implement its sway over the minds and allegiances of citizens. Whatever methods it employed would require the contraction, if not the proscription, of the scientific temper in order to diminish the hazards of belief. The social usefulness of ideas to those who possessed power, and their comfort and consolation to those who did not, would become the criteria of accepted truth. The Protestant Reformation would have succumbed to the Counter-Reformation whose secular form already prevails in totalitarian Europe.

These new currents of Protestantism which profess sincere acceptance of present day democracy employ arguments whose force is drawn from a key assumption. It asserts that modern democracy has been derived from, and can only be justified by, the theological dogmas of Hebraic-Christianity according to which all men are created by God and equal before Him. This assumption is the common ground of unity of all religious and metaphysical rationalizations of democracy. It is the rallying point of the much publicized Conference on Science, Philosophy and Religion in their Relation to the Democratic Way of Life, whose pronouncements indicate that it has officially accepted Maritain's Catholic conception of a pluralistic, hierarchically organized culture, crowned by religion, as "the cornerstone on which human civilization must be erected in our day." Scientific inquiry has a place in it: it will meet the "need for men to attain that increased measure of knowledge, which, according to Francis Bacon, brings men back to God." This Hebraic-Christian philosophy of democracy and culture is presented to a world in which a false conception of scientific knowledge has made it "peculiarly resistant to the teachings of religion. . . ." [8]

It can be briefly demonstrated that the derivation of modern democracy from the dogma that all men are created by God and equal before Him is (1) logically invalid (2) historically false and (3) irrelevant to the pressing problem of democratic defense and reconstruction.

(1) From the alleged fact that all men are equal before God, it does not at all follow logically that they are, or should be, equal before the state or enjoy equal rights in the community. This must be justified by other considerations. Even on the theological scheme, although God is equally the creator of angels, men, animals and things, they are not all equal in value before him. Men are also equal before death, pain, disease and the tax-collector. But how they should be treated often depends upon their relative state of health, their efforts, the consequences of their efforts, and other *differential* features of their behavior. Some Christians have held—with as much logic as their brethren who drew contrary conclusions—that because all men are equally sinners in the sight of the Lord, their social and political inequalities in this transitory life are unimportant. Not infrequently, pious

Christians have believed that these inequalities are our punishment for the sins of our fathers. If men have a common origin, biological or theological, that in itself is not logically sufficient for asserting that they must or should have common opportunities or common education or common citizenship. If we believe that they should have, as we do, then we believe it on grounds whose validity would be unaffected whether they had a common origin or not.

Nor is the alleged fact that man was created by God a logical ground for honoring him. We are told both by the Pope and the Archbishop of Canterbury and the American Institute of Judaism that the dignity of man lies not in himself but in that he is a child of God. In the course of a typical Catholic denunciation of "atheistic saboteurs" who would keep the idea of God separate from our government, Professor Clarence Manion of Notre Dame, at a public meeting sponsored by the Conference, proclaims: "The only reason why we have to respect this so-called dignity of man is because it is God-created." [9] The logic would be just as bad even if the rhetoric were better. As well say that the only reason we have for not lying is that it is forbidden by God. Or that the only reason for appreciating the beauty of a landscape is that it is God's handiwork. The origin of a thing may have a bearing upon its nature. But the value of a thing cannot be inferred from its origin. It is not putative original nature but what emerges in the course of developing nature which is relevant to normative judgment. To judge people not by their origins, for which they are not responsible, but by their efforts, fruits, and achievements is a sound democratic maxim.[10]

(2) There is little warrant for the view that the theological dogmas of Hebraic-Christianity are the historical source of modern democracy. Judaism countenanced slavery while Christianity never condemned it in principle. The Church was one of the mainstays of feudalism; until its real-estate holdings were raided by absolute monarchs, it furnished the chief theoretical justification of the divine right of kings. Ideologically, modern democratic theory owes more to Stoic philosophy and Roman law than to Christian Dogma.

Religious institutions based on supernatural dogmas tend towards theocracy. Priesthoods have often been hereditary, and when not tightly closed corporations, rarely subject to democratic influences. It has sometimes been urged as a mitigating feature of the hierarchical, authoritarian structure of the Church that "a peasant might become a Pope." True, but so can an Austrian housepainter or the son of a Georgian cobbler become a Dictator. Does that alter the character of totalitarianism?

(3) We are asked to accept religious dogmas as true mainly on the grounds of their effectiveness in combating Hitlerism. This in turn rests, as we have seen, upon the notion that Fascism is the consequence not of economic conditions, nationalist tradition, and disastrous political policies inside Germany and out, but of the spread of positivism, secularism, and humanism. Why Fascism should then have arisen in such strongly religious and metaphysical countries as Italy and Germany and not in such scandalously heretical and positivistic countries as England and America, is something that the neo-Thomists and their fellow-travellers do not explain.

None of the specific proposals of social reform that issue from religious conclaves, or even the principles sometimes offered to justify them, follow from the theological dogmas that preface their announcement. This is no more surprising than the absence of connection between the pleas for divine guidance which since the war stud the speeches of *all* statesmen of belligerent countries, except those of Stalin,[11] and the content of the speeches. Specific proposals to insure peace, security and freedom warrant attentive consideration no matter from what quarter they come. But their value in effecting what they claim to accomplish depends not on pious faith and good will but upon their consequences which can be adequately explored only by rigorous scientific thought without benefit of theology. To the extent that the scope of scientific thinking is restricted or limited to judgments of bare fact, the new social consciousness of the Christian churches will have just as little relevance to the future as their old consolatory ideals to the past. At best it will take flight from power politics; at worst it will act as a cover for it.

The new failure of nerve in contemporary culture is compounded of unwarranted hopes and unfounded beliefs. It is a desperate quest for a quick and all-inclusive faith that will save us from the trouble of thinking about difficult problems. These hopes, beliefs and faiths pretend to a knowledge which is not knowledge and to a superior insight not responsible to the checks of intelligence. The more fervently they are held the more complete will be their failure. Out of them will grow a disillusion in the possibility of intelligent human effort so profound that even if Hitler is defeated, the blight of totalitarianism may rot the culture of his enemies.

Religion and the Intellectuals

Several years ago in opening the series of articles on "The New Failure of Nerve," in *Partisan Review,* I offered an explanation of the revival of religion in terms of the decline of capitalism, the rise of totalitarianism, the outbreak of war, and the simultaneous decay of socialist belief.

What then seemed to be a strong current, has now become a tidal wave. Regarded as a social phenomenon, I still believe that the complex of factors described in my earlier article, together with the spirit of *fin du mondisme* generated by the liberation of nuclear energy, is roughly adequate as a causal explanation. But since we are considering the renaissance of religion among intellectuals, certain special features, cultural and psychological, should be noted.

First of all, the intellectuals mainly concerned are literary and political—individuals who are not professionally interested in ideas from the point of view of their validity. With notable exceptions they had never earned their right to religious disbelief to begin with, but had inherited it as a result of the struggle of an earlier generation. They were largely ignorant of theology and philosophy, ignorant of the facts of historical evil, ignorant of the recalcitrance of human habit and of the depth and varieties of human limitation. It would be false to say that any group was properly prepared for the modern world in the sense of anticipating its horrors. But these intellectuals were pitifully unprepared to understand them even after they happened, and to re-examine their assumptions about the modern world in the spirit of critical realism rather than of panic or despair. The shock of recent events bewildered them to such an extent that they have become intellectually, not more skeptical, but more credulous, abandoning beliefs never properly understood, for others understood even less. Some have become so obsessed with the animality of man that they can see no grandeur at all in human life; so fearful of the possibilities of human cruelty, that they are blind to still existing possibilities of human intelligence and courage; so resigned to the betrayal of all ideals, that they can no longer make distinctions and regard all social philosophies which are not theocentric as different roads to the culture of 1984.

It is safe to say that those whom Hitler and Stalin have caused to flee to the arms of God had never read, or seriously reflected upon, such works as Henry C. Lea's *History of the Medieval Inquisition* or Graetz's *History of the Jews* or accounts of the religious wars in France and Germany and other wholesale massacres and mass expulsions in European history in centuries less secular than our own.

The revival of religion today is not due to the discovery of new arguments or evidence for supernaturalism or a profounder analysis of the logic of religious belief. This is apparent in the fact that among intellectuals it is not rational theology but mystical theology, not the principle of objectivity but of subjectivity, not the clear, if defective, arguments of Aquinas but the record of the tormented inner experience of Augustine, Pascal, Kierkegaard which are found most appealing. To the extent that evidence is introduced it is drawn from feeling, the feeling of awe and sublimity, of holiness and humility, dogmatically interpreted as indisputable intimations of divinity. Reason is short-circuited by the assumption that there is a non-propositional truth about the nature of things, obscurely grasped in every intense experience. The re-

ligious renaissance of our time is really part of the more inclusive
movement of irrationalism in modern thought. How irrational
is indicated by the feeble character of the arguments which are
offered by the new converts when they deign to employ them
against their critics.

For example, the admission that the existence of God cannot be
demonstrated is often coupled with the retort that neither can his
non-existence be demonstrated—as if this puts belief and disbelief
on an equally reasonable footing, as if no distinction could be
made between the credibility of purely logical possibilities, *i.e.,*
of all notions that are not self-contradictory. It is a commonplace
that only in logic and mathematics can the non-existence of anything be "demonstrated." If we are unjustified in disbelieving an
assertion save only when its contradictory is demonstrated to be
impossible, we should have to believe that the universe is populated
with the wildest fancies. Many things may exist for which we can
give no adequate evidence, but the burden of proof always rests
upon the individual who asserts their existence.

Or if it is admitted that belief in the existence of God or Divine
governance rests in faith, the answer quickly comes that science,
too, rests on faith—faith in causality or the principle of induction,
or some other fundamental assumption of inquiry. As if all fundamental assumptions are equally valid! But the faith of the scientist
is expressed in what he or *anyone else* cannot help believing if he
wishes to predict or control experience. And no one can continue
to live or choose to die without acting on "faith" in the principle
of causality or its equivalent. This faith is of an altogether different kind from the faith of the believer in something which he
cannot help believing on exclusively personal grounds. No believer can live or die without acting on faith in causality: but the
non-believer can with no difficulty at all live or die without faith
in a single religious dogma.

If one chooses to say that the scientist has "faith" in the power
of the anti-rabies treatment to ward off the consequences of the
bite of a mad dog, there can be no objection to this peculiar language provided it is not regarded as equally justified with the
"faith" that rabies can be prevented by prayer, or with the "faith"
that rabies, when it occurs, serves some purpose in a divinely
ordered economy, or the "faith" that even if prayer is not effica-

cious, its appropriateness or fittingness is in some way analogous to the appropriateness of a scientific conclusion in respect to its evidential premises and the principles of inference.

Nor are the facts of moral experience cogent evidence which testifies to the existence of the objects of religious faith. Even if all naturalistic interpretations of obligation and duty are denied out of hand for some variety of ethical intuitionism, according to which "right" and "wrong" are non-natural predicates, this in no way necessitates belief in the characteristic dogmas of religion. And conversely, neither the goodness nor justice of a supernatural power can be derived from His existence. That God is does not entail that God is good.

Indeed, from the point of view of modern need for religious belief, it is highly questionable whether the existence of supernatural elements, in the conventional sense, would be sufficient. Even if psychical research established the fact that some shreds of personality survived the disintegration of the body, which is all the most sober researchers at the moment claim for it, the genuine God-seekers would find no edification in such a state of affairs any more than they would in an atheistic community of more developed spiritual selves.

For what these God-seeking intellectuals are looking for is not so much a theology but a theodicy, not merely, or even primarily, truth but justification and comfort.

Here is located the perennial and most powerful source of religious belief, not only for these intellectuals but for most men, especially in times of social crisis but also in periods of personal crisis. Naturalism as a philosophy is sufficient to gratify all the legitimate needs of the understanding without yielding to the conceit that human intelligence is omnipotent and that all problems will be solved. But in recognizing the reality of the evil and the horrible in human experience, in accepting the finitude not only of man but of every other creature and power, in refusing to swallow the crude or subtle efforts to picture the cosmic order as a moral order, it cannot provide the consolation which the tender-minded must have, if they are to find their existence meaningful and tolerable. It is not that the believer lacks the tough-mindedness to recognize the existence of evil, but that, if he is not to choke to death on it like Ivan Karamazov, he must blunt its sharp edge and learn to believe on no rational grounds that it fulfills a "higher" purpose he does not see.

An intelligent naturalism, no matter how Promethean, will recognize that in addition to the suffering that flows from social inequalities and injustice, there are major experiences of frustration, grief, and loss from which sensitive human beings cannot escape. In the best of societies death may be conquered, but not tragedy. It is not the poor we will always have with us, but the "Underground Man." Scientific knowledge increases human power at the same time as it brings home to us the fundamental precariousness of human existence. Bertrand Russell to the contrary, the growth of science does not make for cosmic impiety or a decline in intellectual humility. Why should the world appear less wonderful or awesome if some day we step from one planet to another, synthesize protoplasm, or lift the darkness from the minds of the insane?

A seasoned naturalism is not Utopian. It realizes that knowledge and wisdom do not guarantee happiness, that they can do little or nothing to lessen the pangs of the mediocre, of the ugly, of those bereft of love or friendship. It cannot promise total security, even when it understands the needs of those who seek it.

Max Weber somewhere suggests that the great religions are interpretations of the world which try to make sense of the meaningless suffering in human life. Although this is not the whole story, I believe it does express something essential in the attitude of the religious person for whom suffering *must* have a meaning and no good cause ever goes down to final defeat. It is true that some naturalists have been shallow optimists—something easily remediable in the light of more knowledge—but such a charge is peculiarly malapropos coming from religious believers whose emotional compulsions have led them to accept optimism on the vastest scale imaginable.

There are some reluctant naturalists with a hankering for the genteel tradition who blame the "new failure of nerve" on the philosophy of naturalism because it does not offer an adequate analysis of the alienation of the modern intellectual and his moral predicaments. How unwarranted such a view is becomes apparent when we reflect upon the fact that philosophical naturalism has never been so far removed from the crudities of reductive materialism as today. It leaves unexplained why the modern intellectual in search of salvation evinces such an obvious distaste towards the very attempt at scientific explanation in history and psychology, and why he substitutes for it not a more rigorous theoretical scheme, but, as his enthusiasm for Toynbee shows, extravagant myth. His dissatisfaction is not intellectual but emotional. The critics who are homesick for gentility look to naturalism to provide a faith to live by equivalent to religious faith. This is precisely what naturalism cannot do if it is honest to the facts of experience. They forget that religious faith cannot be separated from religious belief or dogma, and ultimately from the question of truth. Otherwise we have a serious fooling or a discussion in religious terms of ethical or aesthetic subject matter.

Pruned of its sentimentalism, there is a deep insight in Feurbach's philosophy of religion according to which the secret of theology is (philosophical) anthropology. What Marx did was not to renounce this insight but to show that the emotional needs of which religion was both an expression and gratification could not be dissociated from their cultural matrix. He overstated his position, and some who imagine themselves his followers have made a grotesquerie of it.

So long as religion is freed from authoritarian institutional forms, and conceived in personal terms, so long as overbeliefs are a source of innocent joy, a way of overcoming cosmic loneliness, a discipline of living with pain and evil, otherwise unendurable and irremediable, so long as what functions as a vital illusion or poetic myth is not represented as a public truth to whose existence the once-born are blind, so long as religion does not paralyze the desire and the will to struggle against unnecessary cruelties of experience, it seems to me to fall in an area of choice in which rational criticism may be suspended. In this sense, a man's personal religion justifies itself to him in the way his love does. Why should he want to make a public cult of it? And why should we want him to prove that the object of his love is the most lovely creature in the world? Nonetheless, it still remains true that as a set of cognitive beliefs, religious doctrines constitute a speculative hypothesis of an extremely low order of probability.

The belief that the acceptance of certain religious beliefs of a non-empirical or transcendental character can be a guide to social reorganization leads to intellectual confusion. It often obscures the fact that a parochial power interest is operating behind a universal claim. The most diverse patterns of social control are equally compatible with the same religious doctrines. There are Christian democrats and Christian totalitarians who are at one in their acceptance of religious mysteries. Who is prepared to show that Hromadka, the Czech theologian on the Communist Action Committee which purged the Charles University, was theologically heterodox? Or that the Dean of Canterbury who bore false witness that the United States had used biological warfare in Korea and who fawned on the Communist Procurators of Hungary was a heretic?

Historically, it is undeniable that prophetic religion in the Judaeo-Christian tradition has on occasions pleaded eloquently for social reform in the *language* of supernatural faith. I submit, however, that if we survey history as a whole we will not appreciably differ with the judgment of Ernst Troeltsch in his summary of "the lasting and eternal content of the Christian Ethos" as expressed in his monumental *The Social Teaching of the Christian Churches*. The Christian Ethos, according to Troeltsch, "recognizes differences in social position, power and capacity, as a condition which has been established by the inscrutable Will of God; and then transforms this condition by the inner upbuilding of the personality, and the development of the mutual sense of obligation, into an ethical cosmos." But my point is not historical but logical. Not only are religious dogmas no guide in settling specific issues of an economic or political character, from a wage dispute to the international control of nuclear energy—they can be squared with any solution. And according to the testimony of the great mystics, the most authentic religious experience is beyond concern with good and evil, right and wrong.

There is something ironical in the plea made by the professional misunderstanders of pragmatism (a philosophy which in Peirce and Dewey is an explication of the logic and ethics of scientific method), for a revival of religion as a bulwark against totalitarianism. When they argue that unless men worship God, they will worship either Hitler or Stalin—whose divinity has just been proclaimed in one of the satellite countries, they are themselves lapsing into the vicious kind of pragmatism they attribute to others. The argument presents alternatives that are certainly not exhaustive, and may not be exclusive. Even if valid, it would be relevant not to the truth of the statement that God exists but to the entirely different statement that belief in Him, whether He actually exists or not, has certain desirable effects of a social and psychological kind. But the argument is not valid.

At the present juncture of world history it is true that what is most precious in human experience is threatened on a global scale not by authoritarian religions, which have been chastened by their sufferings at the hands of their secular rivals, but by the expansion of Communism and its regime of ruthless terror. What we need as a rallying cry is freedom, not salvation. A man can choose to save his soul and count the world well lost for it: and one man's salvation is another's superstition. A sure way to lose the struggle for a democratic world is to permit the Pope to take the lead in a crusade against Bolshevism. The struggle of the unfettered intelligence against institutional orthodoxy must continue despite the fact that conflicting orthodoxies, in the interest of their own religious freedom, find themselves allied for the moment against the political super-orthodoxy that will brook no dissent, not even that of silence.

Just as it is fatal to conduct the international struggle against Communism in the name of capitalism—Communism can more easily come to terms with moribund capitalism than with *democratic* socialism—so with the slogans of the parochial religions of the West which the majority of mankind does not accept. What can unite Christian and non-Christian alike in a common struggle for freedom is only the pluralistic philosophy of democracy. For whatever its program for a more humane control of the material conditions of life, democracy permits each individual "to save" his soul in his own way.

An Open Letter to Sidney Hook:
A defense of religious faith
BY ERNEST VAN DEN HAAG

O navis referent in mare te novi fluctus!
O quid agis? Fortiter occupa portum! *

In your contribution to the *Partisan Review* symposium on "Religion and the Intellectuals" (March 1950) you have convincingly shown that religious beliefs cannot be logically justified.

But when you attempt to show that religion is unnecessary or noxious to society, you require more faith from the reader than any church does. The faithful believe—to paraphrase William James—in something doubtful, unknown or unknowable. You require more. Yours is a faith contrary to the evidence: You believe that most men, if left alone, are as reasonable as you are. This is admirable but also dangerously wrong. I must prefer a belief demanding less of my credulity, for my supply of faith is low and my view of society scientific; further, secular faiths are, in effect, less reasonable than ultra-mundane ones. (A secular religion is faith in redemption on this earth by some human action social or individual. It satisfies the same needs satisfied by belief in celes-

---

* Oh ship! new floods are pulling you back to sea!
  Why do you waver? Stay safely in port!
                    HORACE *Ode to the Republic*

tial salvation. The effects, in terms of social and individual action, tend to be more specific and dangerous to freedom and rational conduct. While Catholicism is an ultra-mundane religion, and Marxism and political antisemitism are two instances of secularized faiths differing in degree of elaborateness and comprehensiveness, Christian Science represents an interesting compromise.)

Perhaps I misinterpret your essay. But if you did not mean that religion is, at best, socially useless, then your essay is a charming but socially irrelevant disquisition in logic. You show that religious doctrines can be used to justify almost anything and therefore have no propositional meaning; and you imply surprisingly that they are not needed to help our society. But it is precisely because it is willing to defend almost any society that tolerates it that the Church is important in ours. Religious sanction is required—just as the police force is—for any society which wishes to be stable without being totalitarian. It is required for ours not logically, but psychologically. (Surely you know that few people hold any belief—right or wrong—for sufficient reasons. Beliefs are held because of more or less institutionalized myths. We must make sure that they permit freedom and reason to survive; and the motley array of "psychologists," "counselors," social workers, etc., who have taken the role played by priests, merely reinforce the popular view that all "bad" things—from death to poverty—are due to remediable mistakes, crookedness, maladjustments or defects in the social system. Such a grotesque myth represents the beginnings of a secularized eschatology. The dangers inherent in this can be averted only by return to a celestial one.)

According to Malinowski, religion differs from magic: it is an attempt to accept the universe as a moral order (comforted by celestial promises) rather than to control it. Science thus, particularly in its application, is nearer magic than religion, though distinguished from both by its method. But where the rational (*i.e.*, achievable) ends of science are replaced by irrational (unattainable) ones, by any kind of this-worldly eschatology, the resulting parascience (or alchemy) tends to prescribe a conduct far less reasonable than the one required by religion; and when this prescription is institutionalized, there is danger that it will be imposed.

Religion is a useful, even a necessary opiate—a sedative protecting us from excessive anxiety and agitation and from those who, like Marx, thrive on agitation and therefore hate the sedative and would replace it by the murderer's hashish. But the sedative is needed not only against Marx's Ismailitic exploitation—it is needed until the patient can take his medicine. There is hardly much danger that we will become overly addicted to it. On the contrary, the difficulty is to evoke the faith that makes religion effective. But this is a different problem. Surely, even if the trend of history is "inevitably" away from religion, you would not be addicted enough to Marxian logic to infer that you have to approve of this trend; and once you see the social danger, you will find a number of policies to oppose the trend.

If religion does not reconcile us to the suffering and the "injustices" inherent in life, men will try to eliminate them. But it is better to promise the meek that they shall inherit the earth than to allow power-hungry fanatics to invite them to conquer it. For the meek will always be with us, but the Utopian attempt and the necessary failure spell tyranny. We may have to admit with Faust:

> *So haben wir mit hoellischen Latwergen*
> *in diesen Thaelern diesen Bergen*
> *weit schlimmer als die Pest getobt.*
> *Ich habe selbst das Gift an tausende gegeben;*
> *Sie welkten hin, ich muss erleben*
> *dass man die frechen Moerder lobt.**

Ignoring the need for a myth—and for an institution to support and render acceptable the values which we must hold to survive in freedom—also conflicts with the external demands of the moment. We need a faith to transcend life, for the survival of our society will require the sacrifice of individual lives. Reason cannot justify the unreasonable and inequitable individual sacrifices which its defense requires. And *non omnis moriar,* or *dulce et decorum est pro patria mori,* are neither comfort nor justification for an anonymous and perhaps unsurvived death. Such sacrifices require either a transcendent myth or a forceful totalitarian propaganda-monopoly. We have neither, and thus we are necessarily on the defensive in this war, risking defeat.

---

* "So thus we raged through these hills and vales doing far more harm with our infernal drugs than the plague itself. I myself gave the poison to thousands; they withered away, yet I must suffer hearing the impudent murderers praised."
Faust, Part I

Except for religion I am aware of no available myth strong
enough to hold against the rival secularized eschatologies (and to
hold us together) while tolerating the freedom which is at stake.
Democracy means to choose freely and to depend on ourselves for
improvement. It does not depend on grace, nor promise perfection
—thus it cannot become the needed myth without becoming un-
democratic. For transcendent myth is required just for the purpose
of making tolerable the difference between even the best of social
systems and eschatological perfection—ultimate justice. (Democracy
requires such a myth more than other systems for it intensifies by
its improvements the wish for perfection.) If this difference is no
longer tolerated by virtue of myth (and people are not ready to
tolerate it otherwise) we will soon lose what liberty we have now.

Not unlike the democratic party, or Marxism, religion and the
Christian church have stood for many things in the course of history. But in any period or place they advance particular policies.
This is what matters. You would not always have wanted to oppose
these policies although you probably would never have wholly approved. But of what actual policy of any group could one approve
wholly? Why would we act as if total approval of each past and
present policy were required? One may oppose some of its policies
without opposing the Church, which more than once defended and
preserved freedom and civilization from external and internal
dangers. Did not the successor of Peter and Pontifex Maximus exe-
cute Girolamo Savonarola, thus saving the culture of the Renaissance—our civilization—from destruction?

It is socially and politically not important whether religious doctrines are true. It matters only that they are believed. This belief is
necessary for the existence of an effective Church (although not
sufficient). And the social effects of the Church today (not in 1600)
are better, not than the blueprints of a mythless society, but than
the existing and threatening alternatives. I will not forsake the
better for the Utopian best and the existing worst. Nor is it important to consider to what extent the current virulent ersatz
religions are due to the weakening of faith, as long as we remember
that, where faith buttresses a strong church and is buttressed by
it, the Ersatz has no entrance.

Don't you think that Dr. Fuchs, Alger Hiss, *et al.* have embraced
Communism not because of but despite what it is, to "live tensely

under the discipline that such a faith instills in them?" Have you not heard with Ortega the "formidable cry rising like the howling of innumerable dogs to the stars, asking for someone or something to impose an occupation, a duty"? What superfaith is required to believe—*quia absurdum*—that religion will be replaced by the reasonable naturalism by which you live! More faith than I have, more, I think, than you can afford and be reasonable.

Max Weber taught us that the institutional structure of the Church is indispensable to absorb or eliminate the charismatic rebels or competing destructive myths which continuously threaten civilization. Emile Durkheim taught us that without a myth around which group-sustained values may center, people find their lives meaningless, their activities futile, their existence fragmented, and their beliefs fragmentary. For a time the institutionalized faith which relates us to each other and to past and future may be replaced by individual compulsions; and for some even by stark acceptance of their aloneness. But without the dikes of the past, left from past floods, the wave of the future soon engulfs those who do not drown themselves voluntarily.

Religion and the Church have greatly weakened their hold on man's mind. But not redemptionism. It has merely been secularized. People no longer place the pie in the sky. They want it here and now; they no longer project their needs, wishes, and confusions onto the heavens but into this mundane universe. They demand specific measures to change it. They want salvation here, now and "scientifically." They come to prefer para-scientific to religious ideologies. Sometimes pseudo-economic, sometimes pseudo-biological, sometimes pseudo-psychological ones. Sometimes only the trivial or sordid: to seek forgiveness and through grace repair their impotence, people continue to appeal to omnipotent panaceas; but what loss of dignity in the change from the cathedral to the "functionalist" soap box or to the orgone box!

Nor are the secular religions confined to trivialities. The replacement of the Holy Father with the father of the people, of the College of Cardinals with the Politburo, involves nothing less than new and indefinitely prolonged dark ages.

We should allow some twilight here and there, even some dark corners, to avoid the total darkness that may follow your insistence on enlightenment. For the blaze of reason which you are inviting is sure to cause an emotional short circuit, or hysterical blindness. The more interested you are in enlightenment, the more you should favor the distribution of obscuring glasses to those otherwise unable to stand the glare. Further, I hold with Leopardi (and perhaps Eliot):

> ed è men vano
> Della menzogna il vero? A noi di lieti
> Inganni e di felici ombre soccorsc
> Natura stessa: e là dove l'insano
> Costume ai forti errori esca non porse,
> Negli ozi oscuri e nudi
> Mutò la gente i gloriosi studi.*

Perhaps in some dim future people will stop believing in redemption altogether; they may learn to accept the inherent features of life without crying "miserere mihi" and "aperite mihi portas iustitiae." They may no longer need to believe that God "justly secret and secretly just" will sometime open the gates to paradise. (They may even give up their faith in "democratic socialism.") There is nothing inevitable in the need for myth. It just exists as a matter of fact, and I see no evidence for its weakening in the proximate future. If that is so, surely the faith propagated by the Church is the best of those available and effective (and just as the Church is the best alternative for those who want freedom to survive, Democracy is the best alternative for those who want the Church to survive). The Church has already lost a great deal of effectiveness. We must do our best to avoid weakening it further. The ancient splendor of that many-layered apostolic rock on which a super-structure of logic and absurdity has accumulated through the ages is now one of the few remaining citadels. Behind it, if not within it, we may be able to preserve some freedom.

Perhaps you will object that I am pragmatic (in Bertrand Russell's crude, but meaningful, interpretation of the word). Indeed in these concrete matters, I tend to be as pragmatic as you are only in abstract ones. But one need not become a camelot du roi nor

---

* Leopardi's lines come from his "Ode to a Ball Player" and may be rendered as follows:

"And are truths less vain than lies? Nature itself helps us with encouraging deceits and comforting illusions: and where unhealthy social ideas do not tolerate fortifying illusions people transmute their glorious endeavors into obscure and futile pastimes."

confide one's mind and soul wholly to the Church to admit what
you are at once too proud and too humble to own up to: that few
men are possessed of the intellectual strength required to give
significance to their lives without having it imposed in some part
from outside.

But then, is this ecclesiastical imposition really universal and
identical for all? Haven't you, yourself, argued that it is not, that
it allows many, if not all interpretations? Is the pattern that God
is supposed to weave for us through the sacred texts really—as Kant
thought—heteronomous? May it not be the pre-text of our autonomy? Without the sacred thread the garment has no texture.
Not autonomy, but anomy is the effect; and then a new collective
myth far more coercive and totalitarian than the one which wisdom
and time have deprived of a great deal of belligerence. In a society
conceiving life as a race, more than ever there is a need for faith
to rationalize "that the race is not to the swift . . . but time and
chance happeneth to them all." Your stark acceptance cannot perform this function for most. (Nor can the desperately trivial and
trivially desperate eudaemonism into which most have fallen.)
Your belief that it can is a testimony to your own moving faith.

Neither Myth nor Utopia
A REJOINDER TO ERNEST VAN DEN HAAG

We are living in a time when not only power corrupts but ideas,
too. It may be that the corruptions of power in the twentieth cen-

tury are not unrelated to the generic contempt for human beings of which, I very much fear, your attitude is an unconscious expression. Everything that can be said for your position has already been said by the Grand Inquisitor in Dostoyevsky's *Brothers Karamazov*. And much more persuasively said because his defense of myth, miracle and priestly authority in social life is motivated by a desire—that often may be quite genuine—for human happiness. But to defend, as you do, organized irrationalism in behalf of human freedom is an intellectual absurdity—a cruel paradox which requires that we forget whatever we know about history, social institutions and human beings.

It is unnecessary to confront those who still have faith in freedom with a choice between Rome and Moscow in order to justify some form of common *political* action in behalf of an imperfectly free society. If it was legitimate to send aid to Stalin to withstand Hitler's onslaught, it is certainly permissible in present historical circumstances to support churchmen against Stalinist terror. Cardinal Mindzenty is a human being like any other, and those miserable "liberals" whose hostility to the Church led them to gloss over his martyrdom as incidental to the hypocritical land reforms of a satellite regime will some day themselves suffer his fate if Soviet expansion is not brought to a halt. But to accept the myths of the Church—not for oneself, of course, but for the herd!—is superfluous folly. It is comparable to the stupendous blunder of those who thought that we couldn't send aid to Stalin without promulgating the lie that the Soviet Union was genuinely interested in the defense or extension of democracy and that therefore public criticism of its terroristic regime should be discouraged.

You remind me that "one may oppose some of its policies without opposing the Church." If this is possible, why is it not equally possible to support some of its policies without supporting the Church? Just think what you are asking of us. We are to evaluate particular Church policies on specific matters—European Union, trade unionism, birth control and divorce, race relations, support of Franco—taking and rejecting what seems to be required in the interests of a free society. But we are not to evaluate the Church myths: we are to accept them and teach them *in toto* (or at least not criticize them) as medicinal lies for the masses. In this you insult those whom you wish to teach, who are not so stupid as to fail to see through your own theology of disbelief, as well as those genuinely pious believers for whom the passion of Christ is not a "pragmatic" fairy tale in the strategy of the cold war.

Even in terms of the narrow, and to genuine believers somewhat cynical, use to which you wish to put faith in Church dogma, your recommendation is self-defeating. You do not explain why the Communist threat is strongest in countries in which the Catholic tradition has the deepest hold. You do not explain the failure of a selective application of Church policies to meet the problems of land reform and overpopulation, in a country like Italy, problems which require something less than Utopia to mitigate if not to solve. You do not explain the disastrous political ineptitude and worse of the Church in Austria and Germany; its role in the Abyssinian War and Franco's rebellion—events which made multitudes an easy prey to Stalinist duplicity; its freedom-loving behavior in Quebec, Boston, and New York City where it led the crusade against the employment of Bertrand Russell.

Your history, it seems to me, is questionable and in no way fortifies the ground for your politics. I hold no brief for Savonarola, but, to do him historic justice, he was no foe of the Renaissance as his friendships with some of its great figures show. And he was a nobler creature than the venal Bishop of Rome who destroyed him after extorting from his racked body Moscow-like confessions. But we do not have to choose between the corruptions and insincere mythology of Alexander VI, and the superstitious prophecies of Savonarola even if we believe that it is far worse to burn human beings than to burn trinkets. In the interests of the scientific truth which leads you to proclaim the necessity of mass belief in scientific untruth, it seems to me you should admit that the history of the Church as a defender of cultural and intellectual freedom is until very recently in the main a history of persecution and heresy hunts. Or are you already rewriting church history for the masses as a corollary of your new insight into the liberating function of vital illusions?

Nor have you properly learned the logic of organization from your unavowed Machiavellian masters. Even if you could guarantee us a free-thinking Pope with a fondness for heretical argument, once the Church was safe from the tidal wave of Bolshevism, what further guarantee is there that he wouldn't throw you and your friends to the dogs of orthodoxy whenever organizational needs demanded it? Viewed empirically, the Church exists for the sake of the Church and not for the sake of your freedom or mine. If the masses of people are as inherently credulous as you suppose, they will always lack the sophistication to tolerate the artful thinking you recommend to their pastors. In the presence of apparent hypocrisy and the ambiguities of poetic faith, with its suspended belief and analogical truth, fanaticism emerges with an exalted sincerity. What you are inviting with your theology of fiction is a recurring alternation of Reformation and Counter-Reformations— a progressive competition in doctrinal absurdities to be used as weapons in a conflict for institutional power.

You misunderstand my position. It is not transcendental dogmas of the Church, which with a little logic can be squared with any practice, that threaten the structure of our intellectual and personal freedoms, but its organizational needs and claims. Santayana, certainly no enemy of the Church, which in its current weakness must tolerate both his materialistic and Platonic heresies, once wrote: "If he Catholic Church ever became dominant in America, it would without doubt, by virtue of its concrete mission, transform American life and institutions. In the measure of its power and prudence, it would abolish religious liberty, the freedom of the press, divorce, and lay education." If Santayana is right, could so many liberties be lost without losing others? You cannot safeguard religious doctrines from dangerous criticism without controlling *more* than religious belief, without invading other domains of thought to keep freedom of inquiry in check. No, the only sure way to make the Church an ally of freedom is to keep it permanentl; weak among a multitude of freely competing religious faiths. I am hopeful that the influence of "the American heresy" on the Church, as well as the evolution of its own doctrine of the relation between state and church in the light of the fight for freedom against modern totalitarianism, will prove Santayana wrong. But we cannot rely only on hope. We must put all thinking minds on guard to resist the first infraction of freedom, and strengthen the institutional and educational safeguards against breaches in the wall separating church and state. The effects of your position, I fear, will undermine not strengthen these safeguards.

Your argument rests upon a too easy identification of "faith" with "myth" and of both with superstition. When I say I have faith in medical science, I do not mean that I am confident that medicine will ever abolish all disease and death but that it will heal more people more often than religious piety, absent prayer, or alternative remedies. When I say I have faith in intelligence or democracy, I do not mean that a society organized on these principles will be one without violence or without inequality but only that there is a much better prospect of substantially diminishing the extent of violence and inequality in social life than would be the case if Church authority and myth or any other known alternatives were to become the operating principles. In other words, my "faith" functions as a regulative principle not as a secularized eschatology. You interpret my faith as if it were a demand for the impossible or for total salvation. By definition that makes it a secular eschatology which you equate with a celestial eschatology, and then add to the absurdity by proclaiming that the latter is less absurd than the former, as if there were a reasonable way of choosing between absurdities. Your procedure here is equivalent to those who interpret the principle of induction as if it were a guarantee that we will some day know everything, and then equate faith in the principle of induction with faith in the existence of God.

You insist that you are talking psychology, not logic, but I find your psychology too crude. It is one thing to say that most human beings cannot build their life on the illusionless methods and results of intelligence alone, that in order to sustain courage and hope in certain critical periods they need some compensatory or consolatory beliefs. It is quite another to assert that only a celestial myth interpreted by a secular Church can supply the need. There is an infinite variety of private myths from among which they can choose. Their very number, and personal character, are usually sufficient to protect us from their vagaries. In this sense, Protestantism as a doctrine which makes religion a private matter is much more appropriate to a democratic culture—because in principle it makes even atheism a legitimate "religious" belief—than Catholicism. But the practices of Protestant *Churches* whenever they enjoy a monopoly of religious control can be just as hostile to democracy as those of any other religious theocracy.

It is perfectly possible to enjoy and celebrate Christmas without believing in the existence of Santa Claus or the historicity of Christ. So much I am sure you will grant. Why, then, deny the possibility of loving one's country without succumbing to the vicious religion of nationalism, or of believing in intelligence and democracy without assuming that their use will transform men into Angels and the Earth into Paradise? Enough that they make men and society more humane.

Modern Knowledge and the Concept of God

1

Many years ago in a discussion with Jacques Maritain he re-
marked that anyone who was as keenly interested in arguments for
the existence of God as I seemed to be was not beyond hope of
redemption. One can with equal justification observe that strong
concern with the validity of the arguments for God's existence
threatens the integrity of belief in him. Some believers have become agnostic when they discovered that the chain of argument
which was the anchor of their faith had defective links.

I owe it to the reader to indicate that the point of view from
which I shall develop my position is that of a still unredeemed,
"skeptical God-seeker." I call myself a "God-seeker" because I am
willing to go a long way, to the very ends of reason itself, to track
down every last semblance of evidence or argument which promises
fulfillment of the quest. I call myself a "skeptical God-seeker" because I have so far returned from previous expeditions empty-
handed. Since I am prepared to undertake the quest anew, I have
not embraced any of the final negations of traditional disbelief

which would forever close off further objective inquiry by metaphysical fiat.

This freedom from question-begging commitment is all the more appropriate because I am primarily concerned with "the concept of God" and only secondarily concerned with the question whether that of which we form or have the concept exists. It is of the utmost importance that we abide by this distinction. Who would dispute for long about whether "snow men" exist or whether a "hippogriff" exists without first defining or indicating in a rough way what the meaning of these terms is? Such definitions or concepts do not have to be very precise, but they cannot be so vague that we are unable to distinguish them from definitions and concepts of quite different terms altogether. The least we must know is what we are to count as "snow man" or "hippogriff" before looking for it.

Although this initial demand for clarity is regarded as legitimate in the analysis of most concepts, there is an extraordinary resistance to following the same procedure in connection with the term "God." Many people will heatedly discuss the question whether God exists—without displaying any concern over the fact that they are encompassing the most heterogeneous notions in the use they make of the word "God." After such discussions, one is tempted to say, "God only knows what 'God' means."

Now this expression "God only knows what 'God' means" is perfectly good theology, for it can be taken as a way of saying that "Only God has complete or perfect knowledge of God." Unfortunately, however, not only "complete or perfect knowledge" of the meaning of God is denied us by some theologians, but even *adequate* knowledge. According to these theologians, the concept of God refers to something "unique," and therefore it is impossible to describe him in terms which are applicable to other things. Otherwise God would merely be another item in the catalogue of common things. But he is *sui generis*. Father Copleston, the able Jesuit philosopher, puts the point explicitly: "God by hypothesis is unique; and it is quite impossible to describe Him adequately by using concepts which normally apply to ordinary objects of experience. If it were possible, He would not be God . . . this must be so, owing to the finitude of the human intellect. . . ."

Now I believe it can be shown that this conclusion is false. The

finitude of the human intellect is no bar to adequate knowledge of
other things, even of things which are not finite; for example, we
can give an adequate account of an infinite series of integers. Nor
can our inability to describe God adequately flow from the presumed uniqueness of God because there are unique things in the
world which we can describe adequately in terms that apply to
other things. If there was a first man in the world, then by definition he is or was certainly unique. There couldn't be two first men.
Nevertheless, we have a rather adequate understanding of what it
would mean for anything to be the first man.

What must be intended by Father Copleston and those who
share his views is that God is uniquely unique. In order to understand why God is considered uniquely unique, we must recognize
the second of the difficulties that are said to be involved in getting
an adequate knowledge of God. This is that the concept of God
refers to something or someone that *necessarily* exists. What does
it mean to say that something necessarily exists? It means that our
knowledge of its existence cannot be the conclusion of an empirical
or inductive argument, for such can only lead to a probability
judgment. Nor can our knowledge be the conclusion of a formal
deductive argument—unless the premises are taken as absolutely
or necessarily true, which is never the case even with propositions
in geometry. The only test which is at all plausible of the necessary truth of an assertion concerning the existence of anything is
that the denial of this assertion is self-contradictory. There are
enormous difficulties here, the upshot of which is that at most and
at best the only assertions which fulfill this requirement are the
laws of logic. Everything else which is given or discovered in the
world can be otherwise. Now if the laws of logic are taken as
formal conditions of discourse they cannot establish the existence
of anything (including God) as necessary. If they are taken as statements about things then they produce an embarrassing richness of
necessary existences. Those who accepted them would be under
the intellectual compulsion of finding a way to distinguish between
God and other necessary existences. This makes it impossible for
believers to use the laws of logic alone, for since they generally
assume that the existence of other things *depends* upon God, they
cannot accept any method of argument which leads to the conclusion that there are other necessary existences as well. Such a con-

clusion would entail that God's power is limited. If, for example, we assert that the world necessarily exists, it would be self-contradictory to bring in God as its necessary creator or sustainer.

It should now be clear why those who talk about the concept of God, especially in traditional terms, have such difficulties, and why their arguments keep breaking down. In intellectual fairness we must recognize that they have embarked upon a project of belief which forces them to use the language of paradox and analogy. What exacerbates their difficulty is that the language of paradox and analogy cannot be the same as the ordinary models of paradoxical or analogical discourse. To do justice to the theologians, imagination must give wings to our understanding and broaden the perspective of our vision. But we must also remain within the horizon of intelligibility or of what makes sense.

If the term "God" has meaning, we must be able to say what it is. If we say what God is, we must be able to describe him in certain distinct combinations of words and sentences, and therefore we must find some principle which controls our statements. No one who regards the term God as meaningful will admit the propriety of *any* statement about God, but at the very least he must recognize *degrees* of appropriateness with respect to language. And the problem with which we are wrestling breaks out all over again when we ask: what principle determines the *appropriateness* of the language? For example, the reflective believer in God knows that the epithet "person" or "father" cannot be literally applied to God, that God isn't a person like other persons or a father like other fathers. Nonetheless he finds no difficulty in praying to "Our Father in Heaven." He would, however, deem it singularly inappropriate for anyone to refer to God in prayer as "Our Nephew in Heaven." Why?

The most plausible answer, based upon a study of the names of God and the attributes predicated of him, suggests that the principle which controls the appropriateness of our utterances is derived from the language of human ideals, in their anthropological and ethical dimensions. The conclusion is incontestable that in some sense every intellectual construction of man will reflect his nature. Nor does this fact necessarily entail subjectivity. For even science (which next to mathematics is most frequently taken as a paradigm of objectivity) can be considered a human enterprise whose propositions are constructions of, or inferences from, the data of ordinary experience, and describable in language either continuous with ordinary language or constructed from terms which are ultimately so derived, no matter how technical. But the great difference between God as an object of religious belief, and the objects of scientific belief, is that assertions about the latter are controlled by familiar rules of discourse, understood by all other investigators, that they are related by logical steps to certain experimental consequences, and that these consequences can be described in such a way that we know roughly what counts as evidence for or against the truth of the assertions in question. Now this is not the case with respect to those statements which affirm the existence of God. Certain observable phenomena will sometimes be cited as evidence *for* the truth of the assertion, but it will not be shown how this evidence follows from God's existence; nor will there ever be any indication of what would constitute evidence *against* its truth.

This is what militates against the so-called experimental arguments for the existence of God, as distinguished from the traditional or rationalistic arguments. It must be acknowledged that there is wisdom in the refusal of the traditional position (except for certain aspects of the argument from design) to *risk* the belief in God's existence on any experimental findings. For if it is the case that God's existence is to be inferred from, or confirmed by, the *presence* of certain experimental findings, then the absence of these findings must be taken insofar forth as evidence against the hypothesis. But in fact those who talk about experimental evidence for the existence of God are obviously prepared to believe in Him no matter what the evidence discloses. It is considered blasphemous in many quarters to put God to any kind of test. Truth or falsity as we use the terms in ordinary discourse about matters of fact or as synonyms for warranted or unwarranted assertions in science are not really intended to apply in the same way to religious assertions.

This brings us back to a consideration of the principle which controls the *appropriateness of our utterances* about God. The most fruitful hypothesis about this principle seems to me to have been formulated by Ludwig Feuerbach, that greatly neglected figure of the nineteenth century, who declared after a study of the predicates attributed to God that they were projections of human needs—not the needs of the understanding but the needs of the heart, not of the human mind but of human feeling: emotions, hopes, and longings. What Feuerbach is saying, as I interpret him, is that the principle which controls the appropriateness of our utterances about God is man's idealized conception of himself, and that the predicates of God, particularly those which make him an object of reverence, worship, and aspiration are objectifications of man's highest ethical ideals.

What I propose to do briefly is to show that certain modern conceptions of knowledge tend to confirm the Feuerbachian hypothesis both negatively and positively. Negatively, I wish to indicate some reasons why the idea of a transcendent God and the idea of an immanent God are intellectually unacceptable, *i.e.*, they cannot give an intelligible account of the concept of God, and *a fortiori*, of his existence. Positively, I shall try to suggest the way in which the concept of God has functioned as a moral ideal without supernaturalism.

2

The idea of God as a transcendent power, independent of the world of nature and man, is perhaps the oldest of the concepts of a divine and supreme Being. Certainly it is the most traditional in the West. It views God as a Creator but in such a way as to make an inexplicable mystery of creation. In this connection, it should be pointed out that the argument from the first cause, even if it were valid, which it obviously is not, would by itself be insufficient to establish the existence of God as a Creator. Aristotle's God is a first cause, too, and is introduced as a support, so to speak, for Aristotle's physics—an Unmoved Mover toward which everything aspires. But Aristotle's God does not create the world which exists with him from eternity. It was none other than Aquinas who taught that on grounds of reason alone we could not tell whether the world had existed from eternity or had been created by God: only revelation or faith could be the source of our knowledge that God created the world. Aquinas, however, also assumed that although the truths of revelation are not the same as the truths of reason, the two must nevertheless be logically compatible. Yet the concept of a creative God has always been a stone of stumbling to the human mind—and with good cause.

"Creation" ordinarily presupposes three things: (a) a plan or purpose; (b) a method and instrument of execution; and (c) an antecedently existing subject matter or material which is reshaped or reworked by the instrument in the light of the design or plan. When we speak of God as "creating" the world, there is no difficulty with the notion of plan or purpose. But there is a grave difficulty with the notions of the instrument and subject matter. For God is supposed to have created the world out of nothing—*ex nihilo*. Now in our experience nothing is or can be created out of nothing. There is always some subject matter, some instrument. How, then, is creation *ex nihilo* to be understood? The common reply is that God creates "analogically" not literally. But analogical creation is like analogical fatherhood. It doesn't explain why one kind of analogical expression is used rather than another. Why can't we say that God coexists with the world—"coexists analogically," of course? The reason, Feuerbach would say, is not to be found in God but in man. He worships in idealized form the fulfillment of conscious or unconscious need, especially his needs as a person threatened in a world of impersonal things. He expresses this in the analogical transfiguration of the concept Creator and in its analogical predication of God.

Does modern knowledge in any way help to explain the notion of a "creative God" or *creatio ex nihilo*. Some have thought that this concept of a creative God can be clarified by suggestions from modern cosmology and modern depth psychology. I should like to say a word about each.

According to the so-called cosmology of "continuous creation" developed by Fred Hoyle, Herman Bondi, and others, new matter is continuously being generated out of nothing and in this way the universe (which is continuously expanding) remains "in a steady-state and at an over-all constant density." As Hoyle puts it, "Matter simply appears—it is created. At one time the various atoms composing the material do not exist *and at a later time they do*."[1] What is true now is presumably true for original matter—for the very first speck of matter that ever appeared. But it should be pointed out that this theory says nothing about the *process* by which matter comes into existence. The expression "appearing suddenly" is certainly not synonymous with "creating." One can speak of "life" spontaneously "appearing" or "emerging" in the past or present without implying that it was "created" or that it is necessarily beyond scientific explanation. Matter is "found" to appear at certain times and under certain conditions. That it is "created" is something to be established only after the expression "creation" is given some determinate meaning. But without reference to plan or purpose, act or instrument, the term "creation" is a misnomer. At any rate, whatever the chaotic state of affairs which is described by the new cosmology as having existed in the universe about five billion years ago when matter was born, it came into being at time t, and therefore *in principle* is open to a scientific explanation in terms of the state of affairs at time, t-1. If it is objected that there was no time before matter came into existence and that therefore t-1 is ruled out, then the objection equally applies to any creative act as well. Hoyle, too, speaks of time *before* and after matter appears. Creation becomes just as mysterious in the new cosmology as in the old theology.

It is a far cry from scientific cosmology to depth psychology. I must content myself with only a passing reference to a recent effort by Professor William Poteat [2] to elucidate the expression "creation out of nothing." He admits that any aspect or piece of behavior of the human body—physical, biological, psychological—can be explained in terms of events which precede it of the same logical order, and that these events constitute a theoretically infinite series without any first term. But, he says, when we speak of the human body or being as a "person," when we add to the language of impersonal behavior the personal pronouns "I" and "my," something radically discontinuous with the rest of the nonpersonal world comes into the picture. The world which is "mine" is altogether different from a world in which "mine" refers to nothing. Now the act of suicide is an act of radical destruction which destroys at one stroke the possibility of any kind of personal experience. "I am not destroying something or other *in* the world (by my act of suicide), I am destroying the world as a whole." This is the exact opposite of the process of radical creation. God creates the world out of nothing in an analogously opposite way to our making nothing out of the existing or created world. Granted, then, that "creation out of nothing" is a queer sort of thing, inexplicable in terms of ordinary language. So is suicide. A similar analysis of the notion "I was born"—a phrase I may use when I become aware of the world as related to myself, a person at whose center is the personal pronoun "I"—reveals that this notion is no less queer than suicide. In one case "I make nothing out of something"; in the other "I make something out of nothing." Both escape explanation by ordinary and scientific modes of speech: both provide the analogy for God as "maker of heaven and earth."

All this seems to me more ingenious than persuasive. The psychological phenomena of suicide and "becoming aware" can be given quite different explanations which make them less mysterious than "creation out of nothing." About the causes, motives, conditions, and consequences of suicide we know quite a little. Suicide phenomenologically blots out the world—but so does sleep and unconsciousness. A man may commit suicide not because he wants to destroy the world but because others have destroyed it for him. And since a man who firmly believes in immortality can commit suicide, Professor Poteat's analysis must be revised. "Becoming aware" or "being born" to myself as a first person singular does not so much create a world as light up an antecedently existing one. I undergo the experience of being-in-the-world, of being treated as object or person, long before I become aware of the world as distinct from myself or of myself as counterposed to the world. The discovery of myself is not primary to everything else in the way in which creation out of nothing must be.

These makeshift attempts to demystify the mystery of *creatio ex nihilo* either call our attention to something which is unusual in speech or action but which is otherwise intelligible, or generate mysteries as dark as the one they would illumine. The concept of a transcendent God who creates the world *ex nihilo,* in time or out of time, can no more be clearly thought than the concept of the last number in a series in which every number has a successor. There is a sort of brutal honesty in Karl Barth's contention that God is "altogether Other" from man and the world, and that philosophic reason is unable to grasp what is "ineffable," "unfathomable," and "inconceivable."

What Barth does not understand, however, is that in applying the axe to human reason, he destroys the possibility of any solid ground for Faith or Revelation. If the concept of God defies adequate grasp by human reason, then what can it mean to say that belief in him rests on Faith or Revelation? Men thirst to know what they have faith in "as the hart pants for water." Man's reason will not be denied, despite the pronouncements of Luther and Barth. It makes sense to say, "My belief that X is my friend is based on faith, not evidence or reason," but only because I know what the phrases "X is a friend" and "X is *my* friend" mean. Similarly the statement "Belief in God's existence is based on faith, not rational evidence or argument" takes on meaning only if I am able to describe what it is I have faith in. But how can anyone who eschews intelligence or reason know or describe what he has faith in? How can he distinguish between the assertion, "I have faith in God" and the assertion "I have faith in Mumbo Jumbo"? Whether we approach divinity by reason or by faith, we cannot escape wrestling with the concept of God, even if we are unsure thereby to win Jacob's blessing.

If the foregoing analysis is sound, then the idea of a transcendent God has certain root logical and linguistic difficulties which are not likely to be affected by the progress of modern knowledge—unless the latter leads to a shift in the basic categories of our understanding. If the concept of a transcendent God is incomprehensible, it is difficult to see what difference it makes whether we declare that he created the earth in six days or six million years, whether he created man in one operation out of dust or through a long series of evolutionary changes. At the Darwin Centennial celebration at the University of Chicago last year, Sir Julian Huxley denied that our earth and its inhabitants were created, and he presented anew the evidence for believing that both evolved out of earlier forms. To which Father J. Franklin Ewing, professor of anthropology at Fordham University, replied in somewhat the same way as other distinguished theologians replied to Huxley's grandfather: "God is the creator of man—body and soul. Whether he used the method of evolution for the preparation of the human body or created it from unorganized matter is not of primary importance. In either case he is the Creator. . . . God created not only all beings but also all potentialities for evolution."

In short, no matter what the findings of science are, they cannot affect the truths of religion. And it is significant that in his address to the Vatican Academy of Sciences on November 22, 1951, Pope

Pius XII without any embarrassment accepted the findings of modern astronomy about the age and evolution of the universe. This withdrawal in advance from any possible conflict with the claims of science to true knowledge of the physical universe makes it difficult to understand the intense warfare waged by religion and theology against science in the past. If it really is the case that the domains of scientific inquiry and religious belief do not touch at any point, and therefore cannot conflict, then it becomes hard to explain why the advance of science should in fact have weakened religious belief and produced periodic crises of faith. Whatever the present situation may be, science was not in the past given such autonomy either by religion or theology.

Feuerbach's interpretation of these periodic crises of belief is that they are nodal points in human consciousness when men become dimly aware that their statements about God are not the same kind of thing as their statements about ordinary matters, but are expressions of need and hope for an absolutely secure source, a power or an Ideal, beyond Nature, yet not foreign to human nature, on which to rely for protection against all the evils that beset them in their precarious careers on earth. "The Creation, like the idea of a personal God in general, is not a scientific, but a personal matter," he writes, "not an object of the free intelligence but of the feelings. . . ." If God is awesome and tremendous and mysterious it is because he has unlimited power over nature—and therefore unlimited Will which is related to human will. God defies rational analysis because his "existence" is postulated not by any imperative of thought but by the anguished feelings of finite, suffering man, who wishes to preserve his "personality or subjectivity" against the forces which reduce him to the level of matter. For him "the belief in God is nothing but the belief in human dignity . . . and the true principle of creation the self-affirmation of subjectivity in distinction from Nature." Religion must find a form in which the dignity of men cannot be destroyed by discoveries about Nature whose creatures men are.

3

So far I have been discussing the concept of a transcendent God and the insuperable intellectual difficulties attached to it—difficulties experienced by reflective religious individuals (among whom even Wittgenstein is to be numbered, according to Professor Malcolm's memoir on him). The concept of an immanent God is much easier to understand, particularly since it contains no reference to personality. In the history of Western religious thought there has always been among the orthodox a deep suspicion of concepts of an immanent God, which are often regarded as sophisticated expressions of religious unbelief masquerading in the language of piety. We may take the God of Spinoza and Hegel as examples. Novalis once referred to Spinoza as a God-intoxicated man, but in his own time Spinoza was denounced as an atheist, for his God was neither the God of Abraham, Isaac, and Jacob, nor the God of Maimonides or Aquinas. Spinoza's God is Substance or Structure conceived as a self-sufficient network of timeless logical relations. This God is one to whom man cannot pray, and who cannot be loved as one loves a father or friend. So, too, with Hegel's God. Hegel gladdened the hearts of the pietists when he declared that "the world cannot exist without God," but he brought down an excommunicatory wrath on his head when he added: "God cannot exist without the world." Hegel's God is the God of Spinoza, except that Substance has been replaced by a timeless process, a dynamic system of evolving logical relations which constitute a great Self. In its strict form the concept of an immanent God (which must not be confused with the idea of an Incarnate God) leads to pantheism, but almost all believers in an immanent God have shrunk from this consequence. They have been reluctant to see Divinity in everything because the feeling of cosmic piety, or what Einstein calls "cosmic religious feeling," cannot be sustained for very long against a close-up view of each and every item in the world: there is too much that is ugly, disordered, and painful. Consequently some selection must be made. God may be *in* the world, but even to a believer in immanence not everything in the world is equally divine, or even divine at all.

Two features of experience have been most commonly identified with God. The first is Reason or Order or the pattern of rationality in things without which, it has been said (by Einstein, among others), the success of human thought in charting the ways of things would be a matter of luck or miracle. Not surprisingly, the scientists who hold to this conviction invariably turn out to be the most religious of men. The God of the scientist is not the God of the prophet, priest, or moralist. "His religious feeling takes the form of rapturous amazement at the harmony of natural law which reveals an intelligence of such superiority that, compared with it, all the systematic thinking and acting of human beings is an utterly insignificant reflection." [3] Helmholtz, however, was amazed that the eye should be so defective an organ of vision, while Heisenberg and Bohr are not prepared to give the universe high marks for the order of rationality found in nuclear behavior.

Some thinkers, however, find their God not in the rationality of the natural order but in its thrust of creativity. A merely rational world to them seems dead—not the ever fresh and blooming world of our experience with its surprises and novelties. Bergson's identification of God with the principle of *élan vital,* Whitehead's identification of God with "the principle of concretion" are strong cases in point. In Whitehead's philosophy, God is introduced to account for the fact that not all eternal objects are found in actuality or experience. Out of the realm of infinite possibilities of what might logically be, we must find some principle of limitation to account for the fact that this possibility comes into being and not that, that this "process of actual occasions" is realized here and now and not then and there. Whitehead admits that no logical reason can be adduced for the givenness, the facticity, the just-so-ness of things. His God is the polar opposite of Einstein's. "God is the ultimate limitation, and his existence is the ultimate irrationality. For no reason can be given for just that limitation which stands in His nature to impose." [4] And lest there is any doubt that he is speaking of an immanent God, he adds in his *Process and Reality:* "In this aspect, He (God) is not *before* all creation but *with* all creation." [5]

An immanent God cannot be plausibly conceived as a personal God, and it is not surprising that so many immanentists wage a fierce polemic against the conception of God as a transcendent person. The boundaries between the natural and supernatural tend to be blurred by this immanentism, and a certain irresolution and ambiguity is introduced into traditional religious faith. For a genuine religious function to be served, it is not sufficient to identify God with logical structure or process or any other generic feature of existence. What must be shown is that the world or cosmos, in virtue of the principle of Incarnate Divinity, has an objective purpose or plan which in some way explains or justifies human suffering. Evil, natural and human, must in the religious perspective appear meaningful and, in some fashion, acceptable. That is why in order to warrant the appellation of "God" or "Divinity," in order to be distinguished from a merely natural force or a purely logical pattern, the immanent Principle must be thought of as working itself out in nature, society, and history in such a way that evil loses its sting. As a rule, the evil of the part is represented as necessary to the good of the whole; God, as it were, uses the Devil for His own purposes.

With respect to the problem of evil, the immanence of God is manifestly superior as a conception to the transcendent God. A transcendent God, no matter how analogically conceived, must be endowed with will or intent. Since his power is such that he can intervene in the order of nature (a small feat to one who is the author of nature), anyone who feels himself an innocent suffering victim of the order of nature is psychologically hopeful that by prayer or petition or sacrifice, he can influence the Divine Will or Intent. But if the all-powerful Divine Will refuses to prevent unjust suffering, he becomes to some extent responsible for that suffering—all the more so since he is also omniscient and cannot like the Epicurean God plead business elsewhere. The agony of the problem of evil consists in not understanding how an all-powerful all-loving Father can permit his innocent children to be tortured in a world he has created. And although every honest theologian must in the end declare that the existence of evil is a Divine Mystery, the agony is not therewith dispelled. It may be attenuated by a temporary mood, but it keeps breaking through in every human being who has sensed in his own life and on his own skin something like the afflictions of Job.

One cannot in the same way question, blame, or complain to an immanent God. If "evil" is represented as a *necessary* element in the cosmic order, one may have difficulty in *comprehending* its necessity, but the premise itself commits one to the belief that it could not be otherwise, and that if we persisted and were keen enough, we would finally understand why it couldn't be otherwise. Consequently the alleged mystery of evil finally dissolves in the blinding vision of its necessity. The psychological ground for this is obvious: for example, we can resign ourselves without defiance or resentment to the weather because we assume that no one controls it. When the weather becomes controllable, the weatherman will have hard questions to answer.

Although the concept of an immanent God does not carry in its train such a cluster of theoretical difficulties as the idea of a transcendent God, its practical availability for the most religious purposes, especially in the Western tradition, is highly limited. Its own theoretical difficulties are grave enough, and its moral consequences are confusing. To interpret the natural cosmos as a moral cosmos is in effect to identify physics with ethics, and the laws of nature with the laws and judgments of morality. This tends to paralyze the nerve of morality, sometimes by identifying the actual with the ideal, the "what is" with the "what should be," and sometimes by suggesting that human judgments of better or worse are altogether irrelevant to the course of affairs—both the course of nature and of history. The pattern of Divinity is to be understood without laughter and without tears, unmoved and immovable by the petty concerns of our petty lives.

4

There is another, modern, view of God which is intermediate between the transcendent and immanent conceptions, and perhaps ultimately unclassifiable in terms of the customary distinction—the idea that God is identical with mystical experience itself. The element of transcendence in this view is that it sees God as beyond ordinary temporal experience—he can only be reached by a *break* in the natural jointures and continuities of things. The element of immanence is that once the breakthrough has been achieved, the experience itself is defined as a manifestation of Divinity. Thus Professor Walter Stace, who is the most gifted expositor of this conception, writes: "Just as Nirvana simply *is* the supreme experience of the Buddhist saint, so God simply *is* the supreme experience of the Christian mystic." And "the mystic experience of the Christian, as well as of the Hindus, is itself identical with God." This experience can be described only in paradoxical terms. It is the experience of "an undifferentiated unity," of the merging of self and non-self, object and subject, an eloquent stillness, a rapturous peace, an awesome joy. No language can be adequate to it, not even the language of oxymoron.

But three important questions must be asked. First, is this a genuine experience in the sense that if one has not been seized or blessed by it oneself, one can still find good reasons for believing that others have? Second, if this experience *is* genuine, is it only a psychological event in a particular individual's biography or does it testify to a cosmological or ontological fact? Third, do any ethical consequences for human life follow from the fact of the experience and/or its variant interpretations?

Short of an entire volume, I must content myself with apparently dogmatic answers, but I believe they can be rationally grounded. On the first question: there is little reason to doubt that this experience occurs and that the descriptions of it are authentic. Personally I think that the experience is quite widespread and that anyone suffering an intense emotion in extreme situations may undergo it. It is felt in moments of great danger, great love, great beauty, great joy—and, I am prepared to believe, even at the height of raging hate and the depths of total despair. The nearest I myself have come to it is when getting an anaesthetic, just before going under, and once when I almost drowned. The answer to the second question is that no experience can itself be conclusive evidence for the truth of an assertion about matters independent of that experience. An overwhelming conviction that an oasis which we see on top of a sand dune will be there when we reach it may be the result of a mirage. Even if several people report seeing the oasis, we are still not justified in assuming its existence, for they may all be common victims of the heat and thirst. The testimony of one man who had followed certain canons and methods of scientific inquiry would count far more, even if we grant that it would not be conclusive. Not everyone has experienced seasickness. Yet it is an authentic experience. But not all the unanimous testimony of the seasick can prove that the terrible vision of a nauseated reality experienced at the time gives an *objective* glimpse of those dread abysses of being by which, according to the existentialists, all of us, seasick or not, are surrounded. As for the third question, whatever consequences for human life follow from the mystic vision must be justified, if they are valid, by their observable effects on ordinary human experience. Whether an actual angel speaks to

me in my beatific vision or whether I only dreamed he spoke, the
truth of what he says can only be tested in the same way as I test
what my neighbor says to me. For even my neighbor may claim
to be a messenger of the Lord.

5

This brings me to the third main conception of God, according
to which God is neither a supernatural power nor a principle of
immanent structure, but a symbolic term for our most inclusive
moral ideals. The "divine" refers to that dimension in human
life which is not reducible *merely* to the physical, the social, and
the psychological, although it emerges from and affects them. It is
a dimension which is experienced whenever ideal ends, justice,
compassion for all suffering creatures, dedication to truth, integrity, move men to change the world and themselves. This is the
humanist conception of God. It is what Feuerbach's God becomes
when men grow aware of the mechanisms of transference and projection by which their needs create the objects of ideal allegiance.

The humanist conception of God, which is suggested by John
Dewey's phrase, "the effective union of the ideal and actual," is
fundamentally opposed to any notion of a supernatural power as
the *source* of human morality or even as the *justification* of morality, although it admits that belief in such a power can serve as a
support of human morality. This entire problem of the relation
between religion and morality, between God and the Good, is
extremely complex. The history of the traditional religions of
transcendence reveals a profound ambiguity in the way God is conceived to be related to the Good—an ambiguity on which I have
dwelt elsewhere, and here briefly mention.

On the one hand, God appears in the traditional religions as
the source and inspirer of the moral ideals which separate men
from beasts of prey. He is the lawgiver from whom Moses received
the tablets at Sinai; the fountain of righteousness from which the
Prophets drank; the infinite sea of mercy and love which Jesus
invoked to dissolve human sinfulness. Religion so conceived is the
shield of morality—so much so that any doubt or disbelief powerful
enough to pierce it strikes down at the same time any possibility
of a good life or a good society.

On the other hand, since God is by definition altogether different from man, he cannot be bound by man's understanding nor his ways judged by human ideas of justice. It is an act of impiety to apply to God and his works the same standards which men apply to each other, even if these standards are derived from him. It would be monstrous on the part of a man to punish an innocent child for a misdeed committed by its grandfather. But when the Lord proclaims, I shall visit the sins of the fathers upon the heads of the children unto the third and fourth generation, the pious man must murmur with a full and loving heart, "Thy will be done."

Social Christianity (like prophetic Judaism before it) is a conspicuous illustration of the first strain of thought—the idea of God as the source of ethical ideals. It leads to a withering away of strictly theological issues, tends to define the religious man not in terms of belief but in terms of action or good works, and interprets the religious consciousness as "a participation in the ideal values of the social consciousness." It is, therefore, always suspect of Pelagianism.

The second strain—which stresses the impiety of applying human standards to God—is exemplified in existentialist theology whose roots go back to Paul, Augustine, Pascal, and Calvin, but which has put forth its finest modern flower in Kierkegaard. In his commentary on the Abraham-Isaac story in the essay *Fear and Trembling,* discussed in the following chapter, Kierkegaard praises Abraham as the most pious of men, greater in his religious heroism than all the tragic figures of history because Abraham was prepared to carry out his absolute duty to God—a duty which as a merely finite creature he could not possibly understand but one which cut sharply across his ethical responsibilities. Kierkegaard calls this "the teleological suspension of the ethical," which means that in serving God, one is beyond all considerations of good and evil. One "acts by virtue of the absurd." In the strongest contrast between the ethical and the religious mode of feeling and conduct which has ever been drawn, Kierkegaard says that Abraham must be regarded either as a "murderer" (the term is his) from the ethical standpoint, or a "true believer" from the standpoint of absolute religion. The truly pious man is prepared to accept any command whatever as a test of his faith.

The position of the religious humanist, whether that of Ludwig Feuerbach or John Dewey, reverses this appraisal in a most dramatic way. Its principle might be called "the ethical suspension of the theological." Religious humanism analyzes the parable of Abraham and Isaac quite differently in order to show that a new moral insight was born when Abraham identified the voice which bade him stay his hand as the voice of God. Thus the parable illustrates the Feuerbachian contention that men create and worship Gods in their own moral image and confirms the Kantian principle of the autonomy of moral reason with respect to traditional conceptions of religion and God.

Feuerbach's insight is sometimes recognized by existentialist theologians, but they then compromise it by bringing in some obscure—and irrelevant—metaphysical or ontological conception. For example, Paul Tillich interprets religion as an expression of man's ultimate concern. God, therefore, can be defined as the object of man's ultimate concern. This means that there are as many Gods as there are objects of ultimate concern, and their existence can be established not in the way we establish the existence of atoms or stars or genes or anything else in nature but only in the way we determine what a man's overriding concern may be. So we say, "He is a worshipper of Mammon" or Venus, or Minerva, or Mars, or Apollo, depending upon whether a man makes a fetish of money, love, knowledge, war, or art. Tillich thus reduces the conflict of Gods to the conflict of moral ideals. This is good as far as it goes, especially because it contains a suggestion of moral pluralism and religious polytheism, and because it is coupled with the explicit denial of God's existence as a supernatural power. Indeed, in this respect Tillich seems to go even further than avowed atheists. Literally construed, he is saying that it is simply meaningless, a confusion of dimensions (or what Ryle calls a category mistake), to affirm that God is an entity among, but greater than, other entities. Such extremism, in my opinion, would make almost all the historical religions irreligious and many forms of irreligion profoundly religious. Moreover, since all human beings are passionately concerned about something— unless they are already half-dead—we must call them all "religious." Because the objects of their ultimate concern are what they are, many people are characterized as "Godless," in accordance with proper English usage. Why, then, give the term "God" to their object of concern, and convert "erring souls" by arbitrary definition? This is not the only difficulty. Matters become even more obscure when God is also identified by Tillich as "the Unconditioned," as "beyond finitude and infinity," as "the ground of Being," as "Being-itself" which "includes both rest and becoming." These terms, as I shall show subsequently, defy logical analysis and require some kind of Feuerbachian resolution to become intelligible.

6

I wish to conclude with a few observations about the humanist conception of God. The great problem which Humanism as a religion must face is not so much the validity of its conception of God but how to justify its use of the term "God." The defense can be made briefly. All large terms in human discourse are historically variable in meaning or actually ambiguous in use: "atom," "substance," "experience," "reason," "love," even "man"—all show this variation in meaning. Each term stands for a family of meanings (like the term "game" in Wittgenstein's analysis) which resemble one another but are nevertheless not completely consonant. Consequently, it is argued that if the same penumbral complex of attitudes (intellectual humility, piety, reverence, wonder, awe, and concern) are manifest in a use of the term "God" which designates no thing or person but our highest ethical commitment, no legitimate objection can be raised—providing, of course, we make it clear that the new use or meaning is different from the old.

The criticism can be made just as briefly. The new use always invites confusion with the old use, and there is, after all, such a thing as the ethics of words. By taking over the word "God" as the religious humanists do, the waters of thought, feeling, and faith are muddied, the issues blurred, the "word" itself becomes the object of interest and not what it signifies. When Marguerite in her simple faith asks Faust whether he believes in God, Faust replies with a kind of pantheistic, pre-Whiteheadian doubletalk about luck, heart, love, and God, call it what you will!

Ich habe keinen Namen
Dafür! Gefühl ist alles;

> *Name ist Schall und Rauch*
> *Umnebelnd Himmelsglut.*

To which Marguerite makes reply:

> *Das ist alles recht schön und gut;*
> *Ungefähr sagt das der Pfarrer auch;*
> *Nur mit ein bischen andern Worten.*

This may be called a paradigm case of religious misunderstanding.

Is, then, the religion of Humanism justified in using the term "God" for its conception of the moral enterprise? John Dewey answered the question affirmatively. I answer it negatively. Each one of my readers must answer it for himself.

Two Types of Existentialist Religion and Ethics

It is commonly assumed that religion and morality reinforce each other's claims and that despite differences in emphasis they express a common outlook which assigns man an intelligible place in an ordered world. Historically the connection between religion and ethics has always been intimate. It is possible, of course, to define religion in such a way that every strong ethical or unethical position is religious and the distinction between the religious and ethical categories disappears. Little is to be gained by such procedure. It does violence to the actual historical materials. Further, the differences between ethics and religion reappear in the recognized differences among religions.

In this chapter I wish to call attention to two types of existentialist religious thinking in the nineteenth and twentieth centuries which point up the difference between the attitude of faith—which I regard as strictly religious, and the attitude of morality which I regard as primarily secular.

By the two types of existentialist religion I mean the types of religious thinking represented by Søren Kierkegaard and Ludwig

Feuerbach. The first is oriented towards some transcendental element which conditions the whole of human experience; the second regards human experience as the matrix of all religion. Although in polar opposition to each other, both were critical reactions to the idealistic pan-logism of Hegel, for whom religion was nothing but an aesthetic or symbolic rendition of the truths discovered by philosophy. Kierkegaard has become the most influential philosopher of religion of the Western world in our time; Feuerbach still awaits his proper recognition.

Kierkegaard is an existentialist who takes his point of departure from man's subjective experience, supposedly universal, of incompleteness, insufficiency, and despair, "an anxious dread of an unknown something." On the basis of this and similar subjective experiences Kierkegaard postulates, he cannot rationally establish the existence beyond an "infinite yawning abyss" of an objective Absolute, completely transcendent to man and therefore essentially unknowable and mysterious. In the words of Karl Barth, a lineal theological descendant of Kierkegaard, God is "wholly other than man."

Feuerbach is an even more radical existentialist than Kierkegaard. He interprets man's religious beliefs as projections of human needs and care. They are either ideal liberations from his most pressing concerns or, when they express longings, ideal fulfillments. For him "the secret of theology is anthropology." This is meant in two senses: the first as a heuristic principle in the study of comparative religion; second, and more important, as a naturalistic interpretation in cultural and psychological terms of belief in the supernatural. "Religion is the dream of the human mind. But even in dreams we do not find ourselves in emptiness or in heaven, but on earth, in the realm of reality."

The school of existential theism from Kierkegaard to Barth recognizes the fact that Man's nature is expressed in his religious beliefs. It places, however, an altogether different interpretation from that of Feuerbach upon this fact. It dismisses the Feuerbachian approach as a stupendous but dangerous commonplace; a commonplace because everything man does and thinks bears witness to his faltering mortality; a dangerous commonplace because unless disciplined by the humble realization that the conceptions of finite, wicked and mortal creatures violently distort the nature of God, they inescapably lead to idolatry, in which the part is worshipped as the whole, and man impiously confused with God. Indeed some modern followers of Kierkegaard regard Feuerbach's existential humanism as a *reductio ad absurdum* of any interpretation which takes its point of departure from the facts of religious experience alone independently of its ontological correlative.

The Kierkegaardian point of view is correct in pointing out that there is an inescapable reference to man in all his works, from art to astronomy and religion. The fact that astronomy is a human enterprise does not preclude our achieving objective knowledge of the behavior of heavenly bodies. But certainly this element of subjectivity is not a sufficient condition of knowledge, else there would be no difference between veridical and hallucinatory experience on any level. The only way objectivity can be established on the basis of human experience is by empirical evidence and/or reasoning, both of which are rejected out of hand by the existentialists of this school. This leaves the only way open to them the unmediated "leap" of faith, the reliance upon "paradox, inaccessible to thought," the glorification of "the absurd," the refusal to apply any categories of reason or logic to "the revealed." Since it disdains human reason, not in the light of a higher Reason, for this, too, is infected with man's imperfect nature, it is impervious to rational criticism. Nonetheless it is not beyond the reach of psychological analysis and social criticism.

The existentialism of Feuerbach denies that human projection in religion distorts "reality" because projections are not literal reports of antecedent existence but a mode of experiencing things. For something to be distorted requires that it have a normal or natural appearance. But if all appearances are essentially related to the finite eye and mind of men, it makes no sense to counterpose what human beings experience to some allegedly objective transcendent entity. The eternal can only be grasped in a temporal frame. The "absurd" for Feuerbach always consists in the negation of human sense and understanding and is therefore rejected by him as a negation of the true nature of religion as he conceives it.

Of the two thinkers, it is apparent that although Feuerbach's development took him further away from the Hegelian philosophy

of religion than did Kierkegaard's, the latter made the more radical
break with the Hegelian tradition of reason and the systematic
unity of the concrete universal. Feuerbach is closer to Hegel because like Hegel he rejects all dualisms, epistemological, metaphysical or theological. For Hegel, Spirit, divine or human, is one,
and it develops by alienating itself into objective forms which
become both temporary obstacles and stimuli to its further advance. Feuerbach interprets the process of human alienation as
consisting in this unconscious worship of its own projections. He
naturalizes and demythologizes the Absolute Spirit of Hegel. He
reinterprets the different stages in the progressive development of
the Idea or Absolute or God as a succession of different *historical*
expressions of the human species or essence. "Man—this is the
mystery of religion—projects his being into objectivity, and then
again makes himself an object to this projected image of himself
thus converted into a subject . . ." Feuerbach's attitude towards
religion is reverential and sensitive. He believes that it is an irreducible aspect of human experience no matter how profoundly
its images, symbols and dogmas change. "What yesterday was still
religion, is no longer such today: and what today is atheism, tomorrow will be religion."

The profoundest difference between the approach of existential
theism and that of existential humanism to religion is in their conceptions of ethics and morality. Existential humanism, especially
in its post-Feuerbachian developments, sees man's moral vocation
in redoing, remaking, reforming the world and self in the light of
consciously held ethical ideals to which religious myths and rituals
can give only emotional and aesthetic support. Existential theism,
aware of human finitude and weakness and self-idolatry, places the
greatest emphasis upon the acceptance of the world and its underlying plan, so unclear to human eyes, upon the explanation and
justification of evil rather than on the duty of eliminating specific
evils. This is sometimes obscured by the fact that the transcendent and Absolute God of existential theism is considered to be
beyond good and evil. Psychologically it is apparent that the belief
that the difference between human good and human evil disappears in the light of the Absolute, or that what appears good or
evil in the sight of Man may be quite different in the sight of the
Lord, cannot serve as a premise for the active transformation of

the world. In effect, it accepts the existing order of things, whatever it is, as a basis of preparation for salvation either by a leap of faith or a transformation of self.

This is brilliantly illustrated in Kierkegaard's remarkable analysis of the Abraham-Isaac story in his *Fear and Trembling*. According to Kierkegaard, God's command to Abraham to sacrifice his only and dearly beloved son, Isaac, to Him as a burnt-offering ran counter to one of the highest ethical principles. The test of Abraham's religious faith was his willingness to violate his duty as a father, husband, citizen and compassionate human being in order to carry out his absolute duty to God. This "teleological suspension of the ethical" raises Abraham in Kierkegaard's eyes above tragic heroes like Agamemnon, Jeptha, and Brutus who sacrificed their children to the common good. They were "tragic heroes," exalting the universal over the particular. Abraham is no tragic hero. He must be regarded, says Kierkegaard, as either "a murderer," from the ethical standpoint, or a true "believer" from the standpoint of absolute religion. Kierkegaard's account is powerful and honest. He admits that Abraham "acts by virtue of the absurd" but claims that although it is ethically wrong to subordinate the universal to the particular, in the case of one's absolute duty to God "the particular is higher than the universal." In serving God one is beyond good and evil. "Hence it is," writes Kierkegaard, "that I can understand the tragic hero but cannot understand Abraham, though in a certain crazy sense I admire him more than all other men."

We can use this parable to point up the difference between the approaches of Kierkegaard and Feuerbach. The latter would interpret the story quite differently. First, he would maintain that despite Kierkegaard there is no escaping the standpoint of morality, that we are all responsible for our judgments, and for the consequences of our judgments, no matter what we believe the external source of our moral duty to be. Here the Feuerbachian view follows the Kantian view. When Abraham, knife in hand, prepared to sacrifice Isaac, the Biblical account says an Angel of the Lord commanded him to stay his hand. How did Abraham know that this message was a message from the Lord and not from Satan, or that it was not the voice of his own longing, the expression of the anguished wish of a loving father not to be bereaved of a son? The existential humanist answers that Abraham attributes the source of this command to God, not to Satan, because it is he who finds it good. Every statement which asserts that the Good is what God commands presupposes that we already have independent knowledge of what is good or bad in order to attribute the good to God and the bad to Satan. The command from the Angel of the Lord represents the birth of a new moral insight in man, in Abraham, according to which it is not necessary to sacrifice human life in thanksgiving to, or in fear of, the imputed author of creation. The earlier injunction to sacrifice Isaac undoubtedly reflected a local religious practice.

Certainly, *after* the Abraham-Isaac episode even Kierkegaard would judge a man willing to sacrifice his son or any other human being on the altar of the Gods, by a different standard. Abraham's resolution to carry out the first Divine Command can be justified only because he knows or believes it is a Divine Command and only because he knows or believes that the Divine Command is the source of good. Feuerbach believed, I think truly, that men create God in their own moral image, that morality is autonomous of religion, and that although religious beliefs and symbols may support moral values the latter can never be derived from the former. Where this is denied or overlooked then the status quo in all its infamy is either accepted in terms of a disguised value judgment or it is ignored as something irrelevant to man's profoundest concern.

It is of course true that even an immanent theology can adopt a morality which leads, as in the Hegelian system, to the belief that whatever is, is right. Such an identification receives a well-merited rebuke from existential theism on the ground that it results in an idolatry of history, especially when, as in Hegel, the path of history is interpreted as the path of divinity. The great paradox of existentialist theism is that it properly perceives the finitude of all human standpoints, the relativity of all philosophical absolutes, but fails to see that a finite creature can criticize the finite only in the light of another finite, the relative (or relational) only from the basis of another relative (or relational) position.

The question remains whether existential humanism is also another form of idolatry. If ethical ideals are related to human interests is not man's pursuit of the good a worship of his own nature? There is no doubt that sometimes this is the case. But it need not be. Men, by projecting their ideals as standards, may appeal from an existing self to a developing self, from what things and men actually are to what they may possibly be or become. They may criticize the structure of the self from the standpoint of shared interests with others, which forms the basis of community. Time guarantees that whatever the world is or may be, new visions of human excellence, whether in conflict or cooperation, will prevent men from identifying their limitations with the limitations of all human possibility.

PART 3

The Quest for "Being"

1

During the last few years there has been a revival of the belief in the cognitive legitimacy of metaphysics and ontology. The positivist ban on expressions once called metaphysical or ontological has been lifted by some of the high priests of positivism themselves. Even in quarters where until recently only the austerities of symbolic logic were practiced, there is talk about ontological reference, ontological factors and entities. A good deal of this is very innocent. The context of the term in the writings of some current logicians seems to indicate that the term "ontological" stands for the existential, or for the objective reference of statements, or the designation of a symbol.

I characterize this usage of the term as innocent because all it seems to do is to call attention to the fact, and, in some situations, to the controlling importance, of subject-matter. Physics, chemistry, sociology have an "ontological" character because their equations or laws describe something or point beyond themselves. Indeed, according to some writers the term "ontological" refers to the content of any communication about anything. This, of course, would mean that the only indisputable parts of ontology are the sciences themselves, because no one doubts that the physics of particles or the chemistry of colloids or the ecology of plants or the biology of mammals has a much more definite content than traditional ontology. Hence when Quine says, "Ontological statements follow immediately from all manner of casual statements of commonplace fact," [1] I cannot see in this anything more than an admission that ontology is a collection of supererogative truisms, some might say verbalisms.

There is another ontological aspect of the world which turns out to be nothing more than the recognition that from the character of a specific instrument in a determinate situation we can infer something about the character of the subject-matter or material on which we use the instrument. Thus one writer says: "Given an iron bar to cut, and a choice between a penknife and a hacksaw as instruments, it will require no great mechanical genius to discover that the hacksaw is much more convenient and suitable. From our knowledge of the instruments, and their different degrees of inadequacy here, we can surely draw the 'ontological' conclusion that the bar is *hard* rather than soft." [2] If this is a piece of ontological knowledge, then the fact that the size of a man's shoe is a good index of the size of his unbunioned foot, is also a piece of ontological knowledge—perfectly trivial and perfectly useless. Before we use the hacksaw we already know that the iron is hard, and don't have to infer that fact from the successful use of the hacksaw in cutting the bar; and that we have feet is not an ontological discovery made consequent upon our being shod.

An even more modest conception of metaphysics is the view that it consists in an analysis of the basic categories by which we seek to organize our experience and the structure of the knowledge derived from it. But unless one is prepared to assert that these categories necessarily reflect the nature of things—a conclusion rendered unplausible by the fact that different categorial schemes have been projected, each of which has undergone historical development without resulting in the convergence of findings which marks the growth of knowledge in other fields—such a conception of ontology is hardly distinguishable from the linguistic and logical analysis of philosophical concepts which is sometimes referred to as the modern "revolution in philosophy."

No, the revival of ontology involves more ambitious claims. Its validity as a systematic discipline rests upon the contention that it gives us a knowledge about something or everything which is not communicated by any particular science or all of the sciences. It either tells us something that we didn't know before or makes us aware in some distinctive way of what in some sense we have already known.

The oldest as well as the most recent ontological claim is that the truths ontology gives us are about Being—about Being *as such.* Yet despite the enormous literature which has been written about Being, it is extremely difficult to find anything clear or intelligible in writings which contain that expression. The reasons are obvious. In ordinary discourse every significant word has an intelligible opposite. Being, however, as an all-inclusive category does not seem to possess an intelligible opposite. Not-Being is not the opposite of Being, because when it is taken as equivalent in meaning to Nothing, and Nothing is interpreted as a substantival entity, then Nothing is a Something (indeed, so concrete that some writers speak of it as an "abyss," others as "Death") and hence possesses Being, too. So that whatever is true of Being as such is true of Nothing, and whatever is true of Nothing is true of Something which has Being. If, on the other hand, non-Being means "falsity" and not a substantival entity, then we are dealing with a property of assertions; its opposite is "truth"; and we can banish the term "Being" from the vocabulary of philosophy.

However "Nothing" be considered, it is a derivative notion from something, related to an act, real or imagined, of negation. Bergson, many years ago, in his striking analysis of "the idea of nothing," wrote: "If suppressing a thing consists in replacing it by another, if thinking the absence of one thing is only possible by the more or less explicit representation of the presence of some other thing, if, in short, annihilation signifies before anything else substitution, the idea of an 'annihilation of everything' is as absurd as that of a square circle." [3] Precisely for this reason the question originally asked by Schelling and repeated in our time by Heidegger: "Why is there something: why is there not nothing?" is devoid of sense except as a sign of emotional anxiety.

The same considerations apply to Tillich's "shock of non-being or being not." He, too, asks: What kind of being must we attribute to non-being? Aware that, to make ordinary sense, we should translate this into what meaning can we attribute to the word or expression "non-being," he rejects the reformulation as an ontological evasion. Any theory, he asserts, according to which negation is a *logical* judgment must be "rooted in an ontological structure." [4]

The only evidence that Tillich gives for this assertion is that there are *expectations* in the world which are sometimes unfulfilled or disappointed. "Thus disappointed, expectation creates the distinction between being and non-being." [5] Expectation, however, is an attitude possible only to man. Where there is no man, there is no expectation, and therefore no non-being. Expectation, and therefore non-being, are purely psychological categories. We should therefore expect Tillich to admit that he is not dealing with a substantial force or power when he refers to "non-being," but with a capacity limited to one species in a "sea of being." Instead, he forgets that he has just told us that human expectation has "created" non-being and maintains that man "*participates* not only in being but in non-being." But one cannot participate in a distinction which one creates unless one, of course, is everywhere, unless one's self with one's power of expectation is always present everywhere. And this is the implication of Tillich's further statement that "there can be no world unless there is a dialectical participation of non-being in being." [6]

One can doubt any particular judgment or assertion but one cannot doubt all possible judgments or assertions because significant doubt always rests upon something we accept. The logic is exactly the same with denial. We may dialectically relate non-being to a specific being but not to everything: non-being cannot be regarded as coeval with being.

Nor is the outcome any different if we define Being as the realm of all possibles and consider the actual as the class of realized possibles. For what on this view is the ontological status of the impossible? If by the impossible we mean only the self-contradictory, then the possible can only mean the self-consistent, and we are dealing merely with logical notions, not ontological entities or traits. And if, by the impossible, we mean only what violates scientific

law or fact, we are dealing with an unrealized or unrealizable possibility after all, and the impossible becomes a species of the possible,
and we are back into the same semantic morass as we were with
the concept of Being.

It seems apparent that only by logical legerdemain can we start
from a conception of Being as such or pure Being, and end up with
meanings or categories that are quite distinct from the *as-suchness*
or purity of *Being*. It is notorious that the Hegelian logic comes
a cropper on its very first triad. Its attempt to derive Becoming,
and then Determinate Being, from Pure Being is even more hope-
less than the attempt to deduce, from the notion of God, the existence of the world—which is the real secret of Hegel's ontology. Nor
is the Thomistic ontology in a better logical position with respect
to Being. Notice the way in which "the good" and "the true" are
identified with Being as transcendental notions equally applicable
to each other. "Being" and "the good" (or "valuable") cannot be
identified with each other without making nonsense of the view
that evils and disvalues are to be found in the world. No matter
what one's ontology, to deny existence or being to the many evils
of the world is so gratuitously arbitrary that any conception of
being from which it is a conclusion cannot be taken seriously. This
conclusion cannot be avoided by the scholastic distinction according to which although "ontological evil must be identical with non-
being or nothingness," [7] yet it is logically distinct from the latter.
For from this it presumably follows that evil is not mere negation
but privation, or absence of a good, and is called a defect or de-
ficiency of being only because by *definition* being and good are
identical. I say by definition because if this view has any empirical
content, then the tiniest twinge of pain is enough to refute it. For
if anything is positive in the world, if anything proclaims itself
with a scream or shout, it is pain. To regard pleasure or happiness
as the absence of pain is mistaken but credible. To regard pain
merely as the absence or privation of the good, no matter in what
we find the good—whether pleasure, happiness, the beatific vision,
—is both mistaken and incredible.

Why is it that the term "Being" generates by illogical fission
so many other characteristics in treatises on ontology—whether
Thomistic, Hegelian, or existentialist? Because it has been surreptitiously endowed with the properties of Mind. This property

is no longer a category of classical ontology but of *Tiefenpsychologie*. This is especially true for Heidegger, the fount of almost all existentialist thinking today. Heidegger asserts that every metaphysical question concerns itself with every other, so that *au fond* there is only one metaphysical question. He also asserts that when a question is raised in metaphysics "the questioner as such is by his very questioning involved in the question." [8] Metaphysics, then, can never tell us anything about the world independent of its relation to us, of what could be true of Being if there were no human beings (or would be if there were no human beings). Its concern is quite different from that of science. The sciences, says Heidegger, "allow the object itself the first and last word," but "no matter where and however deeply science investigates what-is it will never find Being." [9] Why? Because "Being is not an existing quality of what-is, nor, unlike what-is, can Being be conceived and established objectively."

What is Heidegger trying to say? He is trying to say that Being is a product of a Creative Act of an anonymous undifferentiated Ego (although he does not use this term) in a process in which a substantial Nothing is presupposed. It is a pagan and Teutonic rendering of the theological myth of the creation out of nothing, which turns out to be really the mythical process of the self-realization of Mind.

No matter how inquiry is conceived, negation is a process of denying, distinguishing, and contrasting judgments or statements. The term "Nothing" has a meaning because in a given situation certain negations may be validly made, but it does not designate an entity. (It is a syncategorematic expression.) Heidegger asserts, however, that in denying there is such a thing as nothing we are already admitting not only that it is a meaningful term but that it is an entity of sorts. This is an even more fantastic inference than the claim that the assertion that round squares do not exist implies that round squares actually exist, otherwise how could we significantly deny them—a kind of argument which seems to me to have been laid to rest by Russell's theory of descriptions. But independently of the character of Heidegger's argument, he makes it unmistakably clear that for him "Nothing [*Das Nichts*] is the source of negation, not the other way about." [10] The nature of his *Nichts* is as positive as any concrete *Etwas* because it has definite powers. These powers are psychological. Notice the terms from which rational negation is supposed to be derived. "More abysmal than the mere propriety of rational negation is the harshness of *opposition* and the violence of *loathing*. More responsible the pain of *refusal* and the *mercilessness* of an interdict. More oppressive the bitterness of *renunciation*" [11] (my italics).

Opposition, loathing, refusal, mercilessness, renunciation—these are some of the modes in which *Das Nichts* appears. This is neither logic nor classic ontology but an ontologized, pseudo-psychological projection of the aggressions of a self-hating and other-hating Ego. It is not surprising that Heidegger says of Reason, Logic, or Common Sense that it "has no sovereignty in the field of inquiry into Nothing and Being." His work is an invitation to apply not logical analysis to his argument but psychoanalysis to his position. But as philosophers we cannot accept an invitation in these terms.

A less subjective conception of Being than Heidegger's is found in Nicolai Hartmann, who properly points out that Heidegger is concerned not with the nature of Being but with the "meaning of Being," *i.e.*, not with the *Seienden als Seienden* but with the *Sinn von Sein*.[12] Hartmann's own conception of ontology, although less mystical than Heidegger's, is no more satisfactory. For him common-sense knowledge and scientific knowledge are both ontological because they exhibit an *initial* naïve realism towards things as the objects of knowledge. But in this sense the basic ontological structure of "being" can hardly be considered as given in the same way. It requires a pretty sophisticated vision, physical or mental, to grasp the Being of this table over and above what we find in our naïve perception of it as a common-sense thing or in our understanding of it as a scientific object.

The real difficulty is that Hartmann does not establish that there is anything corresponding to "Being" despite his use of the term on almost every page of his *Zur Grundlegung der Ontologie*. To be sure he says that Being is indefinable and not graspable (*begreifbar*); but since this is true in a sense of many other terms, like matter, consciousness, color, or sound, it is not a sufficient characterization. But the more important point is that for these *other* fundamental terms, although formal definitions cannot be offered, we can state the rules or linguistic conventions which guide our usage of them under certain conditions. We cannot do so for Being.

The scholastics were perfectly aware of the difficulty and sought to settle it by asserting that Being is neither a univocal term nor an equivocal term but is predicable of the different modes of Being *by analogy of proportion*. The analogy of proportionality is a technical and very interesting doctrine which calls attention to the familiar linguistic fact that many terms in discourse do not have a univocal meaning and yet cannot be said to be ambiguous. In such cases the context provides a principle of specification so that while we are aware that the shades of meaning in two uses of an expression or utterance are different, nonetheless the meanings are sufficiently similar to make the use of the expression or utterance appropriate. For example, if I say the sea is angry, I am using a metaphor. If challenged, I can say what I want to say without using that word or any synonym. Now, someone pokes a stick at a lion when he is feeding. The lion bares his fangs, roars, and leaps. I say, "The lion is angry." In saying the lion is "angry" I am convinced that it is an appropriate expression, and yet I am not convinced that it means the same thing as when I say of the game warden who comes running that "he is angry," and of the sea that "it is angry," although both expressions are properly used. The rules or conventions which determine the usage of the term "angry" for men, animals, and seas are not the same. This is even true when only feelings or emotions are involved. The mystics and poets tell us that "just as the hart pants for water, so the soul pants for God." The term "pant" has not the same meaning, but certainly there is no ordinary equivocation here, because instead of being confused or puzzled by the sentence, we find it more or less illuminating. And so it is argued that when we speak of God's feeling of wrath, although God is not a Creature, and although he cannot be said to feel angry like men and lions, nonetheless there is a greater appropriateness in referring to his *wrath*, in certain situations in which he presumably reveals himself, than in referring to his *mercy*. And so it is declared that all of God's properties are proportionally, analogically predicated of him—from which one consequence is the rejection of negative theology.

Now even if the doctrine of analogy of proportionality were sound, it cannot be applied to Being. And this, for two reasons. When I say God is a father to man somewhat in the same way as man is father to his family, I have at least a reasonably clear idea

of what it means for a man to be a father, and I extend this notion
to God, where, although it cannot be literally true of him, it still
applies with a greater appropriateness than some other notion like
"nephew." We pray to "Our Father in Heaven," but no one would
be likely to pray to "Our nephew in Heaven." Now, to predicate
Being of some particular mode of Being, whether physical, mental, or logical, whether divine, earthly, or satanic, I must have
at least as correspondingly a clear idea of Being as I had of anger
or mercy *before* I attributed it to the Deity. But this is precisely
what I do *not* have; this is just what I am seeking to make clear
to myself. How, then, can I extend it by an analogy of proportionality from other modes of Being? By this procedure the obscure can only become obscurer. Secondly, we are told that "Being
is affirmed of the finite [being] by its dependence on infinite
being," [13] that infinite being is the ground or cause of finite being,
so that the primary analogue for the proportion is not the Being
of finite Being but the Being of Infinite Being. But the fogginess
of the term Being does not disappear when it is lifted from the
dimension of the Finite to the Infinite.

The main point of this critique of Thomistic ontology has been
recently contested on the ground that it overlooks the interpretation of "Being" which construes it as an *act of existing,* as that
which brings a sort of fulfillment or "perfection" to some essence
which receives it. The term "perfection" in this sense connotes
not an ethical character but an actualizing of a possibility. It
marks the difference between an actual oasis and an idea of one,
an actual feast and a Barmicidean feast. A critic writes: "When
Sidney Hook and company ask St. Thomas what is meant by saying of this table: 'It has being' or 'It is'—the answer is that there
is being predicated of the table the real act and perfection which
is the basic cause of all other perfections and predicates." [14] On
this view Being is not a noun but a verb and modes of Being are
modes of Action. Metaphysics apparently is the study of action
qua action.

This does not escape difficulties. It only multiplies them. It is
just as unclear how we get from the action of *this* and the action of
that to action *qua* action as how we get from the Being of *this* and
the Being of *that* to Being *qua* Being. The terms "act" and "action" are just as systematically ambiguous as the terms "Being" or

"existence." In many, if not most usages, when we speak of the "act" or "action" or behavior of something, it clearly presupposes the antecedent existence of some power, material or subject-matter. And when it does not clearly presuppose this, it sets a problem for inquiry. Otherwise we suspect the presence of mystification. No matter how "pure" the act is conceived to be, it is linked in our understanding to a preposition; it is an act *of*. What acts in the act of Being or existing? Certainly not possibilities, essences, or natures. The meaning of "death" is not lethal: the nature of "fire" burns nothing.

It is further asserted that " 'is' enters every proposition and to know what *is* as against what is not presupposes the intellectual grasp of being." This entails that "all that anyone can think is being." The consequence of this mode of speaking about Being is not mystery but plain absurdity. For concepts, essences, natures, and meanings are obviously objects of thought. We can make true or false statements about them. Therefore they have Being, and on this interpretation, are acts of existing, too. Yet previously we were told that Being is an act which brings a fulfillment or perfection to what is an essence or nature or a mere possibility. But if essences are endowed with Being, too, they already have an appropriate fulfillment or perfection. We are compelled to distinguish between the "Being" of essence and the "essence" of essence. Either the result is a mad-hatter's metaphysical race to complete an infinite regress, or essence and existence are no longer distinct but collapse into each other, a conclusion which is incompatible with other assertions of Thomistic metaphysics.

These difficulties are endemic to the entire system of Thomistic thought because the real secret of its ontology lies in its antecedent commitment to Christian theology. What is really meant by saying of this table, or anything else, "It has being" or "It is" is that God created or sustains it, an assertion which is purely gratuitous to our understanding of any property or trait or behavior exhibited by the table or anything else. It has no bearing on any piece of specific knowledge we have about the table. We can get from tables and other things to God as their creator and sustainer only if the argument from a first cause is valid—which it is not. And even if valid, it would be a necessary condition not a sufficient one, for

the eternity of the world would be compatible with the existence
of its Prime Mover.

Let us recapitulate as simply as possible some of the obvious distinctions we recognize in ordinary language and common-sense
discourse which make the alleged category of "Being" a non-cognitive as well as non-communicative, and therefore perfectly dis-
pensable, term in discourse.

Being is not identical with spatio-temporal existence since there
are many things of which we speak, like plans, meanings, memories,
dimensions, that cannot be called spatio-temporal existences; nor
are they treated as such. Even if we assert that these qualities or
patterns of organization qualify spatio-temporal existences, that
they are adjectival of the world-order which is the subject matter
of physics, biology, and other sciences, we must recognize these
distinctions between quality, pattern, and spatio-temporal existences on pain of lapsing into crude reductive materialism and
therefore into radical incoherence.

Being is not identical with the imaginable, for there are many
things in the world which are unimaginable. No one can actually
imagine a sphere like the earth on which human beings are walking erect at antipodal points or literally imagine the subatomic
particles of present-day physics.

Being is not identical with the intellectually conceivable or intelligible, for, as we have already seen, this means subject to the
law of contradiction. Being would be synonymous with consistency
which is not a category of ontology at all—but of logic or discourse.
As I understand the sense in which C. I. Lewis uses the term
"Being," it is like the expression "either A or not A," possessing
zero connotation and universal comprehension in that it is applicable to anything mentionable or discoursed about.[15]

Finally, Being cannot be exhaustively characterized as that
which is independent of presence, or relation, to the knowing mind
in any or all of its participial modes, knowing, hoping, imagining,
believing, etc. For if this is what is meant by Being—why, we
would have to deny it to pains and aches and feelings and dreams
which are certainly dependent upon presence or relation to "consciousness" or "mind," no matter how these terms are interpreted,
in a way different from the presence or relation of sticks and stones
to consciousness.

Before we abandon any further quest for an account of Being which makes sense, let us look at yet one other attempt by a distinguished theologian whose ontology has been widely acclaimed. I refer to Professor Paul Tillich.

For Tillich, philosophy and theology may be distinguished but not separated, for "whatever the relation of God, world and man may be, it lies in the frame of being." [16] Tillich takes being so seriously that he quotes with approval Heidegger's dictum as a definition of man, "Man is that being who asks what being is," a statement whose cognitive import does not differ from the non-ontological statement that man is the only animal which possesses speech, and therefore asks questions. At the outset it seems as if in his ontology Tillich seeks to escape from the subjectivistic strain in Heidegger. Ontology concerns itself with *Being,* "as it *is,*" while philosophical theology deals with Being "as it is *for us,*" *i.e.,* "what concerns us ultimately, inescapably, unconditionally." This brave differentiation collapses almost at once because, like Heidegger, Tillich takes human existence as paradigmatic of the structure of all Being—so that he is capable of writing: "a self is not a thing that may or may not exist: it is an original phenomenon which logically precedes all questions of existence." [17] This seems to me so patently false, if "logical" means logical not psychological, that I should regard it as much as a *reductio ad absurdum* of a philosophical position as I would solipsism, from which it really does not differ, since the self embraces not only the ego but the non-ego as in romantic post-Kantian idealism.

Now the great limitation of using the technique of the *reductio ad absurdum* in philosophical argument is that there is no absurdity, as Morris Cohen used to say, paraphrasing Cicero, to which a philosopher will not resort to defend another absurdity. So instead of showing to what Tillich's views lead, I shall ask some simple questions about his starting point, the answers to which I have not been able to find either in his writings or in those of his commentators.

Tillich writes: "What is Being itself? What is that which is not a special being or group of beings, not something concrete or something abstract, but rather something which is always thought implicitly, and sometimes explicitly, if something is said to *be?*" [18] In another place, he writes: "Ontology asks: what does it mean that something is and is not *not?* Which [What?] characteristics does everything show that participates in Being?" I found no answers to these questions in Tillich's writings. He asks them and passes on to something else. The reason, it seems to me, that he doesn't answer these questions is that, as his very language shows, he has been misled by the *form* that a significant question has when it is asked about terms that have intelligible opposites, and uses the same *form* with words that have no opposites, and fails to see that when this is done he has not asked a significant question. It is an illustration of the by now familiar story and mistake of assuming that because two sentences have the same grammatical form, they have the same logical form.

Perhaps another way of saying the same thing is that Tillich is using the term Being as if it were an essence or universal, and his employment of the word "participates" suggests that he is treating it as a Platonic essence or universal.

I am going to rewrite the first of the above quotations from Tillich, substituting a term for Being which has an intelligible opposite and which can be treated as a genuine universal.

"What is triangularity itself? What is that which is not a special triangle in a group of triangles, not a concrete triangle or an abstract triangle, but rather what we always think explicitly, if something is said to *be* triangular?"

The answer is a definition of triangularity, not a triangle, or even an image of a triangle. It is a geometrical relation, that can be represented in many different ways, of a plane figure enclosed by three straight lines. That is what we explicitly or implicitly mean if something is said to be triangular. If I substitute the term "humanity" for Being in the above passage, it still makes sense, for I would then be asking for a definition of a predicate "human" which is shared by a number of individuals. Tillich, too, as the passage above shows, is asking for a definition of a predicate, but he is assuming that being (or existence) is a predicate. Now it seems to me that if Kant established anything, he showed that existence is not a predicate, or attribute, or property like triangular or human. By turning his back on Kant at this point (which has nothing to do with Kant's epistemology), Tillich is basing not only his ontology but his theology as well on a demonstrable logical mistake. There is no characteristic, to answer Tillich's question, which everything shows that participates in Being. An electron, a table, a mirage, a pain, a stone, an idea, $\sqrt{-1}$, a power, a dream, a memory, an army, a geological stratum, an after-image, a mirror image, the prime number between 1,001 and 1,011, a corporation, a dynasty, a mode of production—have nothing in common except that they are objects of discourse, or can be thought about. And "being mentionable" or "being thought about" is not a characteristic or property which belongs to anything in the way that triangular or human does.

The distinction Tillich makes between being and existence is irrelevant to the point at issue. For him God "is being-itself beyond essence and existence," so that God cannot be a specific thing or self. But, as we have seen, "being" is inconsistently treated as a predicate in the same way as any essence. And since being is more than the merely logically possible, according to Tillich, but is also necessary, it not only is but necessarily is, so that despite his denial, Being is endowed with a certain kind of existence—that which cannot not be. Tillich conceals this from himself by speaking of Being as the absolutely unconditioned. But as Kant wrote in his critique of the ontological argument: "To use the word *unconditioned,* in order to get rid of all the conditions which the understanding requires, when wishing to conceive something as necessary, does not render it clear to us in the least whether, after that, we are still thinking anything or perhaps nothing, by the concept of unconditionally necessary." [19] This seems quite apt as a commentary on Tillich's procedure.

2

What, then, shall we conclude about Being? After all it is a word in the English language as well as in all other Indo-European languages. But the presence of a word does not require that we build an ontology to explain it any more than the use of the word "God" requires a theology, or an actual god, to explain it or use of the word "infinite" entails the presence of an actual infinite.

I do not believe that the word "being" has the same meaning, even analogically, in all the contexts in which it appears. In the expression "He's being funny," the word "being" does not mean the same as it does when the poet apostrophizes a "glorious being" or when we say "he's being one of the boys" or when Heidegger says man is a being who asks what being is. The question is, however, whether the word "being" has *any* meaning in a philosophical context, and by a philosophical context I mean any activity which inquires into the logic and the *procedures* by which knowledge is built up and described.

In this kind of context, the word "being" seems to function sometimes as an "infinity or zero word," an expression Dewey borrows from a metaphysical mariner by the name of Klyce who having read the *Encyclopedia Britannica* from cover to cover published a book called *Universe,* to which Dewey wrote an introduction.[20]

In this introduction Dewey makes the point that "in actual use names call attention to features of a situation; that they are tools for directing perception or experimental observations." But the situation itself is always taken for granted. It cannot be exhaustively described, so that at any point there is something grasped but unsaid, something given over and beyond what is taken. It is understood implicitly as the background without which what we say would make no sense. When we come across a man talking to himself or when we hear an insane man talk, even if we understand his separate words, or an isolated sentence, we say he is not making sense. All discourse, every gesture, every vehicle of communication, in addition to an explicit implication, has an implicit implication (presupposition) of a background or situation or context, call it what you will, which is ineffable. "It is necessary to have a word," says Dewey, "which reminds us that whatever we explicitly state has this implicit, unstatable, implication."

There is an entire class of "words," according to Dewey, which have no definite meaning, and which are distinguished from "terms" which have, and which function as reminders of the presence of something always referred to, of that which we are discoursing about. In this class of words are the expressions "the world," "everything," "existence," "Universe," "the non-mathematical infinite," and *"Being."* At least *one* of their uses in sentences is not to designate or stand for any identifiable trait but to remind us of *what* we are talking about but which at that moment cannot itself be said.

Dewey's own analysis indicates that we don't need these par-

ticular words and that the background of knowledge can be suggested by the use of other words in the statements we make. His
distinction between the cognitively explicit and the qualitatively
implicit blossoms out later into the distinction between knowing
and having and in his doctrine of the situation as always presupposed by inquiry and yet not statable in inquiry. "The situation,"
Dewey says, "cannot present itself as an element in a proposition
any more than a universe of discourse can appear as a member of
discourse within that universe." [21]

The sentence makes the same point without the use of any
"infinity or zero" words. And it is a point relevant to an inquiry
about the nature of knowing, to an analysis of what it means for
anything to be known, rather than an analysis of what it means
for anything to be.

Dewey never claimed to have an ontology and in his *Logic* de-
fends the view that logical forms need no ontological underpin-
ning. He does claim to have a metaphysics. But he wrote in his
ninetieth year that "nothing can be farther from the facts of the
case" than "that I use the word *metaphysical* in the sense it bears
in the classic tradition based on Aristotle." [22] He vowed at that
time (as if he had all of eternity before him) "never to use the
words [*metaphysics* and *metaphysical*] again in connection with
any aspect of any part of my own position." [23]

When he did use the word "metaphysics," Dewey meant by it
the description "of the generic traits of the natural world" or of
existence. In contradistinction, the specific traits of the world are
the subject-matter of the sciences.

Now I shall argue later that when Dewey spoke of metaphysics
as the description of the generic traits of existence, he had in mind
those pervasive traits of existence-as-experienced which were relevant to the formulation of ideals of human conduct or the charting
of the paths of human wisdom. But he has not always been interpreted as meaning this, and his actual words are sometimes puzzling. Undoubtedly there are places where Dewey does seem to
suggest that there is a subject-matter, *viz.*, generic traits of all
existence, which lends itself to empirical study by the same methods which the sciences use.

This is the notion I want now to examine. There are certain
initial difficulties in understanding what is meant by the view that

metaphysics is a science of existence (or being) as such whose task
is the description of the generic traits exhibited by every field of
knowledge and everything within it. For, as the view is sometimes
formulated, some key ambiguities strike the eye.

(1) One writer tells us that

> If metaphysics be a sound analysis of being *qua* being, it could have
> the same relation to geology or astronomy or physiology that physics
> and chemistry have to each other, or chemistry and biology. Whenever
> scientists other than metaphysicians use such terms as cause or law
> or contingency, they ought to be using them in the same sense in which
> metaphysicians define them.[24]

We are not informed which metaphysician's definitions the scientist is to use—Hegel's, Aristotle's, or Whitehead's (or Hume's).
One would have thought such information necessary in view of the
tiresome habit metaphysicians have of contradicting each other—
but let that pass for a moment. More important is the fact that
the relationship between metaphysics and geology (or any other
special science) will be one thing if it is like the present relationship between physics and chemistry, and something else again if
it is like the *present* relationship between chemistry (or physics)
and biology.

(a) As I understand it the present relationship between physics
and chemistry is such that laws in both sciences are explained in
terms of the same set of theoretical assumptions and basic terms,
and these are the assumptions and terms of physics, so that chemistry roughly speaking consists of that branch of physics which
studies certain special types of phenomenon. If metaphysics were
related to geology as physics to chemistry, we should expect either
that some propositions of geology should be derivable from propositions of metaphysics, or that they should be explicable in metaphysical terms. Now let us take any specific geological proposition, *e.g.*, the principle of "posthumous movement" in structural
geology which asserts that the earth's crust is more likely to
crumple along a fold and particular direction in places where previous crumplings have occurred than in other places. Suppose
that we deny this principle or that it turns out to be false. What
possible difference would it make to any metaphysical theory?
What generic trait of existence would thereby be denied? The

answer, it seems to me, is "none whatsoever." The relation, then, between metaphysics and geology, whatever it is, cannot be like the relation between physics and chemistry, for if certain chemical phenomena accompanying the electrolytic dissociation of liquids and metals uniformly failed to occur, certain modifications in physical theory would be called for.

(b) The present relation between chemistry and biology is something different from that between physics and chemistry because not only are we unable at present to reduce laws of biology (say genetics) to those of chemistry but there are certain terms used in biology which cannot be defined by reduction to chemical terms at present. But no true biological statement is incompatible with any of the statements accepted as true in physics and chemistry. If this is the type of relationship which exists between metaphysics and geology (or any other science), then what is being said is that metaphysically true propositions are necessary conditions for the truths of geological propositions, and that the metaphysician has veto power over the findings of the scientist in the event that they do not square with metaphysical truth. What is ontologically false cannot be scientifically true. (Some philosophers actually said this about the theory of relativity and about certain results in atomic physics.)

But there are two difficulties here. (i) If this is the relation between metaphysics and geology (science), it is not sufficient to distinguish it from the relation between logic and geology (science). For logic, too, exercises veto power over what may be believed in science. It doesn't decree what the scientist must find but insists that what he says must be at least internally self-consistent. (And this is perhaps all the philosophic critics of quantum theory and relativity were protesting—not the discoveries but the needlessly paradoxical ways of formulating the discoveries.) (ii) Few metaphysicians, and none of those who define it as the study of generic traits, have the courage of their imperial claims. For sooner or later every one of them admits that the relation between metaphysics and geology is not asymmetrical, as they boldly claimed at first, but symmetrical. The very same writer from whom we quoted above goes on to say: "Whenever [scientists] reach formulations which show discrepancy with the principles of metaphysics, they either need the correction metaphysics can give or can furnish the correction metaphysics needs." [25] When they contradict each other, metaphysicians may correct the geologists or geologists may correct the metaphysicians! It now appears that they are as much a part of one discipline, after all, as physicists and chemists, and we come back to the first type of relation. But if what we have said is valid, then whether it is asserted that the first relationship between metaphysics and geology holds or that the second relation . holds, both assertions are false.

(2) There is still another interpretation offered of metaphysics conceived as a science interested in the accurate descriptions of the generic traits which existence everywhere and always has. According to this view, what metaphysics does is to analyze the *meanings* of fundamental or generic terms. "Careful formulation of the principle of causality," we are told, "is legitimate metaphysics." [26] Not only is the analysis of the meaning of cause and effect part of metaphysics but also "the sense" in which events are said to be determined or contingent, the relation between necessity and chance, and "the nature of 'law' and its relation to the particular events which are said to 'obey' law." [27] If this is metaphysical analysis, how does it differ from logical analysis of basic concepts or the analysis of the language of science? Hume offered a careful formulation of the principle of causality in order to show that no metaphysical assumptions were involved in its consistent use. If the logical empiricists have been really prosecuting metaphysics in their prolonged discussion of "the nature of 'law' and its relation to the particular events which are said to 'obey' the law," why have they been accused of "persecuting" metaphysics?

If metaphysics consists in the analysis of the *meaning* of "causality" or any other category used to describe or explain events, how can we at the same time claim that "its conclusions will be probabilities with which we approach the future"? [28] Only statements of fact can be probable. Metaphysical statements on this view are presumably statements of empirical, generic fact. But an analysis of a concept is adequate or inadequate, clear or obscure. We may say of an attempted analysis that it is probable that it will be an adequate analysis. But we cannot say that the analysis is probable. And if we say, as does Professor Randall, that the conclusions of the metaphysician are not only probable but corrigible, we are obviously denying that metaphysics has anything to do with the logical analysis of concepts.[29]

(3) Do those who talk about empirical metaphysics really believe what they seem to say? Professor Randall writes:

> Metaphysics, in the light of its long history, is a rather specific scientific inquiry, with a definite field and subject-matter of its own, a science that like any other is cumulative and progressive, which has in fact in our own generation made remarkable progress. It is the science of existence as existence.[30]

I hesitate to take issue with such a distinguished historian of philosophy as Professor Randall but I venture to suggest that if the history of philosophy throws any light on the subject it establishes precisely the opposite of what Professor Randall writes, that far from being cumulative in its results, metaphysics is in a worse state of confusion and disagreement than in many periods of the past, and that far from having made remarkable progress in our generation, metaphysics has received such blows that metaphysicians spend an inordinate amount of their time trying to prove that they are not necessarily talking nonsense.

But the more important point I want to urge here is that just as there is no such thing as "Being," i.e., it is a word that neither designates nor refers to anything observable or discriminable in the world, and has neither a substantive nor attributive character, so there is no such thing as a generic or pervasive trait of existence as Professor Randall describes it. Metaphysics, he says, "analyzes the generic traits manifested by existences of any kind, the characters sure to turn up in any universe of discourse—those traits exhibited in any 'οὐσία' or subject-matter whatever, the fundamental and pervasive distinctions in terms of which any subject-matter may be understood, as they are found within any subject matter." [31]

Very well, we ask him to name one such trait. Is time a category of metaphysics? It is not a generic trait of mathematics. It never turns up as a character in the universe of discourse of mathematics, or of logic either. Take space. It is not a generic trait of consciousness. The consciousness of space does not imply that there is a space of consciousness. Causality. It is completely irrelevant to that generic subject-matter known as the theory of numbers. Chance. Are all subject-matters characterized by "chance"? Depending upon how we define the term, the question is silly or the answer to it is indeterminate. The same is true of the scope of "law" or "necessity." Those traits which we identify as "life," "mind," "consciousness," "matter," "energy," are *not* manifested by existences of every kind, they do *not* turn up in every universe of discourse. I cannot call the roll of all the categories or alleged generic traits, but in almost every case it is obvious that none of them are generic traits as Randall defines them, that some subject-matter can be found in which either it is false to say they apply or it makes no sense even to ask whether they apply or not.

There are some apparent exceptions to this, *e.g.*, individuality. Is individuality a generic trait of all subject-matters and an attribute of all universes of discourse? Before we can answer we must ask what it means for anything to be an individual or have individuality. And if we do so, I believe it can be shown that we are dealing with a cluster of different meanings of the same word. The reason the word "individual" can be meaningfully used in statements that describe certain traits and properties of every universe of discourse is *not* that there exists a generic or pervasive trait, but that as we go from one universe of discourse to another, the rules of usage which determine whether the word is being employed correctly in its appropriate universe of discourse, as well as the psychological and sociological reasons for the development of those rules, vary. The term "individual" (like the term "unity") has the same systematic ambiguity as the term "exists." Thus the considerations which make it correct to speak of an individual atom because it is differentiated in space-time from another atom, vary from the reasons which make it correct for me to speak of an individual form or figure because it is unique, or of an individual number because of its position in a series, or of an individual shade of color of a certain hue and intensity because of its specificity. Have all these meanings, or the rules which determine their different, albeit proper, uses, something in common? I do not see that they have. The most I should be willing to say is that all the problems to which the answer consists in offering definitions, or descriptions, of individuality in any universe of discourse are problems which involve the question of when we are satisfied that we mean the same thing, person, event or class of things, persons, or events. In short, it is only for purposes of communication or identification that we ask the question: In what does its or his individuality consist?

The same analysis can be made of continuity, which is a polar term of individuality. It does not characterize all subject-matters in the same sense. Continuity sometimes means the presence of organization, sometimes quantitative variation, or qualitative variation, sometimes the structure of the mathematical continuum, sometimes evolutionary development, sometimes merely similarity. Where the meaning of the term is reasonably clear and definite it does not hold of all subject-matters; where it seems to be applicable to all subject-matters, we have in reality a cluster of different meanings, only some of which stand in familial relationships to each other.

This tendency to assume that a common term in different contexts means the same thing is the source of much confusion not only in philosophical writing but in the special sciences as well; e.g., terms like "field," "energy," "inertia," are carried over, and used not as helpful metaphors but as if they had some invariant significance. By the same argument by which one reaches the conclusion that "continuity" and "individuality" are generic traits, a metaphysician can establish that "inertia" is a metaphysical trait. After all, we can meaningfully employ statements which describe the inertia of a physical thing; the inertia of a system; the inertia of habits, mind, intelligence; the inertia of style, law, or society. Does this justify me in saying that it turns up in every universe of discourse? If the answer is that despite their variations in meaning each usage of "inertia" fixes our attention on a specific mode of a generic trait itself described by the expression "resistance manifested by anything under discussion to a force which would change the state or position or direction of its motion," this will still not give us anything which satisfies the conditions of a genuine generic trait, for terms like "resistance" and "force" and "motion" are just as ambiguous in these several contexts as the expression "inertia" itself.

That there is something anomalous here is suggested by the fact that some generic traits of subject-matter are discovered apparently by pure dialectical inference or definition by those who speak of empirical metaphysics. For example, Professor Randall tells us that "for the empirical metaphysician, his method is no different from the ordinary experimental methods of observation and tested generalization employed in any existential science, and his conclusions share in the probable and corrigible character of the findings of all experimental science." [82] This does not, however, seem to be an accurate description of the way in which he actually brings some traits to light, *e.g.*, the metaphysical trait of intelligibility or knowability. Thus Professor Randall tells us that "knowability or intelligibility is a trait of every object of inquiry, of every subject-matter," and if we ask: Why? he continues: "else it could not be inquired into or made known." [83] If this statement is true, it certainly has *not* been established by familiar experimental methods of observation but only as a consequence of some unproven postulate or of a definition of what it means to be inquired into. How can we know—and as empirical metaphysicians to boot!— that *every* subject-matter, a term used by Professor Randall interchangeably with existence, is such that it *must* lend itself to inquiry, that it *can* be inquired into? Only, it seems to me, by adopting a procedure different from the one that Professor Randall thinks he is using.

This procedure is suggested by Professor Woodbridge. Professor Woodbridge was convinced that intelligibility is a metaphysical trait but he reached such a conclusion because he believed that although scientific knowledge and metaphysical knowledge are not opposed they are still widely different. "Science," he says, "asks for the laws of existence and discovers them by experiment. Metaphysics asks for the nature of reality and discovers it by definition." [34] If, however, we refuse to settle the generic traits of existence by definitions of the real, then I should say that it is a discoverable fact that not all actions, not all subject-matters, are intelligible, that we sometimes use statements properly which contain the expression "unintelligible," and that there is a fairly clear sense in which we can say of the hermit found dead in the desert or of a drowning man that *whether* he thought of his family just before he died and *what* he thought is practically unknowable.

3

Does it follow from all this that the term "ontological" cannot be consistently and correctly used or that there are no ontological statements of which truth or falsity may be predicated? I am not arguing for such a drastic conclusion. I do not believe that there is any consistent usage for the term "ontological." I therefore wish to propose that we call "ontological" those statements or propositions which we believe to be cognitively valid, or which assert something that is true or false, and yet which are not found in any particular science, whether of physics, psychology, or sociology, but which are obviously taken for granted by the sciences. For example, here are some propositions of this character: There are many colors in the world; Colors have no smell or sound; It is possible to perceive two things at the same time; There are many kinds of processes in the world; Some processes are evolutionary; Thinking creatures inhabit the earth.

Note with reference to the last two sentences that I am not saying that evolution and thinking are generic traits of existence but only that the world is such that evolutionary and thinking processes are exhibited or discovered in it. These facts are ontological only because no science owns them. (I do not even have to say that "the world is such that . . . ," because I am not talking about the whole of the world but only of a particular state of affairs or succession of events denoted by the phrase "evolutionary process.")

It seems to me that there is an indeterminate number of truths of this kind which nobody bothers to make explicit or to analyze unless such truths are denied or appear to be denied. The analysis we make turns out to be a more careful and explicit description of what we already know and the grounds on which we say we know it, without committing us to any specific theory as to how what we know was learned. To the extent that they are about the furniture of heaven and earth in the same sense as astronomical, physical, and biological statements are about that furniture, they may sometimes describe certain massive facts of existence and human experience and constitute a primitive or pre-scientific physics and/or psychology.

What I propose, then, to call ontological statements about the world might loosely be called common-sense statements about the world which all scientists, if not all sciences, take for granted (I say all scientists rather than all sciences because these common-sense truths are not all relevant to all the sciences; *e.g.*, that tears are usually a sign of grief rather than of joy is not relevant to

physics). Recognition of their truth provides the fundamental tests
of normal perception and sanity of behavior.

Pre-scientific or primitive physics and psychology do not give
us statements about being *qua* being, or about the generic traits of
existence. For they always fall short of the fully generic, they
always leave something out. As I interpret Dewey's position on
the nature of the subject-matter of metaphysical inquiry (his language is not always consistent), this is his view, too. He is not
so much interested in the traits that are truly generic but in those
that are *irreducible,* whether generic or not. And he is interested
in our giving intellectual recognition to the irreducible traits of the
world in order to rule out the legitimacy of inquiries into "first
causes" or "ultimate creation," in order to deny that "potenti-
ality" is a causal principle of explanation or a causal immanent
force, and above all in order to oppose reductionism of the materialistic and idealistic varieties. He believes it is possible to
analyze a situation without reducing quality to quantity, without
abolshing the pluralities of the given, without denying the objectivity of relations, and particularly of time and evolution. "Specifically diverse existences, interaction, change," Dewey tells us,
are generic and irreducible traits, but these three traits turn out
to be the irreducible traits "of the subject-matter of inquiry in the
natural sciences," [35] which certainly is not coextensive with all
subject-matters. If there are any doubts about this, his remarks
about evolution should settle them. "Evolution," he tells us,
"appears to be just one of the irreducible traits of the world,"
which constitute the subject-matter of metaphysics. Obviously it
cannot be generic in Professor Randall's meaning because not all
changes are evolutionary.

It seems to me that the first, if not the last, thing Dewey is trying to say about ontology in this sense is that "the attempt to give
an account of any occurrence involves the genuine and irreducible
existence of the thing dealt with." It is a negative counsel of
methodological wisdom: don't call your subject-matter into question as a conclusion of your inquiry into it. The investigation of
the causes and consequences of any phenomenon is not sound if it
denies in the end the phenomenal data which pose the problem,
and the existential data which are truly presupposed by, or given
with, the phenomenal data. Ontology is then a collection of an

indeterminately large number of commonplaces or truisms—*e.g.*,
the world is such that this, that, or something else is found in it,
which has these, those, or some other characteristics—truisms which
have a certain use and point when they are counterposed to absurdities. There will always be a need for such truisms to the
extent that philosophers—and others—keep on uttering absurdities.

There is another class of ontological statements or rather another character that they may have in addition to stocking our
arsenals of sanity. Why, we may ask, do philosophers select some
features about the world for special attention rather than others
out of the infinite range of fact? And I wish to suggest that they
do so because of their belief that these features have especial relevance to the career of human life on earth. Truths about them
constitute what may be called philosophical anthropology. Philosophical anthropology is what Dewey calls metaphysics in *Experience and Nature*. Its subject-matter is not Being *qua* Being but
those features of the world which constitute, to use Dewey's words,
"a ground map of the province of criticism."

It is relevance to the life and death of man and to the whole
gamut of his experience which is the key to the set of traits Dewey
or any other ontologist selects for analysis and description. When
Morris Cohen charges that Dewey's metaphysics is anthropocentric,
echoing Santayana's criticism that Dewey emphasizes the fore-
ground of experience, Dewey replies to both that every metaphysics which is not a pretentious rival to or substitute for science
or religion is inescapably anthropocentric and has its own fore-
ground. Metaphysics in this sense gives us the kind of knowledge
which, to indulge a fancy, a Platonic soul would like to have, after
it has drunk of the waters of Lethe, and before it descends, in
answer to the questions: What kind of a world am I going to live
in? What is the life of man like on earth? The answers to these
questions may be vague but they are significant. And it is arguable
that to the extent that good literature as a vehicle of communication has a cognitive content what it says can be expressed as
answers to such questions. In answering these questions we don't
seek scientific detail nor do we read the *Encyclopedia Britannica*.
We are content with descriptions of life and existence in the large
in which the human predicament, or the life of man, is taken *not*
as analogue of the nature of nature, as in the myths of existential-

ism, but as a reflection, and outgrowth, of certain traits of nature, in which the human spirit although not constitutive or pervasive in nature is just as much a part, just as much at home, just as natural, as any other aspect or expression of nature.

The traits to which Dewey pays the greatest attention show that a standard of selection is at work. Individuality and constant relations; contingency and need; movement and arrest; the stable and precarious. These are not the categories of science but of the cosmic theatre of human destiny. Of all of them one can say what Dewey says of one of them: "Barely to note and register that contingency is a trait of natural events has nothing to do with wisdom. To note, however, contingency in connection with a concrete situation of life is that fear of the Lord which is at least the beginning of wisdom. The detection and definition of nature's end is in itself barren. But the undergoing that actually goes on in the light of this discovery brings one close to supreme issues: life and death." [36]

This is not romantic existentialism but scientifically grounded *Lebensphilosophie*. No verbal bars or taboo will prevent people from discussing questions such as these. The only legitimate goal in this connection is to ask that the questions first make sense, and then to find out whether the answers make good sense.

Naturalism and First Principles

In this chapter I shall discuss what seems to me to be one of the most fundamental problems in the intellectual enterprise which goes by the name of philosophy, *viz.,* what it means for human behavior to be reasonable or rational. It is a question which arises even when we have no doubt that a person is logical in the sense that he draws conclusions which are implied or entailed by certain premises. A paranoiac is nothing if not logical when he spins the strands of unrelated events into a web of conspiracy of which he is the presumed victim. Some philosophers have raised the question in connection with a discussion of the nature of intelligibility when the meaning of the thought or conduct of others is puzzling or in doubt. I have been led to it because of some recent criticisms of naturalism which charge that it arbitrarily imposes its own canons of rationality or intelligibility on human behavior and therefore denies certain important truths about the world and human experience on *a priori* grounds.

A similar question has also been raised by some fashionable sociological views of knowledge according to which there are irreducibly different modes of knowing illustrated in different cultures and which suggest, and sometimes explicitly affirm, that there is no such thing as a universally objective, valid method of determining rational or intelligible conduct, independent of time or society or class, or even of party. On this latter view, it is sometimes argued that moral, social, and political conflicts are the results of conflicting logics of inquiry. Sometimes the converse is argued, *i.e.*, irreducible social conflicts give rise to irreducibly different criteria of truth. In either case no one method can claim universal and exclusive validity. Indeed, to claim that any one method of establishing truths is better than another is to be guilty of philosophical imperialism almost in the same way that the claim of superiority for the institutions of modern western, democratic society evinces cultural imperialism.

My argument will make the following points: (1) despite all the basic conflicts over first principles of thinking or evidence, there are working truths on the level of practical living which are everywhere recognized and which everywhere determine the pattern of reasonable conduct in secular affairs, *viz.*, the effective use of means to achieve ends. Rationality on this level is not merely as Charles Peirce suggests "being governed by final causes" but so using the means and materials of the situation in which final causes are pursued as to achieve a maximum of functional adaptation between means and ends. (2) Second, this conception of rationality is not limited to our culture and to our time but is supported by the available anthropological evidence. The mind of primitive man, medieval man, communist man, for all the claims that have been made about their differences, is no different from our own. This is not incompatible with believing that in respect to discovering new truth one or another group of men, in virtue of *historical*, perhaps genetic reasons, at a given time may be in possession of superior powers. (3) Third, scientific method is the refinement of the canons of rationality and intelligibility exhibited by the techniques of behavior and habits of inference involved in the arts and crafts of men; its pattern is everywhere discernible even when overlaid with myth and ritual. (4) Fourth, the systematization of what is involved in the scientific method of inquiry is what we mean by naturalism, and the characteristic doctrines of naturalism like the denial of disembodied spirits generalize the cumulative evidence won by the use of this method. (5) Fifth, that the criticisms of naturalism from which the paper takes its point of departure can be met by showing that, although the assumptions of naturalism are not necessarily true, they are more reasonable than their alternatives.

If it is true, as Peirce says, that "Every reasoning itself holds out some expectation," the validity of rules of reasoning is not a matter of fiat but depends upon the fruits of inquiry. Ultimately the rules of logic are instruments of discourse which enable us to avoid the shocks and surprises, the disasters and disappointments in attempting to understand the nature of the world and our own intentions and purposes. One method of reasoning is more valid than another because its use enables us to make the knowledge we have today more coherent, and especially because it more easily facilitates adding *new* knowledge to it.

1

That first principles must be justified before we can achieve assured knowledge is a view seemingly held by some philosophers but rarely by anyone else. Scientists, for example, have satisfactorily solved problem after problem without feeling called upon to solve the problem of justifying their first principles. Not only scientists but people of ordinary affairs generally know when something is truer than something else without knowing, or even claiming to know, what is *absolutely* true. To say that we do not have to know what is ultimately or absolutely true or good in order to know what is truer or better, sounds dialectically impossible. But I submit that this is actually the way common sense and science operate. Even the most rationalist of philosophers in their nonprofessional capacity make effective use of everyday knowledge long before they reach their uncertain conclusions about the validity of first principles. It isn't necessary to assert that we know what is absolutely true about the cause of tuberculosis to know that a certain germ has more to do with it than climate. Similarly, few people know what their "ultimate" values are, and yet almost everyone will claim to know that it is better for human beings to do productive labor for a living than to be recipients of charity. Deny propositions of this sort and insist that declarations of the truer or better must wait upon knowledge of *the* true or *the* good, and the whole of human inquiry anywhere would come to a halt.

This is not to assert that there is no problem concerning the justification of first principles or of those rules of procedure which we follow when we reach the knowledge about which there is a maximum of agreement among human beings. What I am asserting is that the justification of rules of procedure in inquiry is not of a different logical order, possessing so to speak another or higher type of necessity than the actions of which they are the rule. More specifically what I am asserting is that there is no such thing as strictly logical justification of first principles in science or common sense since proof by definition involves the reduction of all statements to indefinable terms and undemonstrable propositions or to propositions themselves so reducible. And secondly, what I am further asserting is that in the sense in which justification of first principles is an intelligible question—as when someone asks me why I regard naturalism as a truer or more adequate doctrine than its rivals—the answer will take the same *general* form of the answers given by those who do the world's work—the cobblers, the carpenters and gardeners—when they are asked to justify one set of procedures rather than alternative ones.

In other words I am saying somewhat differently what William James observed in *The Problems of Philosophy* although it is alleged he sometimes sinned against the meaning of his own words. "Philosophy," he there says, "taken as something distinct from science or human affairs, follows no method peculiar to itself. All our thinking today has evolved gradually out of primitive human thought, and the only really important changes that have come over its manner (as distinguished from the matters in which it believes) are a *greater* hesitancy in asserting its convictions, and the *habit* of seeking verification for them when it can." [my italics]

Such an approach, as I understand it, is the only one that can consistently be advanced by naturalists in justifying their first principles. This has provoked the retort that it is essentially question-begging, that since the methods and categories of common day activity and science—upon which naturalism relies—are designed to take note only of the existence of certain things, the existence of other things like immaterial entities, cosmic purposes, Gods, and disembodied souls are ruled out *a priori*. The assertion of their existence on the naturalist's view must therefore be assumed to be not merely false but meaningless or contradictory. Since we are concerned here with questions of existential fact, the naturalist who naïvely believes himself to be imbued with a spirit of natural piety for a world he has not created, is taxed with the ironic charge of legislating for all existence.

Before evaluating the charge of circularity it is important to realize that if valid, it holds for *every* philosophical position. We cannot break out of this circularity by invoking only the law of contradiction, unless we are prepared to hold that all knowledge is analytic and that the differences between nature and history, with all their contingency, and mathematics and logic disappear. Certainly, whatever falls outside the scope of the basic explanatory categories of any philosophical position cannot be recognized. This is a tautology. That these categories are restrictive follows from their claim to be meaningful since a necessary condition of a meaningful statement is that it should be incompatible with its opposite. The only legitimate question here is whether they are narrowly restrictive, whether there are matters of knowledge in common experience which they exclude or whose existence they make unintelligible.

Since every philosophic position must start somewhere and make some preliminary or initial assumptions that can be challenged at least verbally by other philosophers, it is always possible to level the charge of circularity. But what shall we therefore conclude? That these assumptions are mere stipulations or arbitrary postulations which express nothing but the *resolutions* of philosophers? This would be voluntarism gone mad. Philosophers might just as well close up shop insofar as they claim for their position some objective validity in reporting or interpreting the facts of experience. For even voluntarism could not sustain itself against the charge of circularity.

The naturalist does not despair because he cannot demonstrate what is by definition indemonstrable. Nor can he rely upon intuitions or revealed dogmas because of their irreducible plurality. He believes he can show that although not demonstrable, his assumptions can be made reasonable to "reasonable" men. And the mark of a "reasonable" man is his willingness to take responsibility for his actions, to explain why he proceeds to do one thing rather than another, and to recognize that it is his conduct, insofar as it is voluntary, which commits him to a principle or belief rather than any form of words where the two seem at odds with each other. The naturalist does not speak, as one of its critics does, in large terms of "justifying philosophical categories as rationally and comprehensively as possible," and then fail to tell us in what specific ways philosophical rationality and comprehensiveness differ from scientific rationality and comprehensiveness. Are the laws of logic and the canons of evidence and relevance any different in philosophy from what they are in science and common sense?

To every critic of naturalism who has charged it with circularity I propose the following. Consider someone who comes to you and proclaims on the basis of some special personal experience that an all-pervasive R substance exists. It is neither physical nor psychical nor social, neither natural nor divine, nor can it be identified by, defined in, or reduced, in any sense of reduction, to any physical, psychical, or social terms. It is subject, so you are told, to no material conditions of determination whatsoever. The very request that these conditions be indicated is brushed aside as revealing a constitutional incapacity or blindness to grasp this unique entity to which all sorts of edifying qualities are attributed in an analogical sense, including a triune gender. It is granted by the believer in R that its existence cannot be logically inferred from whatever *else* is experienced, but he is quick to add that its existence cannot be logically *disproved* without assuming a question-begging philosophical position which rules out the possibility of this unique cosmic process. The next day he reports personal contact with another presence which he calls the analogical father, and the day after, the analogical grandfather, and so on, until even the most fervent supernaturalist finds himself confronted with an embarrassment of supernatural riches.

Embroider the fancy as you will. It is obvious that he can repeat almost word for word the points in the indictment of those who charge naturalists with circular reasoning.

Even if all philosophical positions are *au fond* question begging, there would still remain the task, pursued by all philosophers of determining which of all question-begging positions is more adequate to the facts of experience. Every philosopher who seriously attempts an answer does assume *in fact* that there is some common method of determining when a position is adequate to the facts of experience and when not. The contention of the naturalist is that this common method is in principle continuous with the method which we ordinarily use to hold individuals to responsible utterance about the existence of things in the world—a method which is pre-eminently illustrated in the ways in which men everywhere solve the problem of adaptation of material means to ends.

2

The procedures which are the matrix of reasonable conduct everywhere seem to me to be clearly involved in what broadly speaking we may call the technological aspect of human culture. It is not necessary to maintain that tool using is the only characteristic which differentiates human society from animal societies to recognize that whereas only some nonhuman animals occasionally use natural objects as tools, all human animals, wherever they are found, *make* their own tools. What distinguishes modern society from primitive society is not the presence of inventions but the organization of inventiveness.

Anthropological evidence leaves no doubt that primitive man wherever found solved tremendous problems of adjustment and survival. With a little imagination we can appreciate that starting from scratch such things as the invention of fire and the wheel, the cultivation of plants, domestication of cattle, and the smelting of metal represent inventive feats of a high order. There is an obvious continuity between our own technology and that of our primitive ancestors. "The sapling," says A. A. Goldenweiser, "bent out of its natural position to provide the dynamic factor in a primitive trap, is the remote forerunner of a spring which runs untold millions of watches and performs numerous other tasks in modern technology. The achievement of Alexander the Great in cutting the Gordian knot, though dramatic, did not equal that other achievement—the tying of the first knot. And this knot, in the midst of an ever-growing family of knots, is still with us." [1]

One can multiply illustrations indefinitely of the ingenious ways in which primitive man everywhere chooses between alternate means to achieve the particular end, improves upon these means and tests them by their relative efficacy in achieving determinate results. What stands out in my mind particularly is the impressive functional economy of the Eskimo's composite harpoon, that marvelous contrivance by which he spears seal, walrus, and whale, and especially the way in which the precious point is recovered. Hundreds of decisions must have been made and tested by their consequences before the instrument finally took shape.

The pattern of rationality does not extend of course to all aspects of primitive life any more than it does to our own life, but it points to a universal pattern of intelligibility understood by everyone who grasps the problem which the tool or technical process is destined to solve. Where religion or myth does not influence technology, the indefinite perfectability, so to speak, of the particular instrument is recognized or another one is substituted which gives more reliable results. Thus, for example, the Eskimo will abandon his ingenious harpoon for a gun when he can procure one.

The contention of Levy-Bruhl that primitive man thinks prelogically, that he denies the law of contradiction, that he is unable to isolate and distinguish logically unrelated things or ideas, that he understands by a kind of "participation" is not borne out by a study of primitive technology. Levy-Bruhl's observations are valid enough for the religious beliefs and social customs of the primitives, for their "collective representations" but not for the individual behavior of the primitive in war or hunt or in the field. One might add that Levy-Bruhl's observations can be extended to much of the religious beliefs and social customs of modern society, too. Even if all of Levy-Bruhl's claims are granted they do not invalidate Franz Boas' plausibly argued conclusion that the mental processes of primitive man in respect to inhibition of impulses, power of attention, logical thinking, and inventiveness seem essentially like our own.[2]

Despite their differences on other questions there is fundamental agreement among Levy-Bruhl, Boas, Goldenweiser and Malinowski concerning the universality of the experimental, commonsensical, practical approach to the environmental challenge. Malinowski points out that the realms of the profane or secular, and the realms of the religious or supernatural are not confused even when their respective activities are conjoined. The native plants his sweet potato with the most exacting care for the conditions of soil, moisture, and other elements which affect its growth: but in addition,

he goes through some religious ritual, supported by a myth, before
he believes he has a right to expect a successful crop.

"Can we regard primitive knowledge," asks Malinowski, "which,
as we found is both empirical and rational, as a rudimentary stage of
science, or is it not at all related to it? If by science be understood a
body of rules and conceptions, based on experience and derived from
it by logical inference, embodied in material achievements and in a
fixed form of tradition and carried on by some sort of social organization—then there is no doubt that even the lowest savage communities
have the beginnings of science, however rudimentary." [3]

Similarly, Goldenweiser:

"Technique on the one hand, and religion and magic, on the other,
present from one angle the opposite poles of the primitive attitude.
Industry stands for common sense, knowledge, skill, objective matter
of fact achievement. Religion stands for mysticism, a subjective translation of experience, a substitution of mental states for external reali-
ties and a reification of such states into presumed existences in a
realm which in part is 'another' world but in part also belongs to
'this' world insofar as the two worlds interpenetrate." [4]

What all modern anthropologists seem to agree on, as I interpret
them, is that the religious or mystical elements in primitive experience, with their myths and religious rites, arise not in competition
with the secular knowledge of technology or as a substitute for
such knowledge but as a "complement" in situations in which all
the available technical means and know-how are not adequate to
a desired end, or where events do not clearly or always prosper
when the proper instrumentalities are employed. In a world full
of dangers and surprises, in a world of time, pain and contingen-
cies, it is not hard to understand the psychological place of religion. It is a safe generalization to say that the depth of the
religious sense is inversely proportionate to the degree of reliable
control man exercises over his environment and culture. In this
sense religion is a form of faith, emotion, not knowledge: when
it is something more than this and competes with science or technology it becomes superstition.

We may restate this a little differently. Science or technology and
religion represent two different attitudes toward the mysterious:

one tries to solve mysteries, the other worships them. The first believes that mysteries may be made less mysterious even when they are not cleared up, and admits that there will always be mysteries. The second believes that some specific mysteries are final.

This relation between technology and religion is not restricted to primitive societies. Somewhere in the Talmud it is written that if a man's son is ill, the correct thing for him to do is not merely to call a doctor or merely to pray to God but to call a doctor *and* pray to God. And in our own culture this seems to be the function of nonsuperstitious religion. The theology comes as an afterthought. Even those who do not believe in God often look around for Him to thank or to blame somewhat like the atheist in the well-known story who when asked why he nailed a horseshoe over his door replied, "I really don't believe in it but I've heard it brings luck even if you don't."

In modern societies our attitudes are more complex. There is religion and religion. If you pray to God expecting rain or a baby boy, that is one thing. It is bad science, although if Rhine establishes the existence of psychokinesis (the PK effect), a power which some subjects allegedly have to influence the way dice will fall by wishing or willing, this kind of praying may not be bad science. If you pray in order to relieve your mind that is another thing. It is good psychology although there may be better psychology. If you pray without any purpose at all but out of a sense of relief, gratitude, awe or fear—that is not science at all but pure religion or art. "If scientific statements are to be called truths, religious statements should be called something else—comforts, perhaps." [5]

3

I turn now to a brief consideration of the nature of technology and technological behavior. All technological behavior is purposive behavior; the purpose provides a test of relevance, and the achievement of purpose, a test of the adequacy of alternative means suggested. Its every feature takes note of the compulsions of the environment as well as the much more limited powers of man over the environment. Its knowledge is a form of *ack*nowledgment—an acknowledgment of the nature of materials, the effect of motor action on the redistribution of materials, the importance of sequential order and spatial configuration. It is obviously reconstructive in intent, and makes of a natural order one that is also reasonable. It discounts the immediate qualities of use and enjoyment for the sake of anticipated consequences. Wherever we have a tool or technique, it refers not to a unique situation but a class of situations so that it has a kind of implicit universal import not separable from ultimate individual applications. The better instrument recommends itself to us to the extent that it enables us to make a more reliable prediction of *observable* effects that bear on the the purpose in hand—the resolution of the problem. Learning from these simple inductions of experience is usually the first manifestation of intelligence. The violation, or rather the attempted violation of established inductions, like walking off a roof or out of a window, is sometimes the first evidence of insanity.

Technological behavior may be overlaid with all sorts of propitiatory rites but it is usually possible to distinguish between the functional and ritualistic aspects of the use of instruments. In its purely functional aspect every feature of the technique can be justified by its normal fruits or consequences. In time the process of adaptation tends to give us structures that are as simple and beautiful in their economy as the axhandle and oar, turbine and jet plane.

An analysis of the implicit logic of technology and the commonsense operations it involves, reveals that no hard and fast line of separation can be drawn between the general pattern of scientific method and reasonable procedures in the primary knowledge-getting activities of men struggling to control their environment. With the development of new instruments of discovery and measurement, and the use of mathematical notation, science becomes more abstract, more systematic, more precise, more complex. But wherever a man has had an idea sufficiently clear to enable him to draw a valid inference from it, the truth of which he sought to test by some controlled observation or experiment, he was proceeding—no matter how primitively—in a scientific way. The continuity between reasonable procedures in reaching conclusions about matters of fact of everyday concern and the procedures by which we make the most esoteric discoveries in the advanced sciences cannot be breached without making the whole enterprise of science a mystery, for every science starts from, and returns to, some of these reasonable procedures. If the common-sense world is radically unreliable or illusory, every theoretical construction which is based upon it or which it tests, is no more credible.

What we might call the first order facts of science are drawn directly from the world of common-sense experience—*e.g.*, that a sponge holds more water than a cloth, that a polished surface is a better reflector than an opaque one, that white clothing is cooler than black—all of which were once discoveries. In the development of science no matter what the succession of theories, these first order facts are the last to be challenged. Whether the wave theory or corpuscular theory or any other theory of light is defended, the law which states the inequality of the angles of incidence and refraction when a ray of light passes from one medium to another is not questioned. For the class of phenomena it characterizes must be accounted for irrespective of what other predictions are made. From this point of view the laws of nature may be plausibly interpreted as instrumental devices to bring within the largest explanatory scheme our empirical knowledge of first order facts and successfully to predict future experiences which then become first order facts for all other theories.

Science differs from technology in two important respects. First in generality, and second in purpose. Technology is restricted in its practical reference to useful results; whereas the practical purpose of science, if we choose to use this language, is "the advancement of knowing apart from concern with other practical affairs," *i.e.*, the building up of a systematic body of knowledge.[6]

4

If there is no break in the continuity between life sustaining technological and vocational activities anywhere, and developed scientific activities, there is still less to be said for the view that science is so intimately tied up with culture that we must in Spenglerian fashion speak of Apollonian science, Magian science, and Faustian science with irreducibly different criteria of scientific validity. This is carried to extreme lengths by the current dialectical materialistic interpretation of science which denies its class-less, international character and asserts that all sciences, social as well as physical, are class sciences and party sciences. More is meant here than the obvious view that social and political circumstances, interests and ideas have influenced the kind of scientific problems considered, and the direction of their application. The actual content of science is allegedly dependent upon a class or party approach, and the philosophy of dialectical materialism is recommended because by following its lead, problems within science can be presumably solved which defy solution on the basis of other philosophies. It would follow from this, to paraphrase Mannheim, that different classes think differently about everything, or at least everything important, which is manifestly false. There are no "national truths" in science, and Pierre Duhem is obviously right in his claim that it is only by its deficiencies that a science can become the science of one nation rather than another. The belief that there are "class truths" or "party truths" in science rests upon the elementary confusion between the objective evidence for a theory, which if warranted, is universally valid, with the uses, good, bad, or indifferent that are made of it.

Much more worthy of notice is the claim made that what constitutes "objective evidence for a theory" is an historical conception. The history of science reveals that the conditions which a scientific theory must fulfill to be accepted have been more rigorous at some times than at others. It becomes pointless to speak, then, of scientific method *überhaupt;* there are only scientific methods.

This is a very difficult and interesting question which I can treat only briefly and with the appearance of a dogmatism I do not feel. As a possible solution of this problem I venture the following: At any given time scientists accept as working truths hypotheses of varying degrees of generality and strength. They are more firmly convinced of the genetic theory of heredity than of the theory of organic evolution. They would be less surprised if the general theory of relativity were abandoned than the special theory. The degree of confirmation which a theory must pass muster at any time seems to be a function of the fruitfulness of previous theories in the field with similar degrees of confirmatory strength in extending our knowledge of the unknown. In addition the strength of an hypothesis is a function of the number of alternative hypotheses that are available as explanations. As a rule the more numerous the confirming instances the stronger the hypothesis. But if there are no alternative hypotheses present, we may be satisfied with far fewer confirming instances than where alternative hypotheses are present.[7] Further, the bearing of an hypothesis upon the direction of inquiry, the leads it opens up to new ways of experiment, must be taken into account.

To use a distinction of Peirce, in science a *valid* reason for believing a theory may not be a conclusive reason or even a strong reason. My contention is that what makes any reason in science a *valid* reason for believing an hypothesis is not historical, but invariant for all historical periods in the growth of science. But whether a reason is a strong reason for believing an hypothesis varies with the presence or absence of other leads and the evidence for them. This is an historical matter since no one can predict how many creative, competing insights will be current when an hypothesis presents its credentials for confirmation. I therefore do not believe that the variations in the degree of confirmatory completeness which scientific hypotheses have had to meet at different times relativizes in any way the logic of scientific method.

In passing it should be noticed that even in the history of mathematics standards of rigor seem to have varied, and for centuries mathematicians believed propositions which were only conclusively proved in the nineteenth and twentieth centuries. No one would infer from this that the notion of mathematical validity is historically conditioned, for despite the variations in rigor they progressively illustrate one underlying logical pattern of proof to which no alternative has ever been formulated.

If the foregoing is sound then I think it constitutes some reason for believing that there is only one reliable method of reaching the truth about the nature of things anywhere and at any time, that this reliable method comes to full fruition in the methods of science, and that a man's normal behavior in adapting means to ends belies his words whenever he denies it. Naturalism as a philosophy not only accepts this method but also the broad generalizations which are established by the use of it; *viz,* that the occurrence of all qualities or events depends upon the organization of a material system in space-time, and that their emergence, development and disappearance are determined by changes in such organization.

Common sense takes the word "material" as loosely equivalent to the *materials* with which men deal as they go from problem to problem; naturalism as a philosophy takes it to refer to the subject matter of the physical sciences. Neither the one nor the other asserts that only what can be observed exists, for many things may be legitimately inferred to exist (electrons, the expanding universe, the past, the other side of the moon) from what is observed; but both hold that there is no evidence for the assertion of the existence of anything which does not rest upon some observed effects.

The objections that have recently been urged against naturalism sometimes proceed from the notion that a philosophical position must justify its general assumption in some absolutely unique way. This is, as we have seen, a blind alley. Naturalism makes no assumptions over and above those that have been made every time the borders of our knowledge have been pushed back. It therefore has the cumulative weight of the historic achievements of common sense and science behind it. *If* we want to acquire new knowledge, the naturalist asserts, we should follow the basic pattern of inquiry —recognize the problem, state the hypotheses, draw the inferences, perform the experiment, and make the observation. There is no logical necessity or guarantee that we will achieve new knowledge this way but it is reasonable to act on the assumption. If one chooses to call this faith, it is certainly of a different order from the faith that new knowledge will suddenly be won in some other way—as different as the faith that "if I sow, reap, mill and bake the wheat, I shall get bread" is from the faith that "manna will fall from heaven." This difference would remain even if men decided not to reach for new knowledge, and depressed by Hiroshima, were to cry "Sufficient unto the day is the knowledge thereof." The connection between the method that one *could* follow and the conclusions that depend upon its being followed, remains unaffected by what one wants or does not want.

It is all the more surprising therefore to hear from one critic that "the most fundamental objection to the naturalist's procedure is that in Peirce's words it 'blocks the path of inquiry' in that it seeks to settle by stipulation the very issue that we need to be reasonable about if we can." Why? Because, he answers, "having committed themselves in advance to a position which identifies reasonable procedure with that which does not differ 'sharply' from that of the more developed sciences, they (the naturalists) will limit the scope of reasonable inquiry to what can be settled by the methods these sciences employ." [8]

This charge rests upon a double confusion—one of interpretation and one of observation. It is not reasonable procedure—what Dewey calls the basic pattern of inquiry—of which the naturalist says that it does not differ sharply from the more developed sciences. It is the techniques and body of knowledge which enable us to control everyday affairs of which he says that they do not differ sharply from the techniques and body of knowledge that the sciences have developed. For some of the techniques and parts of the body of knowledge of the former are always incorporated in the latter. The reasonable procedure—which according to naturalists is emphatically *not* a special technique of any special science—is *identical* in every formal aspect in every field in which we can lay claim to tested and universally agreed on knowledge about the world. How, then, can it serve as an obstacle to further inquiry, unless it is held that some disciplines have a basic pattern of inquiry quite different from that employed by critical common sense and science. What are these disciplines? What is this pattern? And what tested and universally agreed upon knowledge about this world or any other has been won by it? We are not told.

The error of observation derives from the failure to note that the driving motivation of modern naturalism has been not to block but to open up the paths of inquiry into whole fields which until now have not been investigated scientifically—especially the social disciplines. If this criticism of the danger threatened by naturalism were just, we should expect to find naturalists opposing attempts to employ scientific method in anthropology, history and economics on the ground that the methods and techniques of mathematical physics—"the more fully developed sciences"—were not applicable to them. But it is precisely the naturalists who by distinguishing between the basic pattern of inquiry and the special techniques applicable to different subject matters have been trying to banish methodological purism.

It is true that there have been occasions in the past when those concerned with the logic of scientific method have seemed to show excessive caution in evaluating the first efforts of scientific theories struggling to be born. Before the theory of evolution was buttressed by the findings of experimental genetics some biologists regarded its claims as too speculative. Today many scientific psychologists are very dubious about the validity of psychoanalytic theories which are somewhat in the same state as theories of magnetism at the time of Oersted and Oken. But all of these doubts, including those that follow from a too rigorously formulated canon of verifiability, far from obstructing inquiry are a challenge to it, and melt away as fruitful results are achieved and systematized. Such hypercritical doubts about evidence usually lead to suspension of *judgment* not of inquiry; they do not establish or enforce nontrespass signs. The dogmatism of a Comte who ruled out the possibility of our ever learning anything about the internal constitution of the stars, derided the undulatory theory of light, and professed skepticism about the results of microscopic investigation is as rare as it is inconsistent, and was repudiated by his scientific colleagues as soon as his views were made known.

If we take a long view of the history of scientific inquiry, the evidence is overwhelming that it has not been the naturalists who have obstructed investigation into new fields by insisting that the methods of the more advanced sciences be taken as paradigmatic for all inquiry, so much as those who have contested the validity of the naturalist position, particularly in the study of the human body and mind. The deliverances a few years ago by high church dignitaries against psychoanalysis follow a precedent established by a long line of more distinguished predecessors. An interesting chapter remains to be written on the distortion produced in other fields of science by those who took mathematics as the *model* of all knowledge. But the mathematical ideal for all human knowledge was held by comparatively few naturalists. Those thinkers who took it seriously tended to regard scientific knowledge as mere opinion lost in the welter of appearances and unable to grasp reality.

The most powerful opposition to naturalism comes not from those who feel that it obstructs the path of inquiry and closes the gates to new knowledge but from those who fear that it arbitrarily excludes from the realm of existence and knowledge something which we actually have good reason to believe in, *viz.,* God and

man's immortal soul. Naturalism *arbitrarily* excludes the existence
of God and man's immortal soul, it is alleged, because its first
principles and categories of explanation are such as to make the
very assertion of their existence meaningless. If true, this charge
would be serious indeed, for the naturalist professes to be open-
minded about the possibilities of existence in a world in which
his greatest efforts seem so modest in the cosmic scale.

There are many conceptions of God and the soul which are
unintelligible because they involve the attribution of contradictory
qualities to Him; and there are other conceptions which are so
vague and indeterminate in meaning, that nothing significant can
be affirmed or denied of them. But it is not difficult to find conceptions that are sufficiently meaningful to make the contention of
the *impossibility* of their existence arrant dogmatism. Are naturalists guilty of this kind of dogmatism?

I do not believe this to be the case. For one thing this would
remove the sting from naturalism. Its criticisms of the belief in
Deity have not been based on semantic considerations but on what
it presumed to be the weight of scientific discovery. Some theologians and even some Catholic scientists like Duhem have sought to
bolster the beliefs in God precisely on the ground that in relation
to the categories of naturalistic science, the affirmation as well as
the denial of God's existence would be meaningless. Such a view
of naturalism is more devastating to atheism than to theism because the atheist does not profess to have any other categories at
the disposal of his understanding while the theist emphatically
does.

Secondly, wherever declared naturalists assert that the existence
of God is impossible, it will usually be found they are using the
term impossible not in the logical or mathematical sense but in
the physical or medical sense in which we say that it is impossible
for anything to burn or for a man to breathe without oxygen.
Neither Professor Ducasse in his recent discussions of immortality
nor Professor Ewing in his discussions of the body and its mental
attributes have established anything more than what a sophisticated naturalist is prepared to grant them *to begin* with, *viz.*, that
God's existence and personal survival are synthetic propositions
and that therefore their denial cannot be contradictory or a matter
for logic alone to settle. G. E. Moore once observed that the fact

that one needs one's eyes for seeing is an empirical discovery, and
this is obviously true for more recondite matters like the role of the
brain in thinking and of the nerves in feeling. To see without eyes
is physiologically impossible but every believer in immortality
known to me is convinced that in his disembodied state he will
see at least as well as he sees now. The two assertions are not *logically* incompatible for obviously the believer in immortality ex-
pects the laws of physiology to be suspended in the hereafter. This
is not logically impossible but the absence of a logical impossibility
does not constitute a scintilla of evidence against the usual validity
of physiological law as we know it. Every reasonable person in his
behavior denies the assumption "that we have no right to dis-
believe in anything which cannot be logically disproved." [9]

The history of naturalism, it seems to me, has been marked by
two main tendencies. The first has interpreted God in the same
way as the great historical religions; *viz.*, as an omnipotent personal
power who guides the destinies of the world He has created—and
concluded that the evidence does not warrant belief in the existence of anything corresponding to this conception. The second has
reinterpreted the conception of God and used the term "God" to
signify a principle of order in the universe, the totality of all
things, the possibility of good in the world, or the object of human
allegiance. Karl Marx once observed that even the profession of
belief in deism on the part of scientists was motivated by a desire
to win freedom to continue scientific inquiry and to escape molestation from those whom we would today call religious fundamentalists. But in most cases the attribution of such motives seems to be
entirely gratuitous even though a greater freedom from interfer-
ence by revealed religion may have been among the effects of the
profession of deism.

Whatever the historical facts, the charge of dogmatism against
naturalism on the ground that it rules out by definition the possible existence of God and the soul has often been made. Recently
it has been renewed and fortified by quoting from an essay by
Professor W. Dennes some ambiguous passages which are interpreted to mean that all things in the world *must* ultimately be
described and explained in terms of the categories of quality, relation, and event. One critic then asks, "How do we know that the
world consists of events, qualities and relations, and nothing more?

We know that we must so describe it if we are committed to basic categories of a naturalistic philosophy. . . . But would the nature of a spiritual substance be so determinable?" [10] Another critic referring to the same point writes, "If everything has to be an event, the idea of a timeless God is excluded from the outset and without argument. The writer asserts that his list of categories makes no demand upon the metaphysical commitment of the reader, as though giving up one's belief in God were nothing." [11]

These questions seem to me to misconceive both the meaning of the text criticized as well as the position of naturalism. I shall, however, discuss only the latter.

(1) Naturalism is not committed to any theory concerning which categorial *terms* are irreducible or basic in explanation. Naturalists differ among themselves about this in the same way that scientists may differ among themselves as to what terms in the language of science should be taken as primary. What all naturalists agree on is "the irreducibility" of a certain method by which new knowledge is achieved and tested. The analysis of this method may be made in terms of categories like thing, structure, function, power, act, cause, relation, quantity and event. The choice of which categories to take as basic in describing a method depends upon the degree to which they render coherent and fruitful what we learn by the use of the method. Historically, and up to very recently, the most widely used category among naturalistic philosophers has been matter or substance. It is a complete non sequitur to assume that because one asserts that the fundamental categories of description are X and Y and Z, and that they hold universally, he is therefore asserting that the world cannot be significantly described *except* in terms of X, Y, and Z, or as so many critics assume, that the world consists of "nothing but" X and Y and Z. One may use categorial terms A and B and C that are not fundamental and maintain either—what most naturalists do *not*—that they are logically definable in terms of X, Y, and Z or—what most naturalists do—that the conditions under which any existing thing is significantly describable in terms of A, B, and C are such that they are always describable in terms of X, Y, and Z.

This gives us two possibilities in respect to a term like substance. It might be defined as a constellation of events instead of a substratum in which predicates inhere, and all statements about substances translated without loss of meaning into statements about organized sets of events or processes. Or second, an attempt might be made to show that whatever else a substance is, its manifestations or appearances can always be described in terms of activities or operating powers, themselves definable as events or powers. This does not require that substances whether material or spiritual have to be directly observed, but it does require that their presumed manifestations or effects must be observable in our experience, else we can populate the world at will with the creatures of our fancy.

Whether the existence of the identifiable "effects" of an allegedly spiritual substance justifies our belief in the existence of a separable and immortal soul rather than our belief that they are "effects" of a highly organized body in a given culture is something which the naturalist proposes to solve, either (i) by proceeding in the same way and with the same logic that he makes inferences from the presence of certain observable occurrences to the presence of other unobserved occurrences, or (ii) by examining the experimental evidence for the survival of the soul or personality after the death of the body, which brings us into the field of parapsychology and psychical research.

That the choice of which categorial terms to use in description is a problem independent of determining what actually exists in heaven or earth may be clear if we bear in mind that even if we were to conclude that man has an immortal soul, that would not by itself answer the question whether it was to be described as a spiritual substance or an organized set of spiritual functions. Conversely, Whitehead denies the explanatory primacy of the category of substance, and using the categories of event, quality and relation reaches altogether different conclusions from naturalism.

(2) Nor does naturalism exclude the very idea of a "timeless" God at the outset and without argument, as Professor Raphael Demos alleges. Otherwise, as I have already indicated, it could not deny his existence or be denounced for its atheism. Naturalists use the term "timeless" to designate traits and qualities in existence which either do not change or to which the predication of temporal quality is irrelevant. Circular things exist in time but their circularity is timeless. Before we can assert that there are timeless "entities" in existence which do not change, we should need some experience of them in time in order to distinguish them from what lacks

changeless character. The point is not whether timeless nonexisten-
tial entities can be conceived without contradiction. Assume that
they can. But Mr. Demos is talking not of a purely conceptual or
logical construction from whose meaning we can deduce existence.
He is talking about a timeless entity whose existence must be inferred, as in orthodox theology (*e.g.*, the Aquinate proofs of the
existence of God) from a series of temporal and contingent events.
And he must meet the naturalist contention that there is neither
empirical nor logical warrant for the leap from what we can observe in our experience in time to a creature outside of time. That
there must be some disclosure in time of what is presumed to be
outside of time is a starting point of the argument, Mr. Demos
must admit, else the whole concept of God is useless for the purposes for which Mr. Demos and orthodox theology invoke him.

(3) If God and man's immortal soul are so conceived that they
have no empirical effects, then there is nothing to prevent anyone
from imputing any set of logically consistent attributes to them.
They would then take their place with other imaginary creatures
in the realm of mythology. I can very well understand the refusal
of historical religions to take such conceptions of God and the
soul seriously, since it makes them completely otiose in understanding the world, superfluous entities that can be shaved away with
a flick of Occam's razor.

It is of course true that in modern philosophy the term "God"
has stood for many different ideas—natural structure, the order of
cause and consequence, the principle of concretion or logical limitation, the experience of value and righteousness. Avowed atheists,
like Morris R. Cohen, have described their dedication to truth,
and not only out of piety to the memory of Spinoza, as "the intellectual love of God." Naturalists are under no more compulsion
to observe terminological taboos than other philosophers although
one would expect them to be more careful of the context of
familiar terms used to convey new meanings. If anyone gets particular satisfaction out of the use of the term God, then fortunately
or unfortunately, he can find it in the writings of most naturalist
philosophers. Naturalism, as a philosophy, however, has nothing
to do with such linguistic matters important as they may be in
other respects. Naturalism as a philosophy is concerned only with
those assertions about existence from which something empirically

194 △
⊙

observable in the world follows that would not be the case if existence were denied. And it proposes to treat assertions about God's existence in the same generic way that it treats assertions about the existence of invisible stars or hidden motives or after-images or extrasensory perception. Critics of naturalism who regard this as dogmatic might put their charge to the test by furnishing the reasons or evidence which *they* hold warrant belief in the existence of God or gods, cosmic purpose or personal survival after death.

Some beliefs are reasonable even if we cannot finally confirm or disconfirm them. But if we take technological and practical behavior as the matrix of the reasonable, then beliefs in the existence of supernatural entities are not reasonable. They are not warranted even if they turn out to be true, just as a guess is not warranted knowledge even when it turns out to be true. Santayana somewhere suggests that the reason most people believe in immortality is that they cannot imagine themselves dead. This raises an interesting methodological point since only if we are immortal can we prove it, while the naturalists who deny the immortality of the soul will never have the satisfaction of saying, "We were right." "Wouldn't naturalists be surprised," a critic of the position once observed, "if after they died they woke up in the presence of God." They certainly would be surprised. The degree of their surprise would be the measure of the unreasonableness of the belief. Unreasonable behavior or conduct may sometimes turn out right—*e.g.,* if I gave six to one odds on the toss of a well made coin—but it is no less unreasonable for all that. And what is true for conduct is true for belief. Consequently, in respect to the available evidence in our possession, the naturalist is reasonable in his belief even if it turns out he is wrong about God and survival, while the supernaturalist in respect to the same data is unreasonable even if it turns out he is right. "Faith in the supernatural," says Santayana, "is a desperate wager made by man at the lowest ebb of his fortune." The scientist who predicts that life will disappear because of the second law of thermodynamics will never be around when the last flicker of life dims. The logic of the argument is no different in the case of immortality.

In conclusion, the naturalist believes that his assumptions are reasonable because they express, in a more general way, no more than what is expressed by any nonphilosopher as well as by all philosophers, whatever their school, in their successful working practice in solving problems concerning the nature of things. And by successful is meant here something independent of the categorial terms of naturalism or any other philosophy, something as simple, naïve, and indefeasible as discovering a substance that subjected to friction will burst into flame, building a house that will withstand an earthquake, producing a seed that will yield a better harvest. Naturalism, as a philosophy, is a systematic reflection upon, and elaboration of, the procedures man employs in the successful resolution of the problems and difficulties of human experience. To use a phrase of Peirce, without giving it necessarily his special interpretation, it is "critical commonsensism." But it is more than this. It is a proposal. It is a proposal to continue to follow this general pattern of procedure in all fields of inquiry where it has enabled us to build up a body of knowledge, and to extend it to fields where we have not satisfactorily settled questions *of fact* of any kind. As a proposal it seems hardly less reasonable to the naturalist to follow than, when thirsty, under normal circumstances, to look for some liquid to quench one's thirst. Could any other procedure be more reasonable or as reasonable? Or must we solve *the* problem of induction first? But to raise the problem of induction no less than to solve it assumes that we are already in possession of undisputed although not undisputable knowledge. And to facilitate the transition from the problematic to the undisputed in human affairs has been one of the underlying purposes of all historical forms of naturalism.

Nature and the Human Spirit

The present situation in human history is a challenge to philosophers to vindicate their traditional claim to the possession of a vision of man that can help integrate and enrich human experience. What is required of such vision is that it avoid arbitrariness and pretentiousness, and hold out some promise—however modest—of fruitful co-operation among those different peoples and cultures of the world which have a will to co-operate.

Viewed in the light of the history of philosophy, the great danger of all philosophical thought which goes beyond logical analysis of categories is not an excess of speculation—which has at least an imaginative appeal—but an excess of salvationary zeal. The great systems have made promises that they cannot possibly fulfill. For they have ignored the fact that the concrete issues which divide men and inspire conflict have their primary locus in economic, political, and national life. No philosophical vision or synthesis can provide viable answers to them in their own terms. It is well to admit openly that there is no royal philosophical road to social salvation, however it may be with the quest for personal salvation. And if by personal salvation we mean the achievement of a sane and dignified order in the life of individuals, recent history furnishes a grim but conclusive reminder that for the overwhelming majority of men this is impossible until a stable and more equitable social order has been introduced.

Nonetheless it is undeniable that philosophical attitudes have a broad even if indirect bearing upon the problems of human experience. To the extent that they mobilize human attention and effort along some lines and divert them from others, they have practical consequences even when they preach detachment and withdrawal. I am not here maintaining that any *specific* philosophical doctrines have logical consequences for specific problems —in fact I shall be concerned to deny this—but only that certain basic points of view which express value judgments have a selective impact upon the variety of problems given at any moment, and on the possible approaches to these problems.

The position of this chapter is that the philosophy of *naturalistic* humanism, which regards man as an integral but distinctive part of nature, as wholly a creature of natural origin and natural end, offers an adequate and fruitful basis for the social reconstruction which is essential for the emergence of patterns of human dignity on a world-wide scale. This view in recent years has been the object of sustained criticisms from various quarters which have called into question the self-sufficiency of man. Some years ago, adopting a phrase from Gilbert Murray's account of the stages of Greek religion, I referred to this anti-naturalistic movement as "the new failure of nerve." Since then it has taken on the proportions of a tidal wave in philosophy, theology, literature and the philosophy of history. Characteristic of its views are two beliefs: (1) that our time of troubles is primarily an historical and logical consequence of the abandonment of the religious and metaphysical foundations of Western civilization and of a shift to secular life; and (2) that what gives genuine happiness to man, and relief from the multiple alienations which fragmentize both personality and society, in the words of St. Augustine "is something which does not proceed from human nature but which is above human nature." And from these beliefs the criticism follows that naturalism in any form is incapable of doing justice to the actually experienced qualities of human life, particularly the nature of man's moral experience.

Before proceeding to logical analysis of these criticisms a few historical remarks are in order. The notion that the decline of medieval supernaturalism gave rise to a secular naturalistic humanism which enjoyed the same position of authority and prestige as the philosophy it replaced is a legend that will no more bear examination than its countermyth which holds that the rise of Christian supernaturalism resulted not from the bankruptcy of pagan supernaturalism but from the alleged failure of Greco-Roman secularism. The life of a culture is expressed primarily in its institutions, and the *institutional* history of Europe nowhere reveals the presence of a unifying humanistic secular philosophy to integrate with the heritage of the past the radical changes precipitated by war, scientific technology, and the expansion of the capitalist economy. On the contrary, the new tendencies of industrialization, urbanization, and nationalism were neither predicted nor prepared for by any philosophy, either supernaturalist or naturalist. They made their way in the teeth of the old traditions which were helpless to cope with them and which ultimately were compelled by the logic of events to make uneasy compromises with the historical situations they could not exorcise. The defenders of traditional supernaturalism systematically engaged themselves not so much with the social *problems* resulting from the uncontrolled expansion of the new productive forces in Europe as in a furious polemic against the humanistic striving to find the new social forms and institutions which, without aborting the burst of creative energy unleashed by the industrial revolution, would sustain through the operating institutions of a reconstructed society, the dignity of all human beings.

One could make a far better historical case for the contrary view. To the extent that the dilemmas and tragedies of modern culture are attributable to ideological factors, a greater responsibility rests with a supernaturalist philosophy which was powerless to prevent the emergence of the tendencies it deplored or to give them a moral direction once they appeared, than to the chaotic multitude of doctrines—among which naturalistic humanism was the weakest—that sought, often by transparent rationalizations of sectional and class interests, to give some moral meaning and direction to the new social developments.

Nor in face of the assertion that the wars, revolutions, and bestial atrocities of our century are a consequence of the abandonment of the transcendent religious and metaphysical beliefs of the past, must we overlook the significance of the fact that those centuries when European culture rested on religious foundations were marked, once allowance is made for scale, by practices of persecution and extermination almost as inhuman as those committed by modern totalitarianisms.

1. But historical considerations aside, it is demonstrable that no set of metaphysical or theological statements by themselves entail any specific empirical consequences about the life of man or the structure of human society. Without raising the questions here of the criteria of meaningfulness and verification of such statements, it is apparent that they are compatible with mutually inconsistent social beliefs and the most diverse social institutions. For example, the same set of premises about divine existence, immortality, the nature of substance and the self have been held by believers in feudalism, capitalism, and socialism, by democrats as well as by totalitarians. This indicates that belief in the first set of propositions is not a sufficient condition of belief in the second set of propositions. And we are all acquainted with principled advocates of democracy or dictatorship, capitalism or socialism who regard the metaphysical and theological propositions often offered in alleged justification of these institutions as either meaningless or false which establishes that belief in them is certainly not a necessary condition of social doctrine and action. Indeed, *logically*, with sufficient technical ingenuity, allegiance to any social system can be squared with belief in any metaphysical system whatsoever.

This has sometimes been denied by those for whom metaphysical and theological statements are value judgments in disguise. When challenged they retreat to the position that the validity of moral judgments rests upon transcendental truths of a metaphysical or theological nature. Not only does such a position destroy the autonomy of moral experience, it is exposed to the same logical and historical difficulties that we have noted above. To the extent that transcendental beliefs are disguised value judgments, the actual relation between theology and morals is obscured. For, as we have seen in earlier chapters, it is indisputable that far from morals being historically derived from theological beliefs, men have always created their gods in their own moral image.

2. Any attempt to find a basis to improve the human estate by resort to a principle "above human nature" is doomed to failure because it cannot supply definite criteria to guide the construction of the programs of action required to meet the concrete needs, wants, and aspirations of men which are very much part of human nature and in which the most pressing problems of a domestic and international character are rooted. Ideals and ends that are out of time and so lack a natural basis can never be brought into logical and causal continuity with the means recommended to achieve them, for all such means are temporal acts with temporal consequences. The result of postulating ends that are outside of time and of postulating principles above human nature is that the *choice* of means, without which ends cannot be realized or tested, is lamed at the outset. Freed from critical direction, human choice *professedly* oriented to principles above human nature, oscillates between the extremes of dogmatism and opportunism.

The proposal of naturalistic humanism is to approach the problems of men in their natural and social contexts and to test the validity of all theoretical claims, not by examining their presuppositions but by investigating their empirical consequences. In refusing to allow this concern with antecedent presuppositions to dominate intellectual activity, in pointing out that conflicting varieties of presuppositions are equally compatible with verifiable fact, the naturalistic humanists seek to give the criterion of fruitfulness the same standing in all inquiry as it has in inquiry in the natural sciences. There is no guarantee, of course, that human beings, endowed with variant as well as common needs, will agree upon consequences, but a great deal of human experience testifies that in some areas and in some periods this is possible, sometimes even normal. One of the most impressive expressions of that human experience is the existence of democratic communities in which to a large part a consensus of belief and action in respect to political institutions and processes has been established among individuals holding the most varied metaphysical and theological presuppositions. What is being suggested by this proposal to take consequences not presuppositions as a point of departure is that those processes of inquiry by which in some parts of the world idealists and materialists, atheists and theists, Catholics, Protestants, Jews, and Mohammedans have been able to reach a community of working agreement be employed to explore all the empirical problems and difficulties that beset men today.

Where needs are common, there are as a rule much less differences among human beings as to what constitutes endurable or unendurable, satisfactory or unsatisfactory resolutions of problems than there are over metaphysical or theological presuppositions. To wait upon agreement on first or last principles as a precondition for a solution of what may be called "the intermediate" problems of human experience is hardly a counsel of wisdom in view of the fact that there is no accepted method by which the conflict of first or last principles of this type can be settled, whereas objective methods of settling "intermediate problems" exist that can extend the area of *uncoerced* agreement among men. To be sure, the results won in the latter case are tentative and piecemeal but they make up in impressive number for what they lack in pretentious promise. It would hardly be an exaggeration to say that any attempt to make agreement on philosophical presuppositions a condition precedent for co-operative action would hopelessly divide the world and destroy the working unity established in many existing human communities.

The obvious retort to this is that naturalistic humanism has its own presuppositions. Certainly, but what I am urging here is not the acceptance of its presuppositions but of its program of orientation and work, a program which would find justification by its fruitful consequences, and not by its alleged presuppositions. The argument avoids vicious circularity because at the outset it makes no other appeal than to the reasonable procedures recognized not only by philosophers but by all other men in their successful working practice in solving the problems that confront them in daily life.

It is in the light of those reasonable procedures that naturalistic humanism sees no warrant in experience for belief either in two separate worlds or two truths or two generic methods of reaching truths although it recognizes plural modes or levels of association and existence within nature, and a multiplicity of special methods and techniques which reflect the characteristic dif-

202 △
⊙

ferences between the living and the non-living, the purposeful and the non-purposeful, the historical and the non-historical. Just as it refuses to separate man from society and society from nature, so, for reasons already given in previous essays, it refuses to draw a sharp line of separation or opposition between scientific method on the one hand, and the reasonable procedures in the primary knowledge-getting activities of men struggling to control their environment, on the other.

It is in its allegiance to the continuity of scientific analysis from field to field that naturalistic humanism differentiates itself from all other varieties of humanism, and in its insistence on the plurality and qualitative specificity of the different fields of experience that it differentiates itself from all other varieties of naturalism. It is not in virtue of any of its alleged presuppositions but because it follows the lead of scientific method from its primal to advanced stage that it holds that the occurrence of all qualities and events depends upon the organization of a material system in space-time, and that their emergence, development and disappearance are determined by change in such organization.

3. At first blush it would seem that the philosophy of naturalistic humanism would be regarded as not inadequate—in its intention, at least—to encompass the whole life of man. For it recognizes the complex natural interrelations of man—interrelations made even more complex by his behavior as an historical creature in time, with a developing society and consciousness which, within certain limits, can influence the natural conditions of his existence. But for historical reasons which I shall not here examine, such a philosophy has been criticized for impoverishing human experience, denigrating the human status in the cosmos, and closing the avenues to new truths and insights.

The grounds on which such criticisms have been based are many. But I limit myself only to three: (a) that scientific explanation is inadequate to what is distinctly human, (b) that it necessarily entails "reductionism," and (c) that even if everything else distinctively human could be shown to be accessible to scientific analysis, it is, and will remain, helpless before the facts and problems of moral experience.

(a) Scientific explanation is of various kinds but even if we identify it with its ideal type—the legitimacy of which has been sharply disputed—the first objection cannot be sustained. Let us assume that the ideal type of explanation consists in the subsumption under general laws of particular phenomena which have fulfilled certain initial defining conditions, thus enabling us to predict and sometimes to control events. To say, therefore, that scientific explanation cannot account for what is *uniquely* human is in one sense a truism, in another sense false. It is a truism in the sense that we cannot explain any completely unique event, not only in history but in physics. It is false, however, in suggesting that despite its uniqueness, a phenomenon cannot share common traits or relations with other unique phenomena. It is false further in suggesting that any trait which differentiates a class of phenomena from other classes, whether it be the mammary glands of mammals or man's rationality or sense of humor, cannot be correlated with material conditions of determination, physical or social. It is false in suggesting that scientific explanation is concerned with the totality of any event or even with one total event or that it pretends to finality or exhaustiveness in its account of any event or any aspect of any event.

The main question about human motives, for example, which are cited by Professor William Hocking and others as beyond scientific explanation, is not whether their existence can be accounted for in terms of laws about neural impulses or electronic movements. Although highly unlikely, this is not inconceivable. The question is whether determinate relations can be established between the occurrence, variation and intensity of motives and any changes in the historical, material space-time systems in which all individuals develop. A social or historical explanation of the operation of motives is entirely legitimate even if we do not understand very well its physical or biological basis. In biology, for example, the laws of genetics are accepted as explanations of the facts of heredity although we cannot derive them from physical laws governing molecular phenomena. Yet it would be admitted that despite its lack of comparable exactness, biology is no less scientific than physics.

(b) This first criticism of naturalistic humanism is usually a preface to a more comprehensive indictment of scientific explanation as guilty of reductionism, of explaining away the very phenomena, particularly the consciousness of qualities, given in human experience. That some formulations of materialism in the past have given a superficial justification for this charge hardly extenuates this interpretation of modern naturalism. It is true that the language in which the *causes* of changes in qualitative experience is expressed contains terms which differ from those employed in the *descriptions* of human experience. But it is a complete non sequitur to infer that therefore the existence of the qualities of human experience are rendered precarious in any way. The experience of qualities, whether it be the taste of sugar or the sense of awe, is irreducible as an experience. But it is not therefore inexplicable. Whether any particular naturalist is faithful in his descriptions is an empirical matter to be decided by controlled observation. And since the adequacy of his causal explanations depends in part on whether the experience in question can be reduplicated or transformed under certain conditions, it is literally absurd, if we take note of his procedure, to charge him with reductionism.

It is noteworthy that the charge of reductionism is rarely made against the physicist who explains variations in the distinctive properties of physical things, for example, their sound or color by variations in the quantities or qualities of another order. It is only when the distinctive qualities of human experience are explained that we hear the charge that according to naturalists man is "nothing but" this or that, "merely" a handful of salts in a solution of water, etc., despite the fact that he is proceeding no differently from the physicist who explains a snowflake in terms of certain laws of temperature and liquids without "reducing" the geometrical or aesthetic patterns of snowflakes to such laws. It is appropriate to retort here that in virtue of its commitments to the logic of scientific method, naturalism proclaims that "Nothing is *nothing—but*" and "Nothing is *merely* one thing and not anything else."

It is hard to see how any scientific explanation of the qualities of the human spirit can in any way endanger these qualities, no matter how frail and exquisite they are. On the contrary, by revealing the structure of the material patterns in which they are enmeshed, they can, if we wish, be made more secure. Because it refuses to hypostasize these qualities and insists upon exploring their causes and consequences in the same spirit that it explores the qualities of the physical world, naturalistic humanism has from time to time provoked the hostility of those who feared that increasing knowledge might transform the world. Although such opposition asserts in argument that naturalism ignores the qualities of the human spirit, its secret hope is that materialism will ignore these qualities lest the power to control them be exercised in unacceptable ways.

In this connection two other points must be briefly touched upon. Insofar as mechanism is the belief that all human phenomena can be explained or predicted on the basis of the most general laws of physics, naturalistic humanism is not mechanistic. For it, variation, novelty and diversity are not only undeniable facts of experience, it seeks to bring them about in different areas. And in virtue of its efforts, its failures as well as successes, it recognizes that many more things will occur than we can predict or control. It knows that human ideals and human volition, as well as knowledge of what transpired in the past, may enter as contributing conditions in redetermining the movement of events. The *same* antecedent conditions which determine objective alternatives do not determine the human perception and action which alter the probabilities that one or the other alternative will in fact be realized.

Nor is it true that according to naturalistic humanism only what can be observed exists. Both in science and common life many things may be reasonably inferred to exist from what is observed, and then confirmed by further observations. It does hold that where there is no evidence drawn from observed or *observable* effects, existence cannot be responsibly attributed. Otherwise the distinction between fact and fantasy disappears.

(c) As far as the facts of moral experience are concerned, it is clear that we must distinguish between the causal explanation of moral qualities, and the proper analysis of those qualities. Naturalistic humanists differ among themselves as to the proper analysis of moral statements—some maintaining that they are commands without cognitive significance and others that they make a genuine knowledge claim. But it is certainly illegitimate to infer from the fact that one or another school contests the validity of a particular analysis of moral experience that it denies the existence of moral experience. That we experience moral obligation is a fact to be explained. What is denied by all naturalistic schools

is that the explanation requires any transcendent ideal or power.
The alleged requirement cannot be made part of the datum of the
experience of obligation.

The most common objection to naturalistic humanism is not
that it has no place for moral experience but that it has no place
for an *authoritative* moral experience except one which rests
merely on arbitrary preference, habit or force. In consequence, it
is accused of lapsing into the morass of relativism despite its
desire to discover inclusive and enduring ends which will enable
human beings to live harmoniously together. The impression that
relativism is entailed by every form of naturalism is reinforced by
the refusal of current humanists to content themselves with the
affirmation of general ends certified to immediate intuition and by
their insistence that ends must be related to means and both to
determinate conditions of trouble and difficulty in specific historical situations. This makes value judgments in the only form in
which they count, "relative"—but "relative" not in the sense of subjective but rather relational. The opposite of "relative" is not "objective" but "absolute" or "unconditioned." This emphasis upon
relational character reflects the dependence of value qualities, like
all other qualities in nature, upon activities in process of objective
interaction with each other. It should then be clear that the assertion "a value is *related* to a situation of concrete historical interests"—and the further assertion that "a judgment of value is warranted when reflection indicates that what is declared valuable
promises to satisfy these interests," does *not* add up to the view
that anyone can legitimately believe that *anything* is valuable in
any situation. On the contrary. Inquiry into the relational character of values, their historical, cultural and psychological reference, aims to find reliable values to guide action, reliable because
they have objective grounds.

The impression that because values are relational they are
therefore subjective is the consequence of confusing two different
problems. The first is whether values have objective status and
validity; the second is whether in case of conflict, objective values
and the interests to which they are related, can be shared, *i.e.,*
whether a new value situation can be constructed which will transform the conflicting values into a satisfying integrated whole.

One can hold to the belief in the objectivity of values without *guaranteeing* that agreement among conflicting values, all of which are objective from their own point of view, can be won. How far such agreement can be won cannot be foretold until actual investigation into the conditions and consequences of value claims in definite situations is undertaken—and this is precisely what naturalistic humanists propose to do instead of taking moral intuitions as absolute fiats subject to no control. The assumption that in any particular case agreement can be won, that an objective moral resolution of value conflicts is possible, entails the belief that men are sufficiently alike to work out ways of becoming *more* alike, or sufficiently alike to agree about the permissible limits of *being different.*

Rationality or reasonableness in conduct is the ability—which men possess—to envisage alternatives of action, to apply the test of observable consequences to conflicting proposals, and to accept or reconstruct these proposals in the light of consequences. The institutional expression of this rationality is the communal process of deliberation and critical assessment of evidence which alone makes possible a *freely* given consent. The willingness to sit down in the face of differences and reason together is the only categorical imperative a naturalistic humanist recognizes. And reliance upon the rules of the game by which grounded conclusions concerning concrete value judgments are reached is the only methodological absolute to which he is committed. This places authority solely in the untrammeled processes of inquiry and any alleged humanism, whether Thomistic humanism or so-called Soviet humanism, which places primary authority in institutions or dogmas, is guilty of the most transparent kind of semantic corruption.

Insofar as our age requires a unifying faith, it is clear that it cannot be found in any official doctrine or creed but rather in the commitment to the processes and methods of critical intelligence. Just as science made its way without an official metaphysics or theology, so it *may* be possible to build up a body of social science as a guide to action independently of the plural *over-beliefs* which its practitioners entertain provided only that those beliefs do not encourage the erection of non-trespass signs to inquiry about man and all his works.

In the nature of the case the philosophy of naturalistic humanism cannot promise what the facts of human involvement with nature rules out as unlikely. But within the range of possibilities it promises so much that it is wilful romanticism to demand more. It does not deprive human beings of their responsibility but rather brings home to them their own responsibility, within the constraining conditions of nature and social traditions. By nature man is a creature who can make his own history. But he did not make the world in which that history is open to him. Because he did not make the world is not a valid ground for the belief that any other species did—natural or supernatural. Nor does it follow that, because he refuses to worship any supernatural power, he must worship himself or any natural power whether person, force or thing. Man can live with a natural piety for the sources of his being. He can rely upon nature and himself without worshipping them. Man in fact relies only on his own natural and human resources even when he claims to rely on other resources.

Once men realize this then the chances become better—not certain—that these resources will be sufficient to develop a dignified human existence in a just social order. We need not repine that we are not gods or the children of gods. The politics of despair, the philosophy of magical idealism and the theology of consolation forget that although we are not gods, we can still act like men.

Scientific Knowledge and Philosophical "Knowledge"

I propose to raise some fundamental questions about the relation between scientific knowledge and philosophy. I shall begin with some naive observations which although inexact are hardly likely to be contested, and then proceed to issues of a more problematic and controversial character. The advantage of "naive observations" in sophisticated discussions is that they weaken the tendency to settle questions at the outset by definition.

Let us look away for a moment from the multiple ambiguities in the meaning of terms like "know," "knowing" and cognate expressions. It is a matter of common agreement, even among philosophers, that we derive considerable and reliable knowledge of the world and of ourselves from science, and from our own practical experience of everyday affairs. There is far less agreement, however, over whether in addition to this scientific and practical knowledge there is another category that may be called "philosophic knowledge." The reasons for this lack of agreement are not difficult to perceive, considering the chaotic state of philosophic thought, the recurrent controversies and absence of any cumulative or progressive development within it. Philosophers even disagree about the nature of their subject matter (in this they resemble writers and artists), and a good part of their activity consists in extended justifications, even apologies, for their existence (in this they differ from writers and artists). I know of no other reputable field of thought that exists in such chaos; there is more unanimity even in disciplines such as anthropology or meteorology, which have barely reached the stage of fledgling sciences. In no other field of thought are there "perennial" problems. Sciences grow by virtue of the fact that problems are solved, theoretical difficulties mastered, basic distinctions in language recognized. But in the field of philosophy, even distinctions that would appear to be basic, such as that between analytic and synthetic statements, are constantly being challenged. In our own time a mind as honest and acute as that of G. E. Moore has judged that ". . . unless new reasons never urged hitherto can be found, all the most important philosophic doctrines have as little claim to assent as the most superstitious beliefs of the lowest savages." This would seem to suggest that to apply the term "knowledge"—in the sense in which we use it for undisputed conclusions gained through one set of disciplines, the sciences—to the disputed conclusions or claims of philosophers, is only to invite confusion.

It may be argued that such confusion is more apparent than real. All large terms like "experience" and "life," no less than "knowledge," are infected with ambiguities which do not obstruct but facilitate communication. In this they are like terms in ordinary use whose meanings are blurred at the edges. We may say of them what Wittgenstein says of "games" that they are words that designate a *range* of familiar or similar meanings among which a "family resemblance" is present. Provided we recognize that some activities are *not* games, that there are different family-trees of resemblance, so that not everything is classifiable as one family, this observation, already suggested by Peirce, is illuminating. But I do not believe that it vindicates the conception of "philosophical knowledge." And this for two reasons. Some terms seem to possess a "more typical" family resemblance than others, just as we can more easily recognize some individuals as belonging to a certain family than we can others. For example, a basketball game is more clearly a game than is a bull fight which is also played according to rules. And the latter is more clearly a game than is a political contest, or competitive business activity, which are sometimes cited as instances of the game of politics or the game of business. But although we call Russian roulette by the *name* of a game no one in his senses uses it as a game. In the end what determines whether we are to call some marginal activity a game or give it membership in a family of meanings is its resemblance to the most typical case, to the paradigmatic situation, to the best illustration of the family face. If we proceed in this way philosophical knowledge at best is a poor and distant relative of practical and scientific knowledge. Indeed, its legitimacy depends entirely upon its being like the latter, and it is certainly more unlike than like. Is philosophical knowledge a different *kind* of knowledge or is it knowledge of a special *field* or *aspect* of things like astronomy or linguistics? If the first, how can we explain the history of philosophy and its conflicts with scientific knowledge; if the second, how explain that it seems to be in a state more suggestive of astrology or psychoanalysis than of any well-ordered science?

If the state of philosophy today tends to confound those who would speak of "philosophic knowledge," the history of philosophy is an even more damaging witness against them. Philosophy as a subject matter once embraced the logical, physical, biological, social and psychological sciences. As these developed into recognized bodies of knowledge, they declared their independence, changed their names and scorned their origins, leaving philosophy to make *claims* to a special kind of knowledge—claims which many people, including some philosophers, regard merely as wishful, the expression of parochial interests and concerns. This allegedly special knowledge, some say, provides no truths but only guidance, hope or "comforts."

These strong impeachments would be turned aside if it could be established that philosophy, contrary to what most of its practitioners in the past believed, is actually autonomous in relation to science, that the kind of knowledge about nature and men that philosophy gives us is in no way dependent upon the concrete insights gained through science, technology and common sense. There are two hurdles to be cleared in establishing this. The first is the effect certain scientific findings have had in the past upon the philosophical view of man and his place in the universe. It is hard to defend the autonomy of philosophy when we consider the enormous influence of Copernicus, Galileo and Newton, in the seventeenth century, of Darwin in the nineteenth, of Mach and Einstein in the twentieth, on the philosophies of their time. The second hurdle is a potential one: if experimental biologists working today were able to synthesize unmistakably living things from inorganic substances, even those who firmly maintain the independence of philosophy would have a hard time convincing themselves that this particular scientific development had no bearing on the mind-body problem. A similar dilemma has been posed already by Rhine's experiments and investigations of paranormal phenomena, which some believe increase the probability of consciousness surviving bodily disintegration. In order to get past these two obstacles, we would have to redefine philosophy in such a way that, no matter what scientific knowledge disclosed about the world, our philosophical beliefs would not be affected; those beliefs would have to be valid for all possible, indeed, all imaginable worlds. It would then be necessary to show in what way these philosophical beliefs differed from purely logical statements, since they would be valid for worlds with the most contrary properties.

Now it is clear that many of the statements defended in the past as instances of "philosophical knowledge"—for example, that our physical space must be infinite or Euclidean, or that species are fixed and unalterable—have turned out to be incompatible with scientific knowledge. Therefore such statements must be considered false and can be dismissed as not knowledge at all. The history of the relation between what has been called philosophical knowledge and scientific knowledge suggests three general observations:

(a) We cannot know what does not make sense. We cannot have knowledge of the harmony of the spheres or the virtue of triangles if spheres are things that cannot be in harmony or disharmony and if "triangle" means what it means in Euclid. We cannot have knowledge about anything that has no intelligible opposite even though we disguise this fact from ourselves by speaking of analogical knowledge. We have no knowledge of "Being."

(b) We cannot know what isn't so. If there are no leprechauns or elves such as we read about in fairy tales, we cannot have knowledge of them even though we are able to describe the properties their behavior would exhibit if they did exist. Similarly, if there are no angels we cannot have knowledge of them; what is called knowledge of the angelic hierarchy is knowledge only of the classificatory scheme of them as set forth in a certain book or tradition, just as knowledge of the hierarchy of Olympian deities is not knowledge of any divine creatures, discovered or inferred, but only of what is contained in the works of Homer and other writers. (Actually, there is more empirical evidence, although far from convincing, for the existence of ghosts than of angels, for there are more people who claim to have seen, heard, spoken to and even photographed ghosts than angels. Among the mystifying attributes of ghosts that stand in the way of belief in their existence is their strong predilection for English domiciles.)

(c) We cannot know if we are only guessing. If, ignorant of what horses are running or of their past performances, I guess the winner, or if in a random selection or toss I guess the number or card that comes up, I cannot claim to have knowledge. Indeed, it is not likely that we would speak of "a game of chance" if any of the participants had knowledge of how things would turn out. If, however, I keep on guessing and my guesses turn out always or almost always to be right, others will in time be convinced that I have knowledge. At a certain point my success in guessing in itself constitutes a good reason for keeping on guessing in the manner that has proved successful.

Unless we have good reason for a judgment, or are in possession of evidence that warrants giving one particular answer rather than another, it is arbitrary to maintain that we have knowledge of any kind. Where we do not know, we can claim that our belief rests on faith. I shall use the term "faith" in the sense of belief that is not justified by evidence; knowledge, on the other hand, is belief that is so justified. To assert that knowledge, as well as belief, rests on faith is either to use the term "faith" in some special way or not to talk sense. The notion of knowledge as belief based on adequate evidence leaves the term "evidence" undefined, but for our purposes it will suffice to say that where knowledge of fact is claimed, evidence must rest directly or indirectly upon judgments gained by observation and upon such other judgments as may legitimately, or logically, be inferred from them.

The chief issues with which I am here concerned can be brought into focus by stating briefly a position defended by both Dewey and Russell, despite their not inconsiderable differences, to wit: *All knowledge that men have is scientific knowledge.*

This sounds very dogmatic, but is really an expression of intellectual humility that seeks to avoid unlimited credulity. It does not doubt that we possess scientific knowledge but leaves open the question of what we can have knowledge about. Answers to this question are supplied by individual discoveries in the various sciences. Such humility does not assert that the experience of knowledge exhausts all modes of experience or that scientific knowledge is all-knowing. It does not deny that there may be mysteries, but it approaches all alleged mysteries as if they were *gaps* in knowledge instead of unfathomable and unbridgeable abysses. It does not identify scientific method with the particular methods of physics, but rather with the pattern of hypothetico-deductive-experimental observation exhibited in the different sciences in different ways, depending upon the specific subject matter. We can study an individual's neurosis or a nation's history scientifically even if we cannot put it into a test tube.

Broadly speaking there is no opposition between common sense knowledge and scientific knowledge as knowledge, but only a difference in their objects and problems: direct use and enjoyment of things in the realm of common sense, and the winning of new facts, new laws, and a synthesis independent of present, or even of ultimate, use and enjoyment, in the scientific realm.

That the opposition between the two cannot be sustained is apparent from the fact that all scientific procedures that are well grounded take note of common sense identifications, distinctions and generalizations. There is no science whose language can be formalized to a point where it can dispense with everyday language. The scientific entities of theoretical physics could not be discovered, formulated or applied without referring ultimately to the gross objects and qualities of common sense experience. This is not to say that scientific entities are necessarily describable in terms of the qualities of common sense experience. We move from the vague and inexact toward the less vague and more exact. It was necessary to be able roughly to differentiate between colors in use before we could develop a scientific theory of color that would enable us to make finer and subtler differentiations. If we had no perceptions we could not discover the conditions of perception. If we could not distinguish between brain and mind what earthly use would the concept of brain-state have? As Susan Stebbing once put it (in *Philosophy and the Physicists*): "It is only because they (the scientists) are able to perceive the solidity of a piece of iron that they are able to discover that atoms are tenuous." Quantitative scientific determinations may ignore qualitative experiences, but they cannot abolish them, since they take their point of departure from them. Regardless of what the organizing categories of a science are, when its conclusions are applied, or when its rules of operational procedure are stated, they must take note of the catalogue of common things, their varying structures, functions and locations.

It is sometimes said that common sense inquiry operates with concepts that are direct transcripts of things and their qualities, while science uses theoretical constructs that are at best indirectly related to the elements of experience. This statement seems to me to be inadequate, on two counts. First, it overlooks the differing degrees of complexity among the constructs of the different sciences. These range from the relatively simple ones of biology and economics, which are not far removed from the abstractions of ordinary discourse, to the theoretical constructs of modern physics, which are far beyond description in such ordinary terms. Secondly, this distinction does not do justice to the extent to which common sense or ordinary discourse is shot through with theoretical constructs. A man need not be a scientist to talk about the *average* age of his children or the *potential* power of his automobile, the *reliability* of his neighbor's *memory*, the *honor* of his country. Although these instances involve only simple theoretical constructs, they are still constructs. This is not to deny the enormous difference between the language of common sense inquiry and that of science; but the difference is not a principled one, if only because the gradual changes in common sense language reflect the influence of scientific theory and discovery. Ordinary language in its historical growth usually shows the influence of the science of an earlier generation.

There are certain objections that must be dealt with by anyone who asserts that there is no knowledge except scientific knowledge. (1) Is not this view self-refuting? There is no science in which such an assertion is warranted, as a piece of knowledge. And if it is held

to be knowledge nonetheless, is it not an instance of purely philosophical knowledge? (2) If there is no knowledge but scientific
knowledge, are we not ruling out *a priori* the existence of supernatural entities and creatures, playing at being God at the very
moment we are denying the possibility of his existence—a strange
procedure for avowed empiricists? (3) If we recognize that there
is such a thing as common sense knowledge, does this not contain
an implicit admission that we have *some* metaphysical knowledge?
I shall deal with these objections in the order given.

(1) That all human knowledge is scientific knowledge is a statement about human beings and about knowledge. It does not come
from any specific science: it simply means that claims to having
knowledge other than scientific cannot, broadly considered, be sustained. The statement reflects and summarizes an *historical* fact
about certain bodies of knowledge that have been developed to a
point where the control and mastery they make possible in meeting
problems is open, publicly verifiable and, even though limited,
compares favorably with all other methods of solving problems. At
the same time it is not a mere summary of historical fact, but a
proposal to use the term "knowledge" in such a way that all other
claims to knowledge of the world shall be initially assessed as to
validity in the light of criteria drawn from common sense and from
scientific knowledge universally agreed to be highly reliable. It is
true that a certain decision is involved in making such a statement,
but the decision is not arbitrary: one can give good reasons for it
or can point to the historical evidence that makes it a reasonable
decision, show that in the past generalizations supported merely
by hunches, guesses, visions, revelations, *a priori* reasoning, have
turned out to be unreliable, and have failed to predict the occurrences with which they were concerned. In short, the justification
for asserting that all knowledge is scientific is not a matter of definition but is, rather, pragmatic: such a view enables us to achieve
our ends in the world, whatever they are, more effectively.

(2) "Ah! but that's just the rub," say critics of this view. "It
begs the question not only about what can or cannot be knowledge
but also about what can or cannot exist. It rules out of the world
what cannot be scientifically verified. It rules out a timeless God,
immortal souls, and many other things people have believed in."
The basic answer to this serious indictment may take various

forms. First, as we have seen, every conception of knowledge must make assumptions about what constitutes knowledge, and one such set of assumptions will be incompatible with another. My assumptions about the nature of anything, man, rabbits or stars, must exclude some other assumptions about their nature. All assumptions, as *assumptions*, in this respect are on a par. The question once more becomes: are our assumptions arbitrary or reasonable?

Second, the answer may be that this conception of knowledge does not arbitrarily and in advance rule out God, soul, immortality, angels and devils as possible objects of knowledge. Many naturalists have declared that statements asserting the existence of these entities are doubtful or false, and such declarations could not have been made if the very possibility of these entities had been ruled out in advance as meaningless. As we have seen, if it makes no sense to say that we have knowledge of the existence of what is meaningless, it makes no more sense to deny the existence of the meaningless. To most naturalists, in contradistinction to many supernaturalists, the problem is not so much *what* God is as *that* he is. Further, there are some who pledge allegiance to scientific method as the only avenue by which knowledge can be gained who believe that the existence of such entities is still an open question, or who are unabashedly satisfied that the logic of experimental science makes belief in the existence of supernatural powers and entities at least as plausible as belief in electrons, if not more so.

The third, and perhaps most crucial, answer to this objection is that it can be shown that all human beings in their everyday experience are guided by the conception of knowledge as scientific knowledge. To deny this is palpably insincere. A Platonist might invidiously dub all empirical knowledge as "opinion," but no matter what one calls such knowledge, one acts on it, and to achieve one's ends one must necessarily act on it. The burden of proof rests entirely upon those who assert that there exists another kind of knowledge over and above technological, common sense, empirical knowledge, and the scientific knowledge which is an outgrowth and development of it. It is not enough to maintain that such a body of knowledge exists because people claim they are guided by it to solve specific problems. People do not always *do* as they say. It is not even enough to establish that such a body of knowledge exists to show that people *seem* to act on what they say, as do those who profess to be guided by astrology, numerology, angelology and Christian Science. Some connection must be established between the differential behavior of the actors in the concrete situations in which they face problems and the concepts by which they are presumably guided. There must be reasoned grounds for making one prediction about the future rather than another and confirmations greater than what one would expect on the basis of chance.

Fourth, we may answer the indictment by saying that if scientific knowledge is the paradigm of all genuine knowledge, then wherever any body of knowledge exists it should be possible by further inquiry to win *new* knowledge of fact as distinct from what can be learned merely by logical transformation.

(3) Even if the foregoing is granted is it not true that common sense knowledge presupposes a knowledge different from scientific knowledge? Whether this knowledge is called metaphysical or ontological, the claim sometimes made for it is that it grasps the nature of things directly, makes distinctions between kinds and classes of existence, and provides the matrix out of which questions concerning what, where, how, why and when arise and are answered. Now in one sense it is perfectly true to say that common sense knowledge recognizes distinctions and truths that are not part of any particular science. A color is different from a sound, all physical things are more than two-dimensional, full-grown human adults are larger and wiser than infants, water quenches thirst, no one remembers his own birth, dogs are more attached to their masters than cats—all these are instances of knowledge and yet not integrated into a formal science. They may be called pre-scientific: they are not incorrigible, and scientific knowledge may lead to their revision but at any definite time there will be an indeterminate number of items of knowledge of this character accepted as true by all practicing scientists. They are not less certain than scientific knowledge, only less detailed and precise.

Whatever the status of common sense knowledge, we must now come to grips with the claim that scientific knowledge is itself of only dubious validity as compared with two other types of knowledge, philosophy of nature and metaphysics. What we have regarded as scientific knowledge is called by Maritain "empiriological" or "perinoetic" knowledge, inferior in certainty, intelligibility and truth to philosophy of nature and metaphysics. Thinkers of this school are not altogether in agreement among themselves concerning the exact relationships which exist between common sense knowledge, empirical knowledge, physico-mathematical knowledge, philosophy of nature, and metaphysics. But it is with what they have in common that I wish to take issue. And what they have in common is expressed in the following representative comments:

> What is true is that the explanations of science, since they do not bring us into intimate contact with the being of things, and are only explanatory of proximate causes or even simply of that kind of formal cause which is represented by the mathematico-legal option of phenomena (and the entities more or less arbitrarily constructed in support of that system) cannot suffice for the mind, which by necessity, and always, asks questions of a higher order and seeks to enter into regions of intelligibility.[1]

> Superior, therefore independent, at least by its own formal constitution: philosophy (metaphysics and philosophy of nature) is as such independent with regard to the sciences.
> It should be understood: there is no *formal* dependence of philosophy with regard to the sciences. No scientific results, no scientific theory, in short, no science in the exercise of its own proper means, can ever adequately cut the knot of a philosophical problem, for those problems depend both in the origin and their solution on a light which is not in the reach of science.[2]

> For, formally speaking, metaphysics is in no degree an experimental science, but a form of knowledge far more purely rational than mathematics.[3] [On the other hand, physico-mathematical knowledge is referred to as] a well-founded myth which has contributed to build up the structure of that universe and its elements: it cannot endow it with an ontologically explanatory value.[4]

There are several assumptions made by this position about the nature of explanation and the nature of rationality that seem to me to be extremely questionable, but before discussing them I should like to look at some of the specific conclusions reached by this kind of philosophy of nature and metaphysics.

The philosophy of nature is presumably the study of sensible existence or of mobile being. Let us ask the simple question: what does the philosophy of nature tell us about the world of motion which empiriological physics does not? As a source I turn to a book inspired by the conception of the degrees and kinds of knowledge expressed in the citation above from Maritain—*Philosophical Physics* by V. E. Smith. Almost the first thing we are told is that the experimental scientist cannot possibly understand motion: "Motion eludes the empiriological physicist . . . he cannot claim to be a rival of the philosophical physicist in the study of the mobile world." [5] The reason for this is that "time and motion in empiriological physics are not mobile." If this means that the conceptions of time and motion are not mobile, of course they are not. Our concepts do not have to move to understand motion any more than they have to eat to understand eating. If the reference is to the properties and behavior of moving things, this is precisely what physics tries to discover. Apparently, however, the fact that empiriological physics seeks to *discover* truths about motion is a sign that it is not strict science, indeed that it is not even strict physics because it is not a method of proof achieving its fulfillment in speculative knowledge but "only in the order of making inhabited by the engineer."

The criticism that modern physics is interested in discovery rather than in proof is hardly likely to be taken as a defect by those who believe that new discovery, the winning of new knowledge through confirmed prediction, is at least one sign of truth. Even proof ultimately rests on definitions or postulates. And if these refer to the nature of the world, only inductive empirical procedures can tell us whether one set of definitions or postulates is more justifiable than any others that are conceivable. The term "intelligible," when employed by those who criticize both classical mechanics and relativity physics as being ontologically defective, really means "familiar." Thus it is actually a psychological and historical concept. One man's intelligibility is another man's paradox and a third man's absurdity.

At any rate a philosophy of nature which impugns the truth of experimental science not in terms of findings but in terms of previously held metaphysical beliefs is not likely to give us greater insight or more reliable truths than the magical *Natur-philosophie* to which in some ways it is akin. I find the laws of motion, refinements aside, much more comprehensible, much more informative about the nature of bodies at rest and in motion, than such pronouncements of philosophical physics as that "motion is a mixture of act and potency," which seems to be a mixture of tautology and fantasy. I do not see that it follows in the least that a universe in which the principle of inertia holds is one in which no interaction or transaction between different things is possible. Nor do I see that the alleged consequence of such an initial principle—"that there would be no intrinsic causality like that exercised by form" constitutes a *reductio ad absurdum*. The evidence for the principle of inertia is much stronger than that for the belief in intrinsic causality and for the view that form by itself has any influence in the executive order of nature.

The philosophy of nature seems to me to be a composite of Greek physics and Aristotelian metaphysics and to the degree that it is accepted is likely to constitute a psychological obstacle to the experimental study of nature. To object to the latter on the ground that it yields some, but not all, of the secrets of matter, would be permissible if we possessed a science that yielded all knowledge of nature's secrets. But philosophical physics yields no knowledge of nature's secrets whatsoever because it yields no knowledge at all, certainly no genuinely new knowledge. It claims to take its departure from the world of experience. This, of course, would make it empirical. What it actually does, however, is to use illustrations from experience as alleged truths which it maintains would constitute knowledge no matter what the world was like. It speaks of proof, but systematically confuses illustration with proof. Thus it raises and settles questions such as whether a compound is a complex individual body and has an "essential unity" by arbitrary definition, rather than by specific inquiry into chemical elements, mixtures and compounds. If the elements of a compound are "virtually" present in a substance, it is a genuine complex individual body; if not, not. Such distinctions throw absolutely no light on our knowledge of chemical elements and compounds.

As one Thomistic philosopher, Bonnet, puts it,[6] the philosophy of Aquinas "furnishes us with the metaphysical 'rules' which govern the intimate being of any complex individual body." Whether such a complex individual body exists in *fact*, he adds, is not its concern. If it does exist, it can be cited as an illustration. The philosophy of nature, he holds, "has limited itself as it should, to establishing and elaborating the necessary laws of the being of such a (possible) body." All that has been established, however, is a certain way of talking about things, not that there is anything in the world the knowledge of which makes it necessary for us to talk about things this way. It may be a necessary law of the being of a centaur that it should be half man and half beast, but it is not necessary that this be recognized in biology or even in mythology.

There is also a fundamental ambiguity in the formulations of this school of thought which seems to me unresolved. Some—like Father Henle, if I understand him—claim that although the subject matter of the philosophy of nature is the same as that of natural science, *i.e.,* corporeal being, the two disciplines, as bodies of knowledge, are autonomous of each other. Perhaps the autonomy is analogous to the autonomy between physics and economics. We can establish the economic laws that determine the *price* of iron independently of the physical laws that determine its electro-magnetic properties and vice versa. Other representatives of the Thomistic philosophy of nature seem to construe the relation between the philosophy of nature and natural science not as one of autonomy but of subordination, the latter to the former. For example, Bonnet asserts in the same article from which I quoted earlier that the philosophy of nature "can direct him (the scientist) in his experimentation and indicate the presence of error" whereas science can be of aid to the philosopher only in providing "further examples of the universal application of philosophical principles. . . ." It is *not* asserted that facts and hypotheses about nature can be "deduced" from philosophical principles or that they can be "founded" on the latter, so that it is difficult to understand by virtue of what knowledge the philosopher of nature is to direct and correct the natural scientist in his work.

In passing it should be noted that the philosophy of dialectical materialism, which is another variant of a philosophy of nature, makes precisely the same claim, with no better grounds, to direct and correct the experimental work of the natural scientist. Any such claim no matter what its source is in fact an arrogant assertion that the philosopher of nature is really a better scientist than the scientist who pursues scientific truth without benefit of the allegedly necessary truths of philosophy. It seems to me that such an assertion is not only false but vicious, for it provides a convenient premise for political and religious restriction of scientific inquiry.

The most important piece of knowledge allegedly gained by metaphysical rather than scientific method is, of course, the existence of God—most important only if God is conceived as having Personality or Mind. If God lacked Personality or Mind and was just another item in the catalogue of cosmic entities, then, no matter how vast its dimensions, the cosmos would still lack value for man. According to Maritain, whom I quote as representative of a type of thinking, we can have *demonstrative* knowledge that God is an "infinite personality" and "absolute subject." ". . . For we know by certain knowledge, more certain than that of mathematics, that God is simple, one, good, omniscient, all-powerful, free. . . . We are more certain of the divine perfections than of the beating of our own hearts." Since we cannot be certain that any existing thing has any properties unless we are certain that it exists, we must have demonstrative knowledge that God exists.

This calls attention to a fatal ambiguity in the meaning of "demonstrative" and "empirical" in much discussion of the arguments for the existence of God. If "demonstrative" means the use of a deductive method which draws from *a priori* or tautological statements certain implications, then we cannot have demonstrative knowledge of anything but the concepts or meanings of pure logic and mathematics. If one rejects the ontological argument for the existence of God, it is difficult to see how anything can be demonstratively known to exist with a greater certainty than the truths of mathematics. And, although under special conditions I can hear the beating of my own heart, I am more certain that "twice three are six" than that "it is my *heart* I hear beating" or that "it is *my* heart that is beating." It is more likely that I may some day be compelled by evidence to withdraw the latter statements than to deny the former one.

If by "empirical" we mean that we start from the facts of experience, then any explanation of these facts which postulates a transcendent cause is arbitrary, because it is a fact of experience that all *other* causal explanations of the phenomena of experience operate within the realm of experience. The finite is explained by the finite, what is in time now by what was in time then, and so on indefinitely. This seems to me to be true independently of

the nature of our analysis of the concept of cause, whether we
interpret it as a form of invariable association and succession or as
involving efficacy. The chain of causes, on the basis of the *postulate*
that everything has a cause, something *assumed* to be true, extends
infinitely into the past and, like the series of negative numbers,
may not have a final member. That is to say, even if we admit that
everything which comes into existence has a cause, the world may
never have come into existence.

If the existence of God is an empirical hypothesis, then any
statement about him must have the same contingent and probable
character as statements about invisible stars or electrons or any
other entity in whose existence we believe on the basis of what is
observable but which cannot itself in fact be directly experienced.
Thus even if we start from the reported *facts* of mystic experience
and from the conviction of the necessity of God's existence, we
cannot conclude that God *necessarily* exists.

Now if the existence of God is not causally determined in the
way in which science and common sense use the expression "causally determined," and if it is not logically entailed by any fact in
the way logical propositions are said to entail each other, what can
be meant by saying that God's existence is necessary and how can
that fact be established? Father Copleston's recent book on Aquinas
grapples boldly with this difficulty. In it he states that in his argument for the existence of God, Aquinas "was asserting a *unique*
relation between finite things and the transfinite transcendant
cause on which they rest" (my italics).

Now what does it mean to assert that an existential relation
is "unique"? Not necessarily that there is *only* one instance of the
relation or *many* but that there is *at least one* instance. A unique
existential relation between this tree and the apples hanging from
it, this man and his children, this pear and its taste requires at least
the existence of one apple, one child, one experience of tasting the
pear. But in every case the presence of a unique relation is based
on a discovery or an experience exhibited by at least one instance.
The relation in its uniqueness cannot be like something else. And
it cannot be established by argument from canons of general
validity. If the relation between finite things and the transfinite
cause they depend upon is unique, arguments could never prove
it. There would have to be some other way of knowing it even if it

were maintained that the relation between finite things and God was uniquely unique or analogically unique.

We may put the matter another way. According to the position we are examining, reflection on any finite thing encountered in experience reveals that its existence "implies" the existence of an absolutely necessary being. But the existence of no finite thing is itself absolutely necessary. Nonetheless it would still be true to say that no matter what particular finite thing existed, no matter how radically it differed from what is now observable, reflection on it would reveal that its existence "implies" the existence of an absolutely necessary being. No matter what the contingent facts may be, they are said to "imply" not merely a hypothetical but a categorical necessity. An empirical argument starts from contingent premises and results in probable conclusions. A purely rational argument starts from a necessary premise of logic or from a hypothetical assumption and reaches either a formally necessary conclusion or a hypothetically necessary one. However, this particular argument starts from contingent premises and strives to establish a categorically necessary conclusion. It is not a valid empirical argument. It is not a valid rational argument.

The assumptions which are at the basis of this conception of metaphysical knowledge are so far removed from those involved in the theory and practice of modern scientific inquiry that perhaps we should return to the suggestion that we use entirely different vocabularies, to avoid confusion, and insist upon the complete autonomy of metaphysics in relation to science. Not only does history make this difficult, but also those contemporary metaphysicians who regard experimental science as a defective or imperfect kind of philosophy of nature. Consider such a typical attitude as that of V. E. Smith (expressed again in *Philosophical Physics*):

> But how can this procedure (of modern science) meet the classical rigor that a science must be certain, have a knowledge character, and attain to causes? . . . What there is of knowledge proper in empiriological physics is the fruit of philosophy. . . . Truly scientific knowledge can never be purely descriptive since it is only in terms of causes and reasons that science is science.

It is apparent that this school of metaphysical thought cannot let science alone despite its claim that the furthest reaches of science cannot touch it, and that its wisdom is immune to anything the sciences may discover. Because of its animus, the history of science in relation to philosophy has been not so much a *conflict between* science and metaphysics (or religion) as a *battle against* science. Nor is it true that science cannot answer questions about the causes and reasons of things. It cannot answer questions about *ultimate* causes and *ultimate* reasons, not because such questions are too difficult to answer or because they require a special organ of vision, but because if an answer to a causal question is intelligible, we can always ask another causal question about it: and if we can give an intelligible reason for the existence of some state of affairs, we can always ask the reason for it. There is no guarantee at any point that we can answer these questions; nor is it certain that we cannot. To speak paradoxically, there are no ultimate questions: only penultimate ones. Those who are dissatisfied with this, despite what they say, really want answers which will explain why things must logically and necessarily be what they are and not something else. They are seeking more than understanding. They are seeking justification and consolation for the order of things. They are seeking what knowledge and science can never give.

Not every conception of philosophical or metaphysical knowledge claims to establish the existence of God, the soul, the angelic hosts, or a philosophical physics superior to an experimental physics in certainty, universality and reliability. But when it does, the burden of proof that there exist other kinds of knowledge besides scientific knowledge rests upon those making the assertion. In justice, it should be said that even some naturalistic philosophers have developed positions according to which metaphysics yields a knowledge forever beyond the jurisdiction of scientific inquiry. For example, the theory of relativity has been characterized by one naturalist philosopher as "scientifically true but ontologically false." This is almost like saying—not quite—that someone is scientifically dead but ontologically alive.

There are, of course, certain conceptions of philosophical knowledge which are not in sharp conflict with the view of knowledge defended here. It is sometimes claimed that philosophical knowledge is as empirical as scientific knowledge but is expressed in broad and vague generalizations that serve as heuristic principles for the special sciences. This is apparently true of some philosophic systems in the past but current specialization in the sciences and more rigorous criteria of logical analysis make it unlikely that philosophic systems will play the same fructifying role in the future as in the past.

C. D. Broad's conception of critical philosophy makes it ancillary to scientific and common sense knowledge. "The most fundamental task of Philosophy," says Broad in his *Scientific Thought,* "is to take the concepts that we use in daily common life and science, to analyze them, and thus to determine their precise meanings and their mutual relations." This, as he points out, does not make it a merely verbal discipline unrelated to the ways of things and the patterns of events. On the other hand, speculative philosophy for Broad is exciting and important but of a rather ambiguous cognitive character. It is "Man's final view of the Universe as a Whole, and of the position and prospects of himself and his fellows" in it. In the past Speculative Philosophy has been mostly "moonshine." In the present, it must be based on rigorously exercised Critical Philosophy. In the future it can consist only "at best . . . of more or less happy guesses." And at all times it tends to be unduly influenced by one's liver and bank balance. This is hardly an encouraging view of philosophical knowledge.

Although this is not the place to develop the idea, I wish to mention in conclusion a quite different conception of philosophy, which is at once more modest than the view that philosophical knowledge is "superior" to scientific knowledge and yet more comprehensive than Broad's interpretation of "critical philosophy." To the extent that philosophy is not a substitute or rival of the sciences, or an analysis of the categories, the logic, and the language of the sciences, it is a way of looking at the world, a *Lebensphilosophie,* a theory of criticism, ultimately concerned with the better and worse. Philosophy in this sense is wider and more precious than science because in Dewey's words it is "occupied with meaning rather than with truth." It is not a revelation of the physical or metaphysical structure of the universe but of the "predicaments, protests and aspirations of humanity." It was none other than Dewey who deplored "our lack of imagination in generating leading ideas," and who denied that "the scientifically verifiable" at any moment "provides the content of philosophy." Indeed, "as long as we worship science and are afraid of philosophy," he

writes, "we shall have no great science." For philosophy is a vision
of possibility based on actualities and not determined by them; it
reaches beyond fact to values; it exercises "a speculative audacity"
in relating values to each other. It must be consistent with the
findings of science, but outruns and outreaches at any given moment what we strictly know. It is an informed commitment and
an intelligent guide to action on behalf of moral ideals.

Materialism and Idealism

Recent developments in philosophy have suggested that the unanimity and progress long sought for by philosophers may be attained by applying a new method—the operational method of neo-positivism—to allegedly philosophical propositions and problems. This method solves most of the traditional problems of philosophy by discovering why it is irrelevant, or logically meaningless, to ask them. Although I am convinced that this is a fruitful method of solving some questions—at least fruitful for the community if not for the philosopher—I can not believe that there is much enlightenment to be gained by such a method unless it is supplemented by an attempt to show why philosophers and others have persisted, and still persist, in raising these problems. It may be quite true that, *viewed from certain assumptions,* some of the traditional problems can not be meaningfully stated. But it is extremely unplausible to assume that in philosophy, or in any other field of culture, great pother and commotion are made *merely* about words. If philosophical issues are declared to be false and artificial, we must explore the hypothesis that some other issues associated with philosophical issues or cloaked in philosophical symbols were the *actual* issues in dispute.

From this point of view I wish to consider the issue between materialism and idealism. Two tendencies in modern thought have contributed to making focal the question of what it is which distinguishes one philosophical view from the other. On the one hand, the "etherealization" of matter which began in the nineteenth century and dissolved the substantialities of common day experience into complexes of electrical charges and the consequent abandonment of the categories of mechanics as universal explanatory principles, gave rise to the curious belief among physicists, fond of philosophy, that materialism had been "hoist with its own petard," *i.e.*, finally refuted by its own method. On the other hand, in philosophy itself lines and issues have been so blurred that many philosophers refuse to define their position in terms of traditional doctrines and call for the development of a new vocabulary of philosophic classification. Witness, for example, the strenuous contention by contemporary idealists that some of the most illustrious exponents of idealism (Leibniz, Hegel) have been realists in their theory of knowledge, and the merry hunt which this has set up for *the* proposition which is the *sine qua non* of the idealist faith. The upshot of the discussion has revealed what should have been clear to anyone who has read the history of philosophy without epistemological spectacles, *viz.*, that for most idealists, idealism is not a theory of knowledge but a theory of reality. The proper philosophical opposite of idealism, then, is not realism but materialism. (A more inclusive term which prevents the easy and customary identification of the general position of materialism with any specific historical expression of it, is naturalism.)

It is one thing to recognize this, but, as philosophical discussion of the recent past has shown, it is quite another thing to isolate the precise point at issue between idealism and materialism in a way which will express the systematic differences between them and at the same time do justice to the great historic alignments in philosophy with which they are associated. The simple aim of this chapter is to formulate the significant issue, not to settle it. In order to win the right to make such a formulation, it must first be shown why the traditional statements of the issue, and the answers thereto, are inadequate.

(1) The commonest characterization of materialism, one which prefaces most refutations of the doctrine, attributes to it as a cardinal principle, the assertion that "only matter is real" where *matter* is an historical variable with values ranging from Democritus' "atoms in the void" to Dirac's "positron," and where *real* is an ambiguous term meaning either (a) existence, or (b) importance, or (c) necessary condition.

(a) Now it seems impossible for anyone, especially for a philosopher, to have literally or seriously meant that "only matter exists," for the simple and sufficient reason that such a proposition is *obvious* nonsense; and even Wittgenstein must distinguish between the ultimate nonsense which is metaphysics and the ordinary and unblessed kind. Where existence is further defined and identified with spatio-temporal determination, the assertion "only matter exists" becomes clearly tautological; where not, clearly false. No matter what philosophers have *said*, they could not have meant that only material things existed. For the very description of material things involves an inescapable reference to certain qualities and structural relations which can not be reduced to matter in motion although they may be predicated of it. Secondly, the very consciousness of material things, not to speak of the experience of pain, pleasure, memory, and fancy, which have no direct objective reference, can not be dismissed from the realm of existence or degraded to the status of appearance without being recognized. And finally, no materialist of this type can communicate meaningful statements about his position without thereby declaring that there is more in the world than his own system has provided for; since whatever a proposition is, it is something which has implications, and implications are not material things.

Nor is the logic of the situation any different when the idealist proclaims that "only Mind is real" where Mind stands for Reason, Will, Feeling, or Sensation. Here, too, taken literally the proposition represents a violent abuse of terms, for it implies that the conditions of Reason are themselves reasonable, the conditions of Will are endowed with volition, etc. But the proof that the traditional materialist and idealist are not to be taken literally, can be found in their own writings, in which the distinctions drawn by science and common sense are taken over and rebaptized by introducing adjectival differentiations in the Mind or Matter presumed to be exclusively existent. And in truth, when we read how Hobbes distinguishes between different kinds of matter—one of which is identical with what we empirically call mind—or how Berkeley, or Schopenhauer, or Hegel divide perception, will, and reason into kinds or classes—some of which are identical with what we empirically distinguish as non-mental—and further, when we observe the ease with which the verifiable discoveries of the materialist can be translated into the language of the idealists and *vice versa*—is the inference not justifiable that if there is an issue in dispute, it is not adequately expressed in the propositions considered above?

(b) Where real is admitted to be a category of value—of religion, Hegel says—the monistic declarations of both materialists and idealists are therewith removed from the realm of epistemological or scientific discussion. For if value is an expression which may be equated to importance, then to say "only x is real" is to admit the unimportance, and therefore the existence, of other things, and to betray something primarily, even if not exclusively, about the philosopher himself, the structure of his organism, the character of the culture in which he thrives, and the organization of his interests as revealed in his selective activity. If this theory of value is contested, the problem becomes one of analytical ethics.

(c) Where "real" means necessary condition or independent variable, we have an elliptical statement which becomes more complete when we ask "necessary condition for what?" "independent variable in relation to what situation, context, and expected consequence?" In this sense, the statement "x is real" is an assertion that where certain events are expected or certain effects are to be attained, x (which as a meaningful term involves some ultimate denotative reference) is the most reliable sign of the event expected or the most reliable way of securing specific effects. The statement, then, that anything is real in a determinate situation expresses an *order of dependence,* a sequential relation or structure between events. This is what matter and reality mean for the scientist.

It is a methodological commonplace that science is interested in discovering the invariant relations between events and not in the ineffable qualities of the events themselves. For the scientist's purposes the so-called inner nature of the terms of his equations is irrelevant. When he has stated how these terms are related, when he has discovered which are the dependent and independent variables in any law expressing uniform connection, he is describing reality (*a* reality, not *the* reality). Now, there is no sure way of distinguishing between those who have proclaimed themselves to be either materialists or idealists on the basis of their attitude to what we have called the scientists' reality. A great many idealists have accepted a thoroughgoing determinism concerning the ways in which things are *related* even when they have seriously maintained that a chunk of matter is a colony of souls or a complex of sensations. And some materialists have been known who have held to the belief that there are chance events in the world—not merely in the sense that there is an alogical aspect of existence in which structural relations are found—but that structural relations can not always be found everywhere. Determinism, then, is not the issue between materialism and idealism. Nor is nominalism the issue. Although many materialists have simply divided the world, on the one hand, into particular things located in a specific space and time, and, on the other, into concrete mental images, thus denying any objective status to relations and laws, there is nothing in scientific procedure which entails this view and a great deal which is incompatible with it. And that it is possible both to deny materialism and affirm nominalism, Berkeley, Mach, and Pearson bear witness. If idealism be defined as the belief in the objectivity of universals, then every form of non-atomistic materialism is in perfect consonance with it.

(2) Another facet of the historic issue between materialism and idealism appears in the form of the question: what is the relation between matter and consciousness?

The primary contention of materialism is that vital and mental phenomena "arise, develop, and cease" with certain observed, or observable, or legitimately inferable changes in physical phenomena. The evidence is gathered by rigorous scientific method in fields ranging from physics to psychology. The idealists profess not to deny the findings of science, but merely the form in which the materialists have generalized them, as in their statement "consciousness is produced only as a result of a determinate organization of a material system." Here the words "produced" and "only" give offense. "Produced" raises all the difficulties involved in the definition of causation; and "only," the difficulties of induction. But whatever the difficulties may be they are irrelevant to the issue between historic forms of idealism and materialism, for the reason that every positive and consistent system of idealism cannot escape the use of these terms, too. If the production of mind by material changes and *only* by material changes is a mystery, then the production or creation of things by mental activity (whether it be the descent of the soul in the metaphor of Plotinus or the self-alienation of mind in the jargon of Hegel) is no less mysterious. The argument that the disparity between mind and matter is so great that there is no common determinable under which their specific qualitative differences may intelligibly be subsumed—an argument derived from the old superstition that "only like can affect like"— would make causal explanation of any qualitative change within any one realm, mental or material, impossible, so that even if the argument were valid, it operates equally against the materialist and idealist.

Sometimes to the challenge of the empirical data accumulated by the scientific materialist which show the manifold ways in which the mind is dependent upon the organization of the body, the idealists respond that either these bodies themselves can be reduced to states of mind or else the substance of things is not purely material but spiritual. When things have been reduced to states of mind we have merely the familiar transformation of the psychophysical problem into an epistemological one. When things are regarded as essentially spiritual substances, we get a view which is in all verifiable respects the same as that of hylozoism. On the basis of the maxim that there can be no more in the effect than in the cause, the idealist argues that the values of spirit must in some way be potential in the stuff out of which it develops; on the basis of the same maxim, the materialist argues that the distinctive properties of life must be dormant in matter. The result is that it is possible to find in Diderot and Ernst Haeckel sentences which in slightly differently accented form appear in Fechner; sentences of Holbach in Wundt; of de la Mettrie in Clifford.

It remains to inquire why, if the issue between traditional materialism and idealism is neither scientifically statable nor solvable, each party has insisted that the essence of things is matter or mind. The answer it seems to me is this. Among the defining prop-

erties of mind as we know it in the behavior of highly developed
organisms, are purpose and foresight, the capacity to initiate action
in behalf of goals and values. The assertion that mind is a pervasive property of *all* existence means that in some analogical form
or other, teleological reference to values is to be read back into the
structure and function of what is commonly regarded as non-
spiritual. Strictly interpreted, then, the behavior of material particles would have a teleological reference in the light of which
natural laws could be surveyed as in some respects, similar to, or
necessarily involving, human activity in pursuit of ideals. This
would render support to the religious assumption that all the laws
of existence—and therefore the laws of nature—serve some purpose,
that they are not intelligible in their own terms, but only in relation to an all-encompassing end—explicit or hidden. In a more or
less veiled way, this conclusion was actually drawn by all idealists
even when the differences between them were as great as those
between Berkeley and Leibniz and between both of these and
Hegel. I am not asserting that the belief "to be is to be mental"
entailed the belief that the world has an objective purpose, and a
congenial one at that—for not all mentality is purposive. But psychologically it made it easier to believe that man was at home in the
universe, that his brave dreams and ideals were the stuff out of
which existence was made.

For some philosophers and most ordinary men, to make the
hypothesis of universal teleology intelligible, it was necessary to
take refuge in some form of theism. Where theism was openly acknowledged, the crucial contention of idealism was the belief in
the efficacy at some point of disembodied spirit. This was a sophisticated answer to the old theological problem of whether God
created the world or whether the world existed from eternity.
During the middle ages, it will be remembered, materialism meant
belief in the eternity of the world and disbelief in the activity of
final causes. Where theism was not openly acknowledged and the
quest for teleological explanation of specific parts of nature
eschewed, idealists were compelled to interpret the universe as an
harmonious whole, as a cosmic order which was at the same time a
moral order. They attempted to explain why there is a world, what
its meaning is, and what its goal. That is why metaphysical idealism and religion tended to become, so to speak, socially identical

twins. Their purpose was the same: *to justify* the ways of god, or nature, to man. This is not the place to offer detailed historic and contemporary documentation of this, but the evidence seems to me to be overwhelming that the chief difference between material-ism and idealism centers around the question of the *validity* of the arguments for theism or cosmic purpose. We need but point to the fact that almost in every age the terms "atheism" and "material-ism" have been interchangeable. We need but recall that one of the motives of Berkeley—but assuredly only one of them—in his attack upon Newton and other physicists who had taken a mathe-matical approach to nature, was, in his own words "to restore and sustain faith in the constancy and universality of Divine Agency in the world." Interestingly enough, Hegel, too, in his doctoral dissertation, *de Orbitis Planetarum*, and in his later writings, con-demns Newton's physics because in eliminating qualitative con-siderations, it made all of nature appear dead and lifeless, inca-pable of acting as a support for an immanent spiritual principle. And as for contemporary idealism, I find a statement in William McDougall which seems to me to be both typical and revealing. In summarizing the argument for animism, which he identifies with idealism, he says: "animism . . . permits us to hope and even to believe that the world is even better than it seems; that the bitter injustices men suffer are not wholly irreparable and that their moral efforts are not wholly futile." Objective idealists have not infrequently rejected theism but they have held that reality—the systematic structure of things—is rational, and therefore neces-sary, and therefore good.

I would not be misunderstood as saying that belief in cosmic purpose exhausts the wisdom of these men. My point is merely that this faith represents the continuity of the idealist tradition, and that the denial that this faith is necessary for the understand-ing and control of nature and human nature, is central to the materialist or naturalist position. I add further that the great con-tributions to philosophy of Berkeley, Leibniz, Hegel, Whitehead, and others seem to me to be obscured by, and not derivative from, their idealism.

It is interesting to observe that from this point of view some traditional forms of materialism are in actuality species of ideal-ism which have adopted the fighting word "materialism" as a strategic masquerade in their struggle against other varieties of idealism. Orthodox dialectical materialism is a philosophy of this kind. Its belief that there exists a "dialectic" in nature such that it is *logically* related to the dialectic processes in society, and that these social processes must inevitably lead to socialism, entails the view that the structure and development of the cosmos guarantees the advent of the class-less society if not its date.

In this chapter I have tried to re-establish, by a somewhat different line of argument, the thesis laid down a hundred years ago by that much-neglected thinker, Ludwig Feuerbach, that the conflict between materialism and idealism—if and when there *is* a conflict—is the conflict between naturalism and supernaturalism. Here is not the place to debate the issue. But in view of recent discussion, at least this much must be said. If, as some idealists hold, the problem is not accessible to discursive analysis, then it falls out of the realm of philosophy. Where discursive analysis is permitted, it seems to me that the two key concepts are teleology and probability. To a naturalist, evidence for purpose, needs, organization, and ends in nature, is discovered in the behavior of *specific* things and organisms. No reference to the purpose of the whole is *empirically* relevant to the purposes he discovers by natural observation and experiment. And *logically,* no inference to the existence of such a purpose is permissible until it is first shown that the cosmos has the same structure of the finite things and organisms which are the locus of the purposes already discovered. But since the cosmos is declared to be unlimited in space and time, the naturalist denies both the existence of such a purpose and the rationality of its quest. The concept of probability is crucial to the only argument for the divine existence of God which is still recognized in many quarters as having force—the argument from design. This argument in every form presupposes the validity of the *a priori* probability, but not conversely. Most naturalists, however, with respect to the argument from design accept the frequency theory of probability which denies that any unique event or system or totality can be made the subject of a significant probability judgment. Even on the basis of an *a priori* theory of probability the argument from design is far from conclusive.

Where the issues between naturalism and supernaturalism are not resolvable because different criteria of intelligibility are brought to bear upon the argument, I think that further investigation will show that conflicting attitudes, drawn from a non-philosophical context—social or political or cultural—are involved. It is these conflicting attitudes which keep the issues alive. This is largely true, but it cannot be the whole truth. At least two things must be added. There is no *necessary* or logical connection between idealism or materialism and the political or social doctrines which may be grafted upon them. Early Christianity may have been a socially revolutionary force [1] even though its ideology was spiritualistic; the materialism of Hobbes, and in our own day of Santayana, seems perfectly compatible with extreme social conservatism. The nuances and emphases in any philosophical position *may* be historically explained by some political or social motivation, but the logic of any philosophical position, although it may exclude *some* social views, never univocally determines any *one* view. Secondly, social and political attitudes and factors do not *exhaust* the motivations out of which concern with the issue of materialism and idealism arises. No matter what the character of our society may be, it seems to me that the age-old issue between naturalism and supernaturalism will always be freshly discovered when man scans the sky and searches his heart for an answer to the perennial question: how to interpret a world in which he had no making and to organize a life which was not the consequence of his own choosing.

APPENDIX: *Are Religious Dogmas Cognitive?**

I should like to make a few observations on the drift of the discussion, as I recall it, and to raise a lonely voice in defense of Mr. Ducasse's position. Listening to the discussion I wondered whose religious dogmas were being analyzed. It seemed apparent that the "religious dogmas" discussed by Mr. Demos and several other speakers, are not the religious dogmas fervently believed by the overwhelming number of religious people throughout the world. They are not the dogmas of the public, historical religions but the private beliefs of a few which in the past (and in many religious circles of the present) would not have been (and are not) distinguished from disbeliefs. So much Mr. Demos seems prepared to grant. For according to him any representation of God in literal terms is incorrect. It leads to idolatry. Another speaker dismissed such conceptions as superstitions. Now in many religions, idols are openly worshipped and their believers would not regard the charge

* Some remarks contributed to a discussion of the theme "Are Religious Dogmas Cognitive?" before the American Philosophical Association (Eastern Division) in 1953.

of idolatry, even if true, as a *reductio ad absurdum* of their beliefs or a denial of their cognitive character. Some forms of Protestantism regard Catholicism as idolatrous and Judaism characterizes some expressions of Protestantism in the same way. Whether idolatrous or superstitious, such beliefs are at least as genuinely religious as the beliefs of those who repudiate them because they are literal. According to Mr. Demos they are cognitive and false. In calling them false he is using the same criteria of truth which we employ in ordinary experience when we reject statements that a stick became a snake or that a man walked on a lake. But he does not use these criteria in determining the truth of *his* religious dogmas which are descriptive but not literal. It is true that the language of some scientific statements has also been interpreted as descriptive but not literal. In assessing their truth, however, we do not depart from the criteria of truth we use in everyday affairs.

Some speakers have tried to assimilate religious dogmas to aesthetic judgments, but this does not illumine the momentous importance which the question of religious truth has had in the lives of religious believers or explain the fields in which religious truths have been sought. It would be hard to interpret the wars of religious faiths as wars of aesthetic predilection or rewrite the books on The Conflicts between Science and Religion (or Theology) as The Conflicts between Science and Art (or Aesthetics).

If Mr. Demos' religious dogmas are the subject of the discussion, then it would appear to me that his dogmas are religious, to use his own expression, in an analogical sense. But it is difficult to determine the precise meaning of "analogical" in Mr. Demos' paper, particularly when he speaks of God's existence and properties as "analogical," because he denies that analogy is explicable as a likeness in which a common property or element is present. Likeness "is just likeness." Ordinarily the common element is apparent whenever we say that A is to B, as C is to D, *i.e.*, the relation is univocal as soon as the respect or context is specified. (3 is to 6 what 7 is to 14; the sea is to fish what air is to bird; etc.) Mr. Demos believes that although personality cannot be attributed to God in a literal sense but only analogically, nonetheless the "relation of analogy between God and man is known literally." This seems to me an error. In saying "personality is to man,

what Personality is to God" Mr. Demos is saying more than he can
know. For on his own account, Personality and God are analogical
terms while personality and man are literal terms. We can see
the difference at once if we compare it with the expressions above
in which the third and fourth terms of the proportion are known
in a way that Personality and God cannot be known. It would
make no sense to say sea is to fish what air, analogically, is to bird,
analogically. It seems to me that Mr. Demos must hold that the
relation of Analogy between God and man can only be known
analogically. This may generate more Gods or orders of Gods than
one's theology can accommodate.

Mr. Randall suggested that no terms, even in ordinary discourse, have literal meaning, and that this in some way justifies
the symbolic or mythical language employed by Mr. Demos and/or
Mr. Tillich when they speak of God. This reminds me of a symposium I once read on the meaning of democracy by contributors
from both sides of the Iron Curtain. The editors were encouraged
by the fact that all contributors professed belief in democracy.
They noted, however, the glaringly ambiguous way in which the
word "democracy" was used. But they finally consoled themselves with the reflection that the word "ambiguous" was after all
itself ambiguous. I do not believe it makes one a narrow positivist
to hold that unless some words are unambiguous we cannot tell
what we are talking about or whether we are agreeing or disagree-
ing with each other, and that if no words have literal meaning,
then it makes no sense to say that any words have symbolic, meta-
phorical, or analogical meaning. Of course, in ordinary discourse
many words are not used literally ("The light died as the sun
set") but their meaning can often be rendered in literal terms.
More important, however, the rules and contexts which govern the
use of non-literal terms in ordinary discourse cannot be applied
to God without, we are told, falling into idolatry or superstition.

Mr. Demos believes that some words have literal meaning.
Indeed, it is because they use words literally that the religion of
fundamentalists is false. But his contention that not merely the
terms of his own religious dogmas are analogical but also terms
like "discourse," "meaning," "rationality," "meaningfulness," etc.
(which are multiply ambiguous), seems to open up a fathomless
semantic pit in which everyone speaks profoundly and no one

understands his neighbor. In one non-analogical sense of the word, we increase our understanding of the perception of "likeness" by identifying common elements in the field or context, or by distinguishing more carefully between what appears, or is experienced as, "like."

Even if it is granted that God's properties are analogically attributed to him, Mr. Demos believes that some statements about him are true. I suspect that he would not settle for "true analogically." He wants the real article. He believes that it is just as true to say that God cares for us as that a good father cares for his child, even though God cares only analogically. But suppose someone says with Russell "God cares for me" is false because God does not exist, or, with Strawson and Geach, "God cares for me" is neither true nor false but pointless because God does not exist, how would Mr. Demos answer them. By saying, as he does, "in some sense of existence it is false that God exists but in another it is true that God exists; the former is the literal, the latter is the analogical sense"? For would not that response also be appropriate in reply to a question about the existence of Santa Claus (he does not exist as a denizen of the North Pole; he does exist as an idea, a legend, myth, or ideal)? If Santa Claus or any object of discourse exists in an analogical sense, his analogical existence must differ from that of God. Why multiply analogical existences without necessity?

One brief comment on Mr. Demos' view that science (or common sense) and religion rest equally on faith. It is noteworthy that he does not say that science is committed to faith in an analogical sense. He puts the faith of the ordinary man and scientist in the principle of induction and the faith a man has in the resurrection of the dead on all fours. It seems to me that the term "faith" covers two different attitudes here. If behavior is an index of belief, there are some things we can't help believing or having "faith" in. We jump out of the path of a speeding auto unless we want to die; and if we want to die, we can't help but have "faith" in the operation of other physical laws. But men can live or die without having faith in God or the resurrection of the body. Many have. It requires an act of will to have religious faith. When a man tells us that his knowledge that bread will nourish him and stones not, rests on faith, although his behavior would be the same, no matter how much or how little he knows, no matter if he were a pan-logist or complete skeptic, his language is misleading. Science is an elaboration and development of common-sense knowledge which, because it is knowledge, is not faith. If it is retorted that such knowledge rests on "faith" and is therefore no more valid than religious knowledge which rests on "faith," what must first be established is that we have religious knowledge.

Notes

Philosophy and Human Conduct

[1] *Freedom versus Organization*, New York, W. W. Norton, 1934, p. 196.

[2] *Philosophy and Politics*, London, Cambridge University Press, 1947, p. 20.

[3] *Grundlinien des Philosophie des Rechts*, Lasson Ausgabe, pp. 15–16, Leipzig, Felix Meiner, 1920.

[4] *Marx Engels Gesamtausgabe*, Erste Abteiling, Bd. 5, pp. 15–16, Moscow and Berlin, Marx-Engels Verlag, 1932.

[4a] *opus cit.*, p. 27.

[5] One critic says of the identification of the law of nature with the counsels of self-interest "Woe to all the Princes of the earth, if this doctrine be true or become popular; if the multitude believe this, the Prince . . . can never be safe from spears and barbed irons which their ambition and personal interest will provide." *Tenisons Creed of Mr. Hobbes Examined* (1670) p. 156, quoted by Dewey in *Studies in the History of Ideas*, Vol. 1, New York, Columbia University Press, 1918, p. 91.

[6] Robert Hartman, *Journal of Phenomenology and Phenomenological Research*, Vol. XIII, No. 3, March 1953, p. 353.

[7] *The Social Teaching of the Christian Churches*, Eng. trans. London and New York, Macmillan, 1932, p. 1105.

[8] Butterfield, Herbert, *Christianity and History*, London, Macmillan, 1949, p. 175 f.

[9] *Opus cit.*, p. 22.

¹⁰ *German Philosophy and Politics*, New York, Holt & Co., 1915, p. 121.

¹¹ *Opus cit.*, p. 44.

¹² *Reconstruction in Philosophy*, Enlarged edition, Boston, Beacon Press, 1948, p. 191.

¹³ J. S. Mill's *Autobiography*, first unaltered edition, edited by J. J. Coss, New York, Columbia University Press, 1924, p. 158 cf. also pp. 191–4.

¹⁴ Cf. "The Sociology of Philosophic Ideas," *The Pacific Sociological Review*, 1958, p. 77.

¹⁵ *Reason and Law*, Glencoe, Ill., Free Press, 1950, p. 190.

¹⁶ This seems to me to bear upon the contentions of J. W. N. Watkins, "Epistemology and Politics," in *Proceedings of the Aristotelian Society*, Vol. LVIII, 1957–58, pp. 79–102.

Moral Freedom in a Determined World

¹ See *Determinism and Freedom in an Age of Modern Science*, edited by Sidney Hook (New York University Press, 1958), *passim*.

² *Freedom*, London, Longmans, Green & Co., 1954, p. 167.

³ *Mind*, LX (1951), pp. 441–465.

The Ethical Theory of John Dewey

¹ *Ethics*, 2nd ed., New York, 1932, p. 296.

² *Ibid.*, p. 205.

³ Cf. his (1) "Value and Obligation in Dewey and Lewis," *Philosophical Review*, Vol. LVIII, No. 4, July 1949, pp. 321–9; and (2) Chapter XII of his *Social Thought in America*, New York, 1949. I shall refer to these as 1 and 2.

⁴ 1, p. 325.

⁵ 1, p. 324.

⁶ 1, p. 326.

⁷ 2, p. 214.   ⁷ᵃ 2, p. 215.

⁸ *Ethics*, p. 349.

⁹ 2, p. 217.

¹⁰ *Ethics and Language*, New Haven, Yale University Press, 1944, p. 114.

¹¹ "Anthropology and Ethics," *Social Sciences*, p. 34, ed. by Obgurn and Goldenweiser.

¹² *Ethics and Language*, pp. 139–40.

¹³ *Journal of Philosophy*, Dec. 20, 1945, my italics.

The New Failure of Nerve

¹ *The Nature and Destiny of Man*, Vol. I (New York, 1941), p. 73.

² *Modern Monthly*, Vol. 8, p. 712.

³ "Religion and Action," *Religion in the Modern World*, University of Pennsylvania Bicentennial Conference (1941) p. 91.

⁴ *The Nature and Destiny of Man*, New York, Chas. Scribner's Sons, 1941, Vol. I, p. 196.

⁵ For a more extended critique of Niebuhr, cf. my *Social Change and Original Sin*, New Leader, November 11, 1941.

[6] *Opus cit.*, p. 200. It is interesting to note that taxation was one of the means used by the Soviet State to wipe out Russian churches. The curious reasoning by which Msgr. Ryan justifies this position is detailed in another book:

"As we have already pointed out, the men who defend the principle of toleration for all varieties of religious opinion, assume either that all religions are equally true or that the true cannot be distinguished from the false. On no other ground is it logically possible to accept the theory of indiscriminate and universal toleration (*sic!*).

"To the objection that the foregoing argument can be turned against Catholics by a non-Catholic State, there are two replies. First, if such a State should prohibit Catholic worship or preaching on the plea that it was wrong and injurious to the community, the assumption would be false; therefore the two cases are not parallel. Second, a Protestant State could not logically take such an attitude (although many of them did so in former centuries) because no Protestant sect claims to be infallible. Besides, the Protestant principle of private judgment logically implies that Catholics may be right in their religious convictions, and that they have a right to hold and preach them without molestation.

"Such in its ultimate rigor and complete implications is the Catholic position concerning the alliance that should exist between the Church and a Catholic State."

Ryan and Miller *The State and Church*, Macmillan, 1937, pp. 36–37

[7] William Z. Foster, *Toward Soviet America*, p. 275, N.Y., Coward-McCann (1932).

[8] All quotations from the official statement of the Third Annual Conference, New York, September 1, 1942.

[9] Proceedings of Third Conference, p. 538.

[10] For a more detailed refutation of the attempts to ground democracy upon theological and metaphysical foundations, cf. "The Philosophical Presuppositions of Democracy," *Ethics*, April, 1942, pp. 275–296.

[11] For Stalin the dialectic takes the place of Providence. And since June 22, 1941, the Soviet radio has discovered that Nazism is a movement which seeks to destroy Christianity.

Modern Knowledge and the Concept of God

[1] My italics. I am drawing here on the illuminating account of my colleague's exposition and criticism, Milton Munitz, *Space, Time and Creation* (1957). Cf. also for analysis of the concept of creation, the chapter on "The Metaphysics of the Instrument," in my *The Metaphysics of Pragmatism* (1927).

[2] *Mind*, July, 1959.

[3] *The World As I See It*, New York, 1949, p. 29.

[4] *Science and the Modern World*, New York, Macmillan, 1925, p. 249.

[5] New York, 1929, p. 486.

The Quest for "Being"

[1] Willard V. Quine, "On What There Is," *Review of Metaphysics*, Vol. II, No. 5 (September 1948), p. 29.

[2] Irving M. Copi, "Philosophy and Language," *Review of Metaphysics*, Vol. IV, No. 3 (March 1951), p. 435.

[3] Bergson, *Creative Evolution*, Authorized Translation by Arthur Mitchell (New York: Holt, 1911), p. 283.

[4] Paul Tillich, *Systematic Theology*, Vol. I (Chicago: University of Chicago Press, 1951), p. 187.

[5] *Ibid.*, p. 187.

[6] *Ibid.*, p. 189.

[7] P. Coffey, *Ontology* (New York: Peter Smith, 1938), p. 182.

[8] Martin Heidegger, *Existence and Being* (Chicago: Regnery, 1949), p. 355.

[9] *Ibid.*, p. 384.

[10] *Ibid.*, p. 372.

[11] *Ibid.*, p. 373.

[12] Nicolai Hartmann, *Zur Grundlegung der Ontologie*, p. 43.

[13] Coffee, *Ontology, op.cit.*, p. 38.

[14] R. G. Miller "The Empiricists' Dilemma—Either Metaphysics or Nonsense," *Proceedings of the American Catholic Philosophical Association*, 1955, pp. 151–76.

[15] C. I. Lewis, *An Analysis of Knowledge and Valuation* (La Salle, Ill.: Open Court, 1946), p. 48.

[16] Paul Tillich, *The Protestant Era* (Chicago: University of Chicago Press, 1948), p. 86.

[17] *Systematic Theology*, Vol. I, p. 169.

[18] *Ibid.*, p. 163.

[19] *Critique of Pure Reason*, tr. by Max Müller, New York: Macmillan, 1896, 2d ed., p. 478.

[20] Scudder Klyce, *Universe* (Winchester, Mass., 1921), pp.iii ff.

[21] Dewey, *Philosophy and Civilization* (New York: Minton, Balch, 1931), p. 198.

[22] Dewey, "Experience and Existence: A Comment," *Philosophy and Phenomenological Research*, Vol. IX (June 1949), p. 712.

[23] *Ibid.*, p. 713.

[24] Sterling P. Lamprecht, "Metaphysics: Its Function, Consequences, and Criteria," *Journal of Philosophy*, Vol. XLIII (July 18, 1946), pp. 400–401.

[25] *Ibid.*, p. 401.

[26] *Ibid.*, p. 399.

[27] *Ibid.*, p. 396.

[28] *Ibid.*, p. 396.

[29] John Herman Randall, Jr., "Metaphysics: Its Function, Consequences, and Criteria," *Journal of Philosophy*, Vol. XLIII (July 18, 1946), p. 408: "For the empirical metaphysician, his method is no different from the ordinary experimental methods of observation and tested generalization employed in any existential science, and his conclusions share in the probable and corrigible character of the findings of all experimental science." I am assuming that Professor Randall is not using "corrigible" in the sense in which it is applicable to geometrical proof.

[30] *Ibid.*, p. 403.

[31] *Ibid.*, p. 404.

[32] *Ibid.*, p. 408.

[33] *Ibid.*, p. 409.

³⁴ F. J. E. Woodbridge, *Nature and Mind* (New York: Columbia University Press, 1937), pp. 40–41.
³⁵ Dewey, "The Subject-Matter of Metaphysical Inquiry," *Journal of Philosophy*, Vol. XII (June 24, 1915). p. 340.
³⁶ *Experience and Nature,* Lasalle, Open Court Publishing Co., 1925, p. 413.

Naturalism and First Principles

¹ A. A. Goldenweiser, *Anthropology,* New York: Crofts & Co., 1937, p. 134.
² F. Boas, *Mind of Primitive Man,* New York: Macmillan, 2nd ed., p. 131.
³ B. Malinowski, *Science, Religion and Reality,* New York: Macmillan, 1929, p. 35.
⁴ A. A. Goldenweiser, *op. cit.,* pp. 420–21.
⁵ W. Crawshaw-Williams, "True Truth: or the Higher the Deeper," *Rationalist Annual* (London), 1948, p. 28.
⁶ J. Dewey, in *Journal of Philosophy*, Vol. XLII, 1945, p. 206.
⁷ C. Peirce, *Collected Works,* Cambridge, Harvard University Press, Vol. II, Par. 2, p. 780.
⁸ Arthur Murphy, in *Journal of Philosophy*, Vol. XLII, p. 413.
⁹ Crawshaw-Williams, *loc. cit.*
¹⁰ Arthur Murphy, in *Journal of Philosophy*, Vol. XLII, pp. 411, 412.
¹¹ R. Demos, in *Philosophy and Phenomenological Research,* Vol. VII, p. 271.

Scientific Knowledge and Philosophical "Knowledge"

¹ Maritain, *The Degrees of Knowledge,* New York, Charles Scribner's & Sons, 1938, p. 59.
² *Ibid.,* p. 63.
³ *Ibid.,* p. 66.
⁴ *Ibid.,* p. 226.
⁵ Smith, V. E., *Philosophical Physics,* New York: Harper & Bros., 1950, p. 34.
⁶ *The Modern Schoolman,* January, 1944.

Materialism and Idealism

¹ This is still an open question. Insofar as the modification of property relations is concerned, it seems to me highly questionable that Christianity at any time was a revolutionary movement.

Index